The Worlds
of André Maurois

André Maurois as an octogenarian. Inscription: *"Pour Jack Kolbert, mon biographe et mon ami."* **(Photo by Foto Adelman.)**

The Worlds
of André Maurois

Jack Kolbert

Selinsgrove: Susquehanna University Press
London and Toronto: Associated University Presses

Associated University Presses
440 Forsgate Drive
Cranbury, NJ 08512

Associated University Presses
25 Sicilian Avenue
London WC1A 2QH, England

Associated University Presses
2133 Royal Windsor Drive
Unit 1
Mississauga, Ontario
Canada L5J 1K5

The paper used in this publication meets the minimum requirements of the American
National Standard for Permanence of Paper for Printed Library Materials
Z39.48-1984.

Library of Congress Cataloging in Publication Data

Kolbert, Jack, 1927–
  The worlds of André Maurois.

  Bibliography: p.
  Includes index.
  1. Maurois, André, 1885–1967—Criticism and
interpretation.   I. Title.
PQ2625.A95Z694   1985   848'.91209   85-40033
ISBN 0-941664-16-3 (alkaline paper.)

Printed in the United States of America

For Ruth
Also, in Memoriam of Dora, Sophie, and Anna
and
In Anticipation of great things from Aaron, Adam, Aden, Shayna,
Max and Dana

Contents

Preface

The works of André Maurois had originally attracted me when, as a high school student some forty years ago, I enjoyed reading his short stories in second-year-French textbooks. His works continued to play an important part in my educational formation at the University. I suspect this to have been true for many students of French in my age group. Later, as a college professor I noted the sense of pleasure Maurois's prose gave to students in my own classes.

Despite Maurois's pervasive presence in French literature during the period between World War I and the first two decades following the Second World War, relatively few major monographs have been devoted to him. Most of the works dealing exclusively with André Maurois were either limited to a specific phase of this author or else they were small in physical scope or are by now somewhat dated. The most significant works on Maurois were written by Georges Lemaitre, Victor Dupuis, Amélie Fillon, L. Clark Keating, Michel Droit, and Jacques Suffel. Most recently, Judith Kaufmann published her superb dissertation, *Aspects d'André Maurois Biographe.* I have derived much information from all of these works and quote from them extensively. Each of them sheds light on Maurois's place under the sun, but none is in itself the total, comprehensive, large-scaled monograph that this writer deserves. The time has come for Maurois at long last to be studied in a global way, that is, as an interesting literary human being, as a novelist and short-story writer, as a biographer, historian, critic, essayist, moralist, science-fiction author, and as a man whose career intersected the lives of some of the leading figures of his day. Some two decades ago I decided that I would someday attempt to fill this void. The ensuing work, written on and off again in several revised versions and during several stages in my professional life, is the result.

A Fulbright postdoctoral fellowship in 1963–64, coupled with a sabbatical leave from the University of Pittsburgh, enabled me to establish initial personal contact with André Maurois and his wife. The author, Madame Maurois, his children, and his circle of friends provided me with generous assistance: access to their private papers, correspondence, and manuscripts. We spent countless hours together in personal interviews. My research reflected the Mauroisean methodology of writing biographies and literary studies. He once wrote:

> Having reread a fine book, let them [the readers] go and see the country where this book was conceived; let them take pleasure in finding again the natural landscapes, the first sketches, or the pretexts for the paintings created

9

by the artists whom they admire; let them retrace the footsteps and life of a
great man through a province, from house to house, from village to town. I
believe that they will find in such promenades an inimitable charm, because
the beauty of nature will find itself animated and heightened by the memory
of the emotions that it engendered, and that page, which for a long time had
been the object of their predilection, will assume for them much more value,
for they will have reread it in the decor in which it was written.[1]

For several years I too retraced Maurois's footsteps in Normandy, Paris, the
Riviera, Périgord, Mills College in Oakland, California, Kansas City, Princeton, and elsewhere. I have attempted to imbue my own text on Maurois with
the "decor" that was such an integral part of his writings.

In the end, André and Simone Maurois transformed themselves from subjects of what was to have been a scholarly study into close personal associates.
Maurois, in fact, once gave me a book in which he wrote "For Jack Kolbert,
who on making himself my biographer became a friend." ("Pour Jacques Kolbert qui, en se faisant mon biographe, est devenu un ami.")[2]

I must confess that the more I read Maurois, the more I enjoyed his writings.
Alain, Maurois's great teacher, contended that to like something constituted a
precondition for understanding it: "Aimer c'est comprendre." ("To like is to
understand.") I am convinced that Alain was at least partially right.

My objective here is to describe and to evaluate the place André Maurois's
collective works have occupied and will continue to occupy within the fabric
that is French literature of the twentieth century. In providing descriptive and
analytical exegeses of the major and some of the lesser texts, I hope to underscore the chief virtues and some of the defects in them.

Maurois's friend, literary critic Robert Kemp, once wrote that this author
"seems simple, and he is complex. He might fool those with geometrical
minds, who are ever impatient to discern the lines of a face; but those who
possess minds of finesse become attached to the nuances in him and recognize
that he is multiple."[3] Maurois was indeed both a *solitary* figure and one who
enjoyed *solidarity* with the literary world (to use Albert Camus's words).
Though his texts stand out for their facility and succinctness, he defied facile
categorizations and succinct formulae. While he belonged to no literary school
(his solitary side), he was an active participant in the social, intellectual, and
political life of his times (the solidarity in him). He participated actively in the
life of the French Academy, but he attracted few disciples or apologists. If he
wrote with utter simplicity, his thought processes were often complicated.
While he personally observed in his fiction the traditional canons of writing,
most of which he inherited from the previous century, his two most important
posthumous volumes deal with his futuristic views of the universe and the
human race: *Le Chapitre suivant* (*The Next Chapter*, 1979) and *Les Illusions*
(*Illusions*, 1968).

My book on Maurois falls into the time-honored tradition of "Hommes et

Oeuvres" ("Men and Their Writings") studies, and my text is structured accordingly. After tracing a detailed portrait of Maurois's life and his character, I have composed a series of chapters devoted to the genres in which he published.

Portions of this book have already appeared in different form in some earlier articles, especially the sections on biography (in the *French Review*) and on short stories (in *Studies on Short Fiction*). The bulk of the material appears here for the first time.

I am grateful to many persons for having assisted me during the preparatory phases of my research. To name them all would extend the length of these remarks beyond reasonable proportions. But several names cannot go unmentioned: the author's three children, Michelle, Gérald, and Olivier Maurois; Jacques Suffel of the Bibliothèque Nationale; Dr. Albert Delaunay of the Institut Pasteur; the late Nobel Laureate François Mauriac; former Minister of Culture Maurice Druon; Maurice Genevoix, the then Perpetual Secretary of the French Academy; Professor Maurice Coindreau of Princeton University; the Duchesse de la Rochefoucauld and her daughter, the Comtesse de la Rochefoucauld; Michel Droit, former editor of *Le Figaro Littéraire;* André Gillon, the owner of *Les Nouvelles Littéraires;* authors Vercors and Jean Dutourd. My many colleagues in French at the University of Pittsburgh, the University of New Mexico, Pomona College, the Monterey Institute, and elsewhere also offered me much-appreciated counsel. Dean Robert G. Templin, Jr., of Piedmont Virginia Community College provided me with indispensable support during the last stages of preparation. Professor Nancy Cairns of Susquehanna University (one of my most able students in literary criticism at Pitt) was a most critical reader and persuaded me to exercise the courage necessary to eliminate huge chunks of extraneous material. In some respects, this work would not have appeared without her intervention during the last stages of production.

Finally, I would like to express thanks to my patient wife, Ruth, and to my two sons, Harry and Shelley, all three of whom shared with me some of the daily trials of writing a difficult series of drafts on a most difficult subject. And to Max Wiczer, special appreciation for his warm and generous support.

In June of 1965 I was present when all of France seemed to have joined hands in marking the eightieth birthday of André Maurois, then one of France's most distinguished men of letters. Then in October of 1967, the printed and electronic media throughout the world joined in paying lavish tribute to this Academician on the occasion of his death. Exactly ten years later, various ceremonies took place throughout France marking the tenth anniversary of Maurois's death. Although by then he seemed to have plummeted into the recesses of purgatory, streets and city squares were named after him. Plaques and monuments were unveiled in his honor. The Bibliothèque Nationale in

Paris held a major colloquium and exposition, which attracted scholars from throughout the world. Despite all of this fanfare Maurois has not yet emerged from his purgatory.

The year 1985 marks the centennial of André Maurois's birth. My volume is being published now to serve as a timely reminder of his importance. Surely he deserves a monograph that honors his contributions as a writer who once enjoyed prominence throughout the civilized world. Perhaps as a result of my work, new generations of readers will hurry to their nearest libraries to borrow some of Maurois's finest books, or they will persuade the publishing industry to reissue his many discontinued titles.

Posterity has thus far played unfair tricks on Maurois, something that could never have been predicted during his lifetime, when most of his books were read by millions of readers around the world. Perhaps my study on *The Worlds of André Maurois* will rectify this unfairness. To restore André Maurois to his rightful place in the history of French literature—that is my central purpose here.

The Worlds
of André Maurois

Part I
The World
of André Maurois—the Man

1
Maurois's Eight Decades

Nothing is more surprising than to see oneself through the
eyes of another. In the brief account of my life which I have
just read, all the facts are exact and yet . . .

Maurois

His was a full life. He had participated in two world wars, made dozens of trips
and lecture tours throughout the world, written scores of best-selling books.
Yet, of such a life, he inaccurately wrote that "I know of no life more simple, or
more integrated than my own."[1]

Superficially he could view his life as being placid, even unified, covered by
layers of good fortune, honors, international recognition, encomiums and successes of all sorts. In reality he knew that his was "a most difficult human
existence,"[2] as he once referred to it in a moment of truth. It is that existence
which I now begin to retrace.

A. *The World of Emile Herzog*

The story begins fifteen years prior to Maurois's birth, in 1870, in Bischwiller, a thriving Alsatian town of ten thousand inhabitants, situated not far from
the great city of Strasbourg. This region had for centuries been the tolerant
haven for significant concentrations of Jewish families. Among the most indus-
trious of these were the Herzogs (Maurois's father's name) and the Lévy-
Rueffs (the name of his maternal family). After the defeat of the French in 1870,
all of Alsace and parts of Lorraine were forcibly annexed by the victorious
Prussians, who remained there until 1918. Many of the Alsatian Jewish industrialists, rejecting German citizenship, liquidated their holdings and moved
into the heartland of France. The Herzogs, for instance, closed their sizable
wool mill in Bischwiller and moved both their home and business to the
unpicturesque, unattractive milltown of Elbeuf, Normandy. They brought
with them many of their faithful employees and their dependents.

The lone attractive trait of Elbeuf is its proximity to the magnificent Norman
capital and cathedral city of Rouen. Maurois's ancestors introduced into the
ancient province of Normandy the earliest modern methods of mass produc-

17

tion of woolen cloths. Today, few of their original enterprises exist, though Elbeuf continues to survive as an industrial community.[3]

In 1884 Ernest Herzog, Maurois's father (1865–1925) married Alice Lévy-Rueff, his mother (1865–1944). From his photographs, the former appeared to be a distinguished-looking gentleman with a pronouncedly Semitic profile adorned by a curious fan-shaped mustache. As for Alice Lévy-Rueff, the daughter of one of the most prominent textile families in France, she displays the countenance of a refined and attractive young woman. After the merger of these two Jewish mercantile families, their joint wool enterprise expanded and even prospered.

One year after the marriage, to be exact on July 26, 1885, Ernest and Alice Herzog had their first child, a son named Emile. Later he would be known around the world under the pseudonym of André Maurois. At the time of his birth, the young family lived in a triangular, unpretentious abode at the corner of the rue Henry and the Place du Champ de Foire, near Elbeuf's town center.

The future writer was the oldest of three children. Maurois's sister Marguerite was born one year after him, and his sister Germaine arrived four years later.[4] For a family of five, the small house of the rue Henry soon became too cluttered, so the Herzogs purchased a more commodious place on the rue Magenta (no. 3), situated a bit farther from the center of town in a slightly more stately residential quarter. André Maurois spent most of his childhood and adolescence in this relatively charming home and especially within the high-walled garden.

Photographs, almost the sole source of data concerning Maurois's earliest childhood, reveal that at the age of eighteen months this plump baby possessed a round face and a thick head of long, unruly, blond hair. Already obvious in the photo are the penetrating, alert eyes that both impressed and disconcerted his interlocutors eighty years later. A second equally quaint photograph, taken of him at the age of twelve years, shows him with a handsome, angular face, with neatly parted, thick, and darker hair. The meticulous grooming that characterized his later life was already manifest. And always the same piercing dark eyes!

Young Herzog enjoyed a happy, uneventful childhood. His parents—decent, sober, respectable, and hardworking—could not have been more colorless. Above all, they were honest. Their son never forgot his father's untypical (for a Frenchman) obsession with completing his tax returns with fanatic scrupulousness. Later, when filing his own tax forms, Maurois emulated the example of his father, from whom he learned "the respect for laws and discipline."[5]

Elbeuf did not claim enough Jews to form an active religious congregation, so Maurois learned many of the tenets of his parents' faith from the Jewish ethical values that prevailed in the Herzog household. He received no formal religious instruction. Actually, he observed at home not so much the religious practices as the traditional daily conduct of life that one finds so often in many Jewish homes: respect for learning; a lofty sense of charity; sobriety with

Alice Ernest Herzog (1865–1944), André Maurois's mother. (Courtesy, Estate of André Maurois.)

Ernest Herzog (1850–1925), André Maurois's father. (Courtesy, Estate of André Maurois.)

André Maurois at the age of eighteen months. Photo taken in January 1887. (Courtesy, Estate of André Maurois.)

André Maurois, twelve years old. Photo taken in 1897. (Courtesy, Estate of André Maurois.)

regard to alcoholic beverages; strong faith in middle-class standards of respectability; especially the willingness to work indefatigably both in the home and in business. Never feeling the need to rebel against his parents and family, as did Gide for instance, never going so far as Proust in his veneration of his mother, Maurois always padded his later autobiographical publications with lengthy enunciations of esteem for his mother and father: "They were, he and my mother, admirable human beings, both endowed with a purity, a modesty which everyone around them recognized."[6]

Subjected to the usual lessons of patriotism in the Petit Lycée d'Elbeuf, Maurois learned at home that one must be a loyal son of France. He was exposed to reading for the first time in a chauvinistic primer of sorts on the Franco-German debacle: *Français et Allemands*. Before television's advent, families still took walks together. Whenever he strolled with his father and sisters, they sang and walked to the martial pace of the national hymns of France. The first poems Emile Herzog memorized were imbued with patriotic zeal. Later, André Maurois ranked among some of the more fervent author-apologists of France. Three times he had volunteered in the army and thus was never blasé in proclaiming the glory of his native land in his essays, discourses, and lectures.

The Herzog household bathed in a strange aura of reserve and an unusual degree of discreetness. This family could not bear to discuss embarrassing topics with brutal frankness. His parents' taciturnity Maurois often characterized by the word *pudeur* (a blend of modesty and discretion). Life in his clan was governed by an inability to resort to spoken words. After all, once uttered, words could no longer be effaced. Because this "pudeur" dominated his day-to-day existence, Maurois inevitably colored his later literature with themes based on silence and an exaggerated sense of discretion. What is most significant in his books is often not to be found on the printed page; for him the ellipses between words and paragraphs often speak more eloquently than do the written terms.

At the Petit Lycée d'Elbeuf the precocious youngster demonstrated his first real assiduity. When he was six he learned from an Irish girl residing in Elbeuf his earliest words of English. He excelled in Latin, and throughout his published texts we encounter sprinklings of Latin phraseology. His extracurricular activities consisted of horseback riding and piano. He admitted to expertise in the former and to a total lack of talent in the latter. Although he later learned to appreciate serious music, he did so more as a passive auditor than as an active performer.

From the very start, Maurois demonstrated a fondness of books and at an early point in life he wanted to produce his own: "I do not remember a time when I did not dream of writing."[7] At the age of ten he surprised his French instructor Kittel with his talent for writing short compositions. Kittel was, in fact, the first to predict that young Herzog would develop into a master author. That same year Maurois heard the eminent literary critic Ferdinand Brunetière deliver an unforgettable lecture in Rouen on the comedies of Corneille. After that, Maurois dreamed of becoming a famous public lecturer. Both Kittel's prediction and Maurois's dream of emulating Brunetière would someday become a reality.

The youth would often accompany his father and uncles to the wool mill, then known as Fraenckel et Blin. He was fascinated by the hum of the looms, the buzzing activity of the employees, the animation at the loading docks, and the intricate relations between employers and employees that comprised the whole field of employee management. Later, in his novel *Bernard Quesnay*, he vividly recaptured this same industrial atmosphere. Maurois transposed the occasionally bitter commercial rivalries between the two main Elbeuf mills, Fraenckel et Blin and Blin et Blin into a similar rivalry between the fictitious firms of Pascal-Bouchet and Quesnay. The salty old character in *Bernard Quesnay*, Monsieur Achille, with his monomania for work, reincarnates Maurois's own great-uncle Henry, a man who lived, thought, dreamed, and breathed shop.

Maurois's childhood was fed by the marrow of provincial France: its sights, songs, smells, and bourgeois values. He enjoyed intimate rapports with the inhabitants of his province: "For twelve years, at dawn," he reminisced, "with my briefcase under my arm, I would cross Elbeuf mingling with the laborers going back to work."[8] These ordinary people and landscapes inspired his best works: "even today, I can't think of those railroad stations, which were so ugly, or those charming landscapes with their rivers and forests, without believing that I hear *Polyeucte*, "La Jeune Captive," "La Nuit de mai. . . ."[9]

If Emile Herzog witnessed no exciting dramas during his childhood, he did learn one great indelible lesson from his parents, a lesson that became the epicenter of his philosophy of life. He describes in *Ce que je crois (What I Believe)* how his parents taught by deed, not by preaching. Thus what mattered most was not what men said they had accomplished, but rather what men had actually accomplished.

When Emile Herzog graduated from the Petit Lycée d'Elbeuf, where he had been introduced to Latin, mathematics, and French literature, his grades placed him first in his class. Maurois—and later his ambitious second wife—had addicted themselves to being first in everything. Being first was both the boon and bane of his life. Then, as later on in life, he appeared to be endowed with an almost inhuman capacity to get things done with little ostensible effort. The ease with which he seemed later in life to fulfill his Promethean dreams made some critics dismiss his accomplishments with something less than full admiration.

Maurois's secondary education flowered in the Lycée Corneille in Rouen. This lycée, one of the four or five most distinguished in provincial France, had produced a host of famous graduates. Named after the seventeenth-century playwright Pierre Corneille, who attended the Jesuit school which later evolved into a lycée, it produced writers like Maupassant and Flaubert. An impressive structure, built around a great courtyard in the center of which rises a statue of Corneille, the Lycée crowns a hill overlooking some of the most awesome Gothic spires in the world. In contrast with the magnificence of the site, the classrooms in which Emile Herzog studied at the turn of the century, were shabby and bleak. The gallery of portraits in the main hall proudly displays all of the famous national prize winners who graduated from the Lycée, including that of young Herzog.

The four years spent by Emile Herzog at the Lycée Corneille were conceivably the most pivotal in his life. From a certain professor Nebout he learned to appreciate the French Romantic movement, especially the writings of Hugo and Vigny. As a biographer he excelled later in writing the biographies of the great Romantics (Sand, Dumas père, Hugo, Chateaubriand, Balzac, Byron, etc.). His teacher of rhetoric, Texcier, taught him to view the stylistic purity and moderation of Voltaire and Anatole France as a welcome contrast to the bombastic verbosity of certain other writers. Maurois never forgot his indebtedness to his physics teacher, Lecaplain, and to his professors of mathematics, Mouchel and Lelieuvre, all three of whom had instilled in him an undying interest in science and a fascination with the precision and rigor of algebraic and geometrical formulae. Later in life Maurois would turn to science fiction and to popularized presentations of scientific subjects (e.g., the *Life of Alexander Fleming*).

The year 1901 represented the climax of Herzog's education. A senior, he entered his "année de philosophie," that is, the year in French education when philosophy reigned supreme in the curriculum, allowing Herzog to synthesize all that he had learned to date. "The greatest event in my life," Maurois once confessed, "was, in the philosophy class, the contact with Alain, who was then called Emile Chartier."[10] The latter shaped the entire existence of his most impressionable disciple.

If most of the virtues Alain taught were consistent with those Emile Herzog had observed in his home, one lesson did indeed contradict the principles held by his puritanical parents: the teacher of philosophy advocated total openness with respect to questions of sensuality and love. Alain contended that at moments some of the most sensitive questions, even those dealing with sexuality, needed to be confronted head-on. An anecdote from Maurois's days in the lycée discloses the naive shock of the younger students at Alain's blunt frankness. Once, when the teacher was discussing the obligation of young men to respect the dignity of prostitutes, the director of the national system of secondary education walked unexpectedly into the classroom, in fact precisely at the moment when Alain had reached the most embarrassing point in his thesis. All of the pupils wondered how Alain might extricate himself from a most delicate crisis. To their surprise—and admiration!—he greeted the director affably, invited him to a seat, and continued in a natural manner: "I was in the process of explaining to these young men their duties with regard to prostitutes."[11]

How novel this straightforwardness must have seemed to young Herzog, nurtured as he had been at home on a steady diet of "pudeur" and reticence!

At Rouen Herzog ranked first in his school's competition in Latin, Greek, French, mathematics, and philosophy; oddly enough he excelled also in physical prowess. In America he would have been a natural candidate for a Rhodes Scholarship; in France he had to resign himself eventually to writing the biography of Cecil Rhodes instead. As a *lycéen*, he was short, scrawny, and had a slightly deviated vertebral column. But this puniness represented for him only one additional challenge. He *decided* to overcome his physical handicaps, even to win first prize in some area of physical education. Following a period of intensive exercises designed to strengthen and develop his physique, he did in fact win the first medal in gymnastics. [12]

In the Lycée Corneille Herzog learned still one other human lesson: the difficulty of being a Jewish boy in a predominantly Gentile world. At the turn of the century, students in the public schools of France customarily attended daily mass in the school auditorium or chapel. On the opening day of the academic year, Maurois realized that by birth and family-origin he was a "dissident" in a Christian universe. All non-Catholics, excused from the otherwise obligatory mass, were requested by the school authorities to step out of the ranks of the student body that had been lined up in the courtyard. Some twenty Protestants and three or four Jewish boys stepped aside. "We did not feel any shame at being Protestant or Jewish," writes Maurois; "but we felt, at that solemn moment [that we were] on the outside of a community which was nonetheless ours, and unhappy, very unhappy, without knowing why." [13] Later, when dealing with virtually identical events in the lives of Proust and Disraeli, Maurois, thanks to his own poignant boyhood remembrances, analyzed the Jewishness of these two figures with a very special insight.

Émile Herzog commuted between the secondary school in Rouen and his home in Elbeuf. Each morning he took the rickety train before six o'clock and arrived at the lycée by eight-thirty. Rising at five-thirty, he seemed to have enjoyed the ninety-minute ride to Rouen; it enabled him to review his homework from the night before as well as to chat with a few fellow students who shared the same daily ordeal. Why was this minor incident important in his life? Precisely because it was there and then that Maurois developed his lifelong habit of producing his finest work during the early hours of the morning. Besides, the daily train ride forms the basis for several interesting passages in *Cercle de famille (Family Circle)* one of his finest novels. As an adolescent, Maurois had already learned to function like a clocklike mechanism. His literary career was made possible by a most scrupulous arrangement of his time, especially by his efficient management of his morning hours.

Herzog's four-year stint at the Lycée Corneille came to an end in 1902. He graduated with the first prize in philosophy for all of France. Alain had taught him well! Herzog also obtained the first prize in the whole nation in Latin and

Greek "versions," and honorable mention in history. In the entire history of French education only two men have to date simultaneously earned four prizes in the rigorously stiff national competition: former prime minister André Tardieu and André Maurois.

B. *The World of Business and Industry (1903–1909)*

A universal problem is faced by most graduates: the selection of a career. Herzog weighed the alternatives. If he became a pedagogue, at least he could try to emulate his hero, Alain. This was a most tempting option. So he seriously considered presenting himself as a candidate for admission to the Ecole Normale Supérieure, France's most prestigious institution for teacher preparation. But his counselor Alain emphatically cautioned him against this too obvious choice. Citing his student's redoubtable facility in vanquishing all academic obstacles, Alain insisted that the hermetic Ecole Normale would separate the young man from the vibrant mainstream of life. There, his former teacher insisted, Herzog would develop into just another distinguished educator and would inevitably immerse himself in the sophisticated trends of an overly cynical Parisian intelligentsia. The master challenged his disciple to penetrate instead the arena of life and reality, to struggle and suffer, to watch the struggling and suffering of others. Alain advised his pupil to enter his father's wool mill, to climb the ladder of the family enterprise, from apprentice to executive, to work side by side with laborer and foreman, to seek to formulate a sympathetic understanding of the causes of employee discontent, to fathom the laws of finance, profit, investment. The obedient pupil obeyed.

First, Herzog obtained at the Université de Caën—with honorable mention—a Licence ès Lettres, with a major in philosophy. This episode of his life he completed with such ease that it fills no more than a brief parenthesis in his personal biography. Then he owed his country a year of obligatory military service. Actually, because his torso was "thin as a nail,"[14] and he had a deviated spinal column, he could readily have been classified unfit for military service. This disqualification he would have found revolting. Thus he vowed to follow the patriotic example not only of his father, but also of his uncles, all of whom had served in the armed services at one time or other. In 1903—three years prior to the date when he would normally have had to serve—he rushed to the enlistment center and persuaded the skeptical medical examiners to declare him medically fit for army service. He spent one year in the seventy-fourth infantry regiment, stationed near Rouen. In a chapter entitled "Ecole de Campagne,"[15] "Country School", he vividly recaptures some of the comical and quasi-tragic tribulations of garrison life. After four months he became a corporal; after eight, a sergeant. The army provided this frail and bookish fellow with the physical and psychological fortification he would later need for the subsequent rigors of life. He actually became more robust and gained weight, so much so that those who knew him in ensuing periods of life were incredulous at the thought that he had once been so fragile.

After his stint in the army, the wool mill at Elbeuf awaited his return to civilian status. There he was immediately thrust into the feverish universe of commerce. Learning to give orders to his subordinates and to implement orders from his superiors, he learned the relationship between the formulation, execution, and realization of top-level decisions. Out of his fascination with the tenuous equilibrium between those who govern and those who serve, there later emerged a number of works on the question of management, not the least important of which is a full-length treatise entitled *Dialogues sur le commandement (Dialogues on Commanding).*

Ernest Herzog retired in 1912, leaving the management of the wool mill in the hands of his son Emile, as well as to two of the latter's cousins, Pierre Herzog and André Fraenckel. Like his fictional heroes Bernard and Antoine Quesnay, this future author found his commitments divided awkwardly between his filial obligation to serve the family business, on the one hand, and his basic love of literature, education, and the arts, on the other. Every evening the exhausted young administrator returned home to spend his leisure hours locked in his room reading the classics of French and foreign letters. He could not extinguish within his soul the dream of becoming a writer. But, he never believed that someday he would have the leisure to develop into a creative artist. The poetry of the wool mill seemed mightier than the poetry of words.

Competition from abroad and from within France proved extremely menacing. Business was declining. Rising costs of labor were affecting profits adversely. Little money remained for expansion or modernization of the plant, or even for the development of new commercially more attractive products. Maurois set about overcoming these fiscal obstacles. To the surprise of everyone in the mill, he succeeded in rejuvenating his family's faltering company by pioneering in more efficient methods of weaving and production, by finding hitherto unexplored markets for French woolens, and above all by abandoning the fabrication of the conventional solid black woolens in favor of an original line of "fantaisie" or textured fabrics.

This period of life with the family firm added to his formative existence still another layer of educational values and worthwhile lessons. He learned not only how to deal with various highly competitive human beings; he mastered also some of the laws of economics and above all what he refers to as "the rules of action,"[16] that is, the desirability of making swift decisions, of avoiding the pitfalls of excessive analysis, and the necessity of taking concrete steps.

C. The World of Janine (1909–1914)

The year 1909 was another fateful one in his life. During a brief vacation in Geneva, Switzerland, Emile Herzog went backstage at the Théâtre des Eaux-

Vives to congratulate a brilliant French actress, Maggy Bertin, for her splendid performance. In Mlle Bertin's dressing-room he met a stunning blond woman with captivating eyes and a non-Gallic name, Janine de Szymkiewicz. The latter, a Russian girl of Polish descent, had been raised in French-speaking Switzerland. The young industrialist from grimy Elbeuf described this apparently sylphlike woman with words like "surprising beauty," "a perfect face," "a precise voice," "gently lunar burst of light."[17] His photographs of Janine, usually clad in white ermine, attest to his enthusiasm for her loveliness. Until his vacation in Geneva, Maurois, who had always believed himself to be master of his actions, now felt quite helpless in the presence of her charm. The real-life situation of Maurois paralleled that of Proust's character, Charles Swann: what began as a lofty love soon developed into the desire for undivided possession of the person loved and ultimately ended up in the most horrible jealousy and suspicion. The author's reticence, his denials notwithstanding, and the joys and anguish of Maurois's relationship with Janine de Szymkiewicz, form the basis for his finest novel, *Climats* (translated as *Atmospheres of Love*).

For months Emile Herzog spent his weekends traveling from Paris to Geneva to court the seductive Janine. Later she moved to Paris. Of course, he needed little excuse to escape from Elbeuf to rush to the capital where he even rented a small bachelor apartment on the rue de Madrid, a kind of foothold from which ostensibly he could conduct business, see an occasional play, concert or opera, and especially do so in the company of his sweetheart. So enamored was the future author with Janine that he was instrumental in arranging for her to get a proper education, first in a private secondary school in Brighton, England, then during a second year in another school in Oxford.

Marriage seemed at first to be out of the question. She was only eighteen years old, he twenty-seven. Imbued with a strong sense of practical philosophy, he knew that he should first be more solidly established in his family's business before marriage. Janine's education in the then remote English countryside proved to be the perfect pretext for Emile Herzog to take "business" trips to expand his firm's international market. Visiting Janine frequently in Oxford, he posed as her brother: the son of the very proper Alice and Ernest Herzog did not wish to violate British decorum. It was during these oxonion jaunts that the future author of *La Vie de Disraeli* learned to love not merely the ancient university town but also all of the English countryside.

How could he "sell" marriage with a Catholic girl from an unstable, even uncertain family background to his conventional, unromantic Jewish parents? In reality, the problem was aggravated more by the question of unlike family and social backgrounds than by that of religious disparities. How could he even discuss this kind of marriage in this family of extreme "pudeur?" "It was a trait of my family," he wrote once, "this impossibility of transmitting directly a painful message, or simply an important one, to the person for whom it was destined."[18] In the end love triumphed over all hurdles of reason and logic, and the faithful son obtained (through delicate and circuitous strategems) his parents' permission to marry the blond Janine.

Civil records certify that on October 30, 1912, Emil Herzog married Jeanne-Marie-Wande de Szymkiewicz. The civil marriage took place at the *Mairie* of the ninth *arrondissement* of the City of Paris. Later that day, to placate Janine's family, the wedding was blessed in the Church of the Trinity, situated in the parish in which Maurois had just rented a small apartment (4, rue Blanche, Paris IX). Soon the couple moved to the Elbeufean suburb of Caudebec-lès-Elbeuf, where they rented a small house. After several pleasant months there, Janine began to manifest signs of restiveness at the monotony of life in a small provincial town. Her husband, like most of the men in the Herzog and Fraenckel clans, was so devoted to his business enterprises that he was absent from the house most of the time. Nor did Janine feel especially at ease in the company of the Herzog family. She found them too staid, too unlike the more flamboyant types of her own family and former circle of friends. The atmosphere of inordinate discretion among the Herzogs proved overpowering for her. If 1913–14 were essentially happy years of life for the couple, slight crevices of discontent began gradually to crack the walls of their relationship during the war years of 1914–18, especially afterwards. Maurois himself confessed that ". . . we lived there, she and I, under the constant menace of Things Not Said. Mute monsters floated, unseen, among our vases of flowers and our shelves laden with books."[19]

Janine became pregnant in 1913. Her husband hoped that maternity might dispel the boredom of life for her in Elbeuf. But she longed for the more interesting life of Paris and persuaded her spouse to rent a ground-floor flat at no. 16, rue Ampère, in the seventeenth *arrondissement*. After all, she argued that she would require the expertise of Parisian doctors to take care of her coming delivery. The following year, their daughter, Michelle, was born. The tender Janine suffered a most difficult confinement and an even more painful childbirth, during which she almost died from a massive hemorrhage and was debilitated physically for a long time afterward. Less than three months later, World War I was declared.

D. The World of Barracks and Trenches (1914–18)

At the outbreak of hostilities in 1914, and with French soil once more subjected to German invasion, Emile Herzog—at the age of twenty-nine—felt morally compelled to leave his wife and child in order to enlist in the defense of his nation. Losing no time, on the very first day of the war, he enlisted once again in the army. After two years of marital bliss and three months of fatherhood, he knew intuitively that an era had come to a halt: "I felt that these hours, which were so cruelly and so tenderly rapid, were the last ones of my

Jeanne-Marie (Janine) Wanda de Szymkiewicz (1892–1924), first wife of André Maurois. (Photo by Otto and Pirou. Courtesy, Estate of André Maurois.)

youth."[20] And what a contrast between the climate of white flowers and white silken dresses in which Janine floated and that of the crude, coarse, and totally masculine life of the barracks and the mud of the trenches during the ensuing four years!

Janine saw Maurois's departure for the battlefield as her golden opportunity to extricate herself once and for all from the dismal life of Elbeuf and to settle down on a permanent basis in the more ebullient world of Paris. Besides, Maurois himself knew that there was no point in his family remaining in Elbeuf, since for the duration of hostilities he could not possibly hope to spend time at the wool mill of Fraenckel et Blin. So the couple abandoned their home in Elbeuf, never to return there as residents again. During the war years Janine divided her life between her Parisian apartment on the rue Ampère and rented houses in Rouen or in Le Havre, where her husband visited her during military passes. Then, between May and November of 1918, she moved to a rented villa, the Villa Calm'Abri on the picturesque Cap d'Ail, not far from Ville-franche on the Côte d'Azur.

Unable to adapt herself to a husbandless existence, and confused before the spectacle of a topsy-turvy world of wartime with its confused moral values,

Janine fell prey to a complex network of temptations and divided fidelities. Eventually, she suffered a nervous breakdown in her Riviera villa in November of 1918. A similar crisis of a woman in the throes of a breakdown is depicted in Maurois's novel *Cercle de famille.*

In the meantime, the life of the soldier-husband was no calmer. At the enlistment center he was stunned by the barking voice of an officer who assigned him, not to the French military forces but to the British Expeditionary Army in Flanders. Overestimating Herzog's knowledge of English, the army made of him a liaison officer and interpreter whose duty it was to link the two Allied commands. At first indignant at such a desk assignment, Maurois learned English on the job.

From curious twists like these, careers are made and broken. This participation as liaison officer had a marked influence on the career of the future author. Maurois developed such a fascination with the customs and eccentricities of his English military friends that he soon began to take notes daily on their behavior. Out of the threads of these notes he later wove his famous literary tapestries about the customs and people of the British Empire. He also learned to appreciate the traditional British virtues of stoicism and silence in the face of

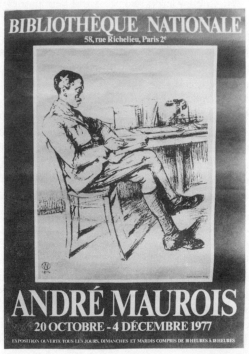

Official poster for the André Maurois Exposition and Colloquium at the Bibliothèque Nationale in Paris. Portrait of Maurois made in 1916. (Courtesy, Estate of André Maurois.)

adversity coupled with a subtle blend of humor and irony. These wartime literary experiences provided him with the incentive to write. Twenty years later André Maurois wrote of Chateaubriand words that aptly describe his own personal situation during 1914: "If he did not write his book, already he had a presentiment of it, he caressed it, he accumulated the materials for it."[21] Maurois's earliest titles, *Les Silences du Colonel Bramble* and *Les Discours du Docteur O'Grady*, express what he saw, heard, did, and felt in the company of his newfound British friends:

> I did not tell myself consciously: "I want to write a book on the English." It took form by itself. Slowly out of this poetic and warlike rumbling, there emerged a few types: the silent colonel whose name would one day be Bramble, I no longer know why; Major Parker, an aristocrat and a tory; Doctor O'Grady, a brilliant and paradoxical Irish fellow; the Padre, a militant Scotchman who was more combative than devout; finally the interpreter Aurelle, who resembled me like a brother and who wrote to his wife the verses which I composed for mine. All of that gave shape, about 1917, to a strange book which was neither a novel nor an essay, but which the few friends who read the manuscript loved.[22]

A whole world of British characters was born. Their names have since joined the repertory of the best-known characters of modern literature. Maurois later expanded his British repertory with real figures from the British past, for eventually he wrote the biographies of Shelley, Byron, Edward VII, Disraeli, Dickens, Browning, Rhodes. He also published abundantly on Shakespeare and Shaw, and on every conceivable aspect of British life and tradition. So firm was his appreciation of English culture that he later wrote a popular *History of England.* Would Maurois have become an author if he had not accidentally, so it seems, been assigned to Mission H of the British Army? Even if his irrepressible urge to write had later exteriorized itself one way or the other, the nature of his literature would probably have assumed a different form. Parenthetically, Maurois's first novel, *Ni ange, ni bête, (Neither Angel, Nor Beast)*, takes place in Abbeville, in northeastern France, a town in which he had been stationed with the British Army.

The budding writer permitted his close friend, Captain de Mun, to read his manuscript. The latter wept and laughed at the antics of Maurois's vividly caricatured English soldiers, their hilarious pranks, their rare moments of relaxation around the old hand-cranked victrola that churned out over and over again the catchy tune of "Destiny Waltz," their valorous deeds on the blood-stained battlefields, and their calm before the tragedies of war. So favorably impressed was De Mun that he urged Maurois immediately to publish the manuscript, especially while the civilian populations in France and England were psychologically prepared to appreciate these tales concerning the lives of their relatives at the front. Herzog's modesty prevented him from thinking that any publisher might be interested in his earliest literary undertaking. Nor did he know a single publisher to whom he could turn. De Mun offered to take the manuscript personally to a publisher friend, Bernard Grasset. Soon afterward, Emile Herzog learned to his astonishment that not only did Grasset accept the manuscript, but he actually planned to publish it immediately.

A new name rose in the literary skies of 1917, but it was not that of Emile Herzog. Fearful that the book might embarrass some of the British soldiers described there, the French military authorities insisted that the identity of the author not be disclosed, at least during the period of hostilities. Lieutenant Herzog thus was forced to drop coincidentally an obviously Jewish name in order to adopt a pen-name that was at once more euphonic, less ethnic, and above all an effective concealment of his identity. Emile selected "André," in memory of his beloved cousin who had recently been slain in battle. And "Maurois" was the name of a village near Cambrai where he had recently engaged in combat. "I like the sad sonority of this name . . . André Maurois. . . . How strange and new these syllables seemed to me then."[23] To a large proportion of his foreign readers, however, his choice of a pen-name was unfortunate: his name would be forever confused by many laymen with those of two other French authors, Mauriac and Malraux.

Bernard Grasset's publication of the *Bramble* in 1918 launched a close and lifelong affiliation between Maurois and this publisher. Always recalling that Grasset had been the one to give him his first chance, Maurois later allowed him to publish many of his finest titles, this in preference to making use of some of the more prestigious firms in the French publishing world. Maurois became one of the big five in Bernard Grasset's stable of "M's," along with Paul Morand, Henry de Montherlant, François Mauriac, and later André Malraux.

André Maurois, né Emile Herzog, learned with genuine amazement that *Les Silences du Colonel Bramble* was a spectacular success on both sides of the Channel. Tens of thousands of readers flocked to the bookstores to purchase this human wartime novel. The book was instantly translated into the world's major languages. So huge were the sales that Grasset commissioned Maurois to write a sequel to the *Bramble*. The now more confident Maurois gladly accepted. Four years later he produced *Les Discours du Docteur O'Grady*. Whereas the first book accentuated the reticence of the hero, the second depicts a garrulous British military physician expounding contentious arguments on virtually every major aspect of human life. Maurois never vanquished his obsession with the Bramble and O'Grady legends that he had created: two decades later he wrote an English-language article called "Colonel Bramble Up-To-Date,"[24] and again in 1950 he published a whole book-length dialogue *Les Nouveaux Discours du Docteur O'Grady (The New Discourses of Doctor O'Grady)*, a near masterpiece, in my judgment, in which he transports his English heroes into the nuclear age.

The *Bramble* and *O'Grady* were best-sellers in every sense of the term. The professional critics, Daniel Halévy, Abel Hermant, Lucien Descaves, and most of the others, wrote ecstatic reviews. Some of the major literary figures of the decade, to whom he had courageously asked Grasset to mail complimentary copies (Anatole France, Rudyard Kipling, Georges Clémenceau, Marshal Lyautey), were equally enthusiastic and responded to the young author with invitations to visit them following his release from military service.

Emile Herzog, industrialist, had entered the army in 1914. Following the armistice of November 11, 1918, André Maurois, budding author, returned to an ailing, disturbed wife, to a child whom he only partially knew, and to a family wool mill that had badly declined.

E. The World of the Widower (1918–25)

A confused soul returned to a confused world. At age thirty-three, his hair had turned completely white. In spite of his lingering devotion to the family business, it did not attract him any longer. Smitten by success as a writer, hardened by the experiences at the front, Maurois was eager to embark upon more ambitious literary ventures. Yet, because he continued to feel a sense of commitment to the family wool mill—then known as Fraenckel et Herzog—he decided to return to Elbeuf at least long enough to get some of its war-neglected activities back on a firm footing. "For five years still, I lived on the frontier of the industrial and the literary worlds."[25] It was not until 1923 that he mustered the courage to make his final rupture with industry.

Maurois had hoped to share the reins of industrial management with two of his cousins, but both (including his namesake André Herzog) had been killed in the war. Somehow the mill without these two men now seemed empty. This provided all the more reason to withdraw from an enterprise that had little appeal for him, especially now that he knew that he could be a successful author.

Furthermore, he knew that Janine could never be persuaded to return to Elbeuf. Paris truly attracted him; after all, he had acquired quite a reputation there and was welcomed warmly by some of the most prestigious literary figures. He wrote: ". . . I formed the project, which four years earlier would have seemed inconceivable, of leaving the factory, my town, my province, and go and rebuild, on a new plane, a life which the war had sown with ruins."[26] He moved to Paris in 1919. The landlord of his rue Ampère apartment offered him a much more spacious ground-floor residence with a private garden, a rarity in Paris, located in the fashionable west suburban extension of Paris, Neuilly-sur-Seine. This apartment, situated in a well-appointed building at the corner of the stately tree-lined boulevard Victor Hugo and the rue Borghèse. For twelve years the author of *Bramble* resided at that address. It was there that two sons were born: Gérald and Olivier (born on September 8, 1920, and October 10, 1921, respectively).

Maurois opened the first phase of his new literary career with the novel *Ni ange ni bête,* published in 1919. Devoid of the vividness of his first wartime books, lacking a clearly delineated central character, and too heavily reminiscent of the nineteenth-century novelist Stendhal, it is understandable why *Ni ange ni bête* should have enjoyed such scant success. However, Maurois was undaunted by his first less-than-successful book. Realizing that his forte lay not in novels about past eras, he returned to the form in which he excelled: the fictional representation of contemporaneous events that he had personally witnessed during the war. In his third title, *Les Discours du Docteur O'Grady,* he regained the verve of the Bramble, and its success was both immediate and impressive.

In 1920 and again in 1921 Maurois traveled to London to renew old wartime associations with his British friends of the battlefield. But he also did research in preparation for a projected biography of the poet Shelley. Observing closely the vagaries of British life, he met for the first time the novelist Maurice Baring, who remained a lifelong friend and whose novels in French translation he promoted in France with the utmost fervor. Through the intercession of Baring, Maurois met the biographer Harold Nicolson, the critic Desmond MacCarthy, and above all the well-known Bloomsbury circle of writers. With these English authors he spent days exchanging ideas about the art of writing biography. It was Nicolson in particular who must have played some part in turning Maurois toward biography. Through Baring he also met Hilaire Belloc, Lady Wilson, Duff Cooper, and other notables of high British society. General Byng, whom he had already known during the Great War, introduced him to the eminent statesman Sir Austen Chamberlain. Someday Maurois would write laudatory essays about him in the French press. Through Lady Colefax, one of the leading ladies of British aristocracy, the society in which Maurois learned to feel most at home, he finally met Rudyard Kipling, one of his real idols, with whom he remained associated until the British author's death in 1936. During the twenties, the French author spent a significant part of his time sojourning in a charming English manor, Avebury, in the Wiltshire countryside, the atmosphere of which pervades many of his books and articles.

Meanwhile in France, Paul Desjardins, the respected French writer and professor of literature at the Ecole Normale de Sèvres, invited André Maurois in 1922 to spend "une décade" (a sojourn of ten days) as his guest in the ancient Abbaye de Pontigny. This restored monastery had been regularly used by French intellectuals as a center in which to debate the burning topics of literary creativity. It was at Pontigny that Maurois, a writer entirely formed outside of the ultra-sophisticated literary milieux of Paris, first encountered en masse the Parisian and international snobbish society of creative artists who consumed their time not only in writing but also in debating methods of writing. At the time the group consisted of men like André Gide, Edmond Jaloux, Robert de Traz, Jean Schlumberger, Roger Fry, Lytton Strachey, Ernest-Robert Curtius. Once, while en route to Pontigny in a train, he accidentally shared his seat in the same compartment with the distinguished critic Charles Du Bos and his wife. Out of this chance encounter the three developed a long, intimate friendship.

But Pontigny was not Maurois's cup of tea. He found that he could not endure the pontifications and endless analyses of super-intellectuals. Essentially a doer, not a talker, Maurois preferred to write, not to discuss writing. Verbose exchange, he believed, led away from, rather than toward, real productivity. His novelette *Voyage au pays des Articoles (Trip to the Country of the Art-Lovers)* satirizes the men of Pontigny and represents about the only tangible piece of writing he could draw out of his own "voyage to the land of Pontigny." Later in life Maurois seemed to have mellowed in his attitude toward Pontigny and stressed not the artificiality and snobbishness of the men he saw there but rather something more positive: he insisted that it was the first time he had personally come into contact with creative artists of real intellectual caliber. A few he even befriended and came to admire both as persons and as artists.

In contrast with the external successes of his literary career, Maurois and his wife had serious problems of personal adjustment. The flighty Janine provoked great uneasiness in him, even jealousy and anger. However, she contracted the fatal blood disease of septicemia. The lovely Janine died at the tender age of thirty-one, on February 26, 1924, leaving behind three young children and a profoundly grief-stricken husband. It is difficult to predict what might have happened to this marriage had she lived longer. Maurois had never ceased to adore her, in spite of all of their domestic tensions. Janine de Szymkiewicz Herzog-Maurois lies buried today in the quaint parish cemetery of La Saussaye, near the spot where Maurois had owned a vacation manor. Ironically, this lovely Norman cemetery is not far from Janine's hated Elbeuf.

Maurois was left with only "the enchantment of that which had been" and "the bitter regret of that which might have been."[27] Never had he experienced a more total despondency. Tormented by his many confused emotions, this winner of first prizes even considered suicide as a possible escape from his sorrow. The tragic wound caused by the death of Janine he describes candidly in the *Mémoires* (chapter entitled "Il faut tenter de vivre ["One must attempt to live"], vol. 2) and also in the fictional transposition of the event in the sad pages devoted to the death of his nymphlike character, Odile, in the novel *Climats*.

For months the romantic widower continued to fill the vases of his Neuilly home with white flowers, just as Janine had done. He displayed photographs of her in every cranny of the flat. But Maurois was not one to yield to the inaction of despair for too long a time. He was reminded of the voice of his teacher Alain, who had exhorted his pupils never to fall victim to the forces of emotion, never to lose hope in the battle of life. Happiness, Alain taught, was the prize gained only following a courageous, incessant struggle against the obstacles from within and without. Parenthetically, one of the most constantly repeated themes in Maurois's literature is that of the necessity of suffering in order to gain happiness.

Maurois's closest friends, Gide, Du Bos, Madame Du Bos, Anne Desjardins, and more especially the faithful Bernard Grasset, continued to console him during their frequent visits to his rue Borghèse apartment. Grasset even tried to inject in Maurois a taste for life by taking him occasionally away from the apartment so pervasively filled with the phantoms of Janine. A writer-friend, Alfred Fabre-Luce, whom he had met at Pontigny, forcefully took him to two flourishing literary salons, the Wednesdays at the home of the Duchesse de la Rochefoucauld and the Mondays at the home of the Comtesse de Fels. There he met many of the major writers of the day.

F. The World of Simone de Caillavet (1925–26)

The enterprising publisher Bernard Grasset, interested in promoting the career of one of his best-selling authors, did what he could to draw the writer outside his syndrome of mourning by pushing him increasingly into the web of literary society. Charles du Bos, too, trying to sublimate the widower's bereavement, led him into the company of the witty critic Edmond Jaloux, who at that time exercised significant power over the literary world by virtue of his position as chief critic for the influential weekly *Les Nouvelles Littéraires*. Maurois found Jaloux's intellectually and artistically oriented wife, Germaine, to be equally stimulating company. Thanks to du Bos too, Maurois involved himself in a close friendship with Jean-Louis Vaudoyer. The Jaloux couple "had become precious friends," and it was Madame Jaloux in fact who introduced him to what would become for him the irresistible universe of Wagnerian music.[28] This fact is not insignificant: in Wagner he learned how to adapt to literature the principle of the leitmotiv, a literary device which manifested itself in many of his biographies and in at least one of his novels. Also, he made frequent reference to Wagnerian operas in the novels *Climats* and *Cercle de famille*, and in the short story "Tu ne commettras pas l'adultère" ("Thou Shalt Not Commit Adultery") in *Les Dix Commandements (The Ten Commandments.)* Later, when he met the woman destined to become his second wife, another Wagnerian worshiper, the links between the two were cemented through their shared enthusiasm for this composer.

On December 2, 1924, the publisher Grasset introduced the widower to the salon of Madame Simone de Caillavet. Maurois consented to go there for one single reason: he expected to meet Marshal Pétain, the then highly esteemed hero of World War I. He wished to discuss with the Marshal his own recently published book *Les Dialogues sur le Commandement*. Maurois was curious to learn how the Marshal had reacted to his treatise. The military hero never appeared. Instead the author met equally fascinating people, among whom were Robert de Flers, the successful playwright, and Paul Valéry, the renowned poet. From the hostess of this literary salon he expected little but the usual gracious but ritualistic hospitality that one came to expect from those several reigning elderly dowagers of Paris society who had taken it upon themselves to preside over weekly salons. He had assumed that his hostess, Madame de Caillavet, would be the legendary lady friend of Anatole France, the same socialite who had inspired this Nobel Prize winner to compose some of his most noteworthy pages. Instead, Maurois confessed that "I was delightfuly surprised when . . . I was introduced to a young woman. My hostess was pretty, dressed in a stunning manner in a black and white dress."[29]

In reality, Madame Simone de Caillavet was the granddaughter of Anatole France's "friend," Madame Arman de Caillavet. She was also the daughter of the playwright Gaston de Caillavet (celebrated because of his collaboration with Flers in the theatrical partnership of Flers et Caillavet), and of the former Jeanne Pouquet, who figured so importantly in the career of Marcel Proust. At one time Proust even claimed that he loved no woman more deeply than Jeanne Pouquet. When the latter married Gaston de Caillavet, Proust insisted— though we may easily question his sincerity—that he was totally heartbroken. One may safely contend that Jeanne Pouquet served as the likeliest inspiration for Proust's famous character Gilberte Swann in *A la recherche du temps perdu.* *(In Remembrance of Things Past).* And Simone de Caillavet, as a young girl, surely must have been the model for the youthful Mademoiselle de Saint-Loup. The fabulous salon of Madame Arman de Caillavet inspired many of the salon scenes in Proust's vast novel.

André Maurois and Simone de Caillavet met each other at a favorable psychological moment. Both had recently left behind them tragic experiences of terminated marital life; he as the result of the ultimely death of his spouse, and she becuase of the recent annulment of her short-lived marriage to a prominent Rumanian diplomat stationed in Paris. Maurois was immediately attracted to the rich literary atmosphere in which Simone was nurtured. Literature seemed virtually to flow in her veins, as he once put it. With her he had much in common. He and she both adored Wagner; both adored Proust. She had been trying to meet Maurois for some time, having recently devoured his latest books.

A true lady of the salons, Simone tried to draw into her weekly coterie not only the beautiful people of high Parisian society (for there is no doubt that her snobbish taste gravitated toward the habitués of the salons of Paris), but as the stellar attractions for this special clan she sought out as guests the brightest names of the creative arts. During the mid-nineteen-twenties Maurois was such a bright name. The moment she met him she realized that he would be more than a compatible literary associate: "We had the same tastes in literature, the same preference for the genius of the English people. Music also brought us closer: two years later he was my husband."[30] Following one unhappy marriage with a nonliterary husband, Simone, who had been virtually raised on the laps of Marcel Proust and Anatole France, vowed that she would devote herself to literature as a nun consecrates herself to faith.

The handsome, slender Maurois still presented a youthful appearance. Having freshly acquired the reputation of a world-famous author, he fitted in very nicely indeed with her intentions to confine herself to a literary existence. Maurois continued to frequent Simone's salon and also that of her mother, Jeanne Pouquet, on the avenue Hoche. It was there that he established close friendships with Admiral Lacaze, the two Poincarés, General Weygand, the poetess Anna de Noailles, the critic Paul Souday. Later, in *Choses nues (Bare Facts)* and in other journalistic writings, he chronicled the thoughts and activities of these celebrated personalities.

The year 1925 was one of the truly peripatetic moments in Maurois's life. Alone he took a trip through Italy in nostalgic search of records of the lives of Lord Byron and Chateaubriand, whose biographies he planned to write one day. During his Roman holiday he had a lengthy meeting with a then promising Italian leader named Benito Mussolini. In March of that same year, in the company of Emile Henriot the critic, he traveled to Casablanca to attend, as the personal guest of the governor-general and conqueror of Morocco, Marshal Lyautey, the inaugural ceremonies of the newly installed national railroad system. With Lyautey he launched a particularly intimate relationship, which culminated one day in his writing of the definitive biography of this soldier.

His father, Ernest Herzog, whom he had continued to visit with frequency, died that same year as the result of postsurgical complications. "Never did a more pure heart cease to beat," wrote the grief-stricken son.[31] The death of his father shattered most of the links between the world of Elbeuf and that of Paris. Only his mother remained in Elbeuf, and even she, several years later (in 1932), moved to a small apartment in Neuilly so that she could be close to Maurois, her son, and to her two daughters.

In the meantime Maurois continued sporadically to visit with Simone de Caillavet. After a year of courtship, to be exact on September 6, 1926, André Maurois and Simone de Caillavet were married in the tiny stone Catholic church of St. Médard d'Excideuil, located in the heartland of the ancient province of Périgord, where the bride's family had had a chateau and estate. Immediately following the wedding, the couple visited the family graves of the new Simone Maurois, to pay tribute to her late father, Gaston Arman de Caillavet, buried in the little parish cemetery a stone's throw from the church.[32]

The marriage of Simone and André Maurois formed one of the most remarkable literary collaborations in French history. Michel Droit former editor of *Le Figaro Littéraire*, once described this unique relationship like this: "In contemporary literature, there exists no example of a union of two beings as perfect as this one, two beings who were predestined for each other, even in their world."[33]

Refusing the role of homemaker in charge of the domestic routine of her household, Simone Maurois chose instead to play an active part in orchestrating her husband's professional career. She could make this choice because both she and her husband could afford to keep in their employ a team of faithful servants: housekeepers, cooks, a chauffeur, a valet de chambre, a governess for the children. Her days—and indeed, large segments of her nights—she spent working on various literary projects for her husband.[34] Maurois was the artist; Madame the scholar, the seeker of facts, documents, statistics; the one who tracked down sources at the Bibliothèque Nationale, the Spoelberch de Louvenjoul Collection in Chantilly, the Commissariat de Police, the department of vital statistics at the Paris Morgue, even the cellars and attics of old chateaus and museums where she would accidentally stumble upon old chests filled with valuable manuscripts, Simone Maurois was indeed a superb genealogist! Gifted with a rare tenacity for ferreting out necessary facts and possessor of a highly systematic mind, she was endowed with what Maurois once characterized as "a merciless memory." The usefulness of such talents cannot be overemphasized, especially when they were placed at the disposal of a biographer and historian. Without his wife's support, Maurois simply could never have found the time necessary to do both the research and the artistic formulation of his major works.

As a hobby—and an expensive one—Madame Maurois collected autographed letters of famous men and women from around the world. Hers eventually became one of the finest privately held epistolary collections in Europe. It included missives by George Sand, Balzac, Musset, Dumas père and fils, Victor Hugo, and hundreds of other literati, artists, statesmen, and aristocrats. Needless to say, this collection proved to be most serviceable to the future biographer of the great French romantic authors. Besides aiding her husband in the documentation of his historical and biographical publications, Simone Maurois learned to type with astonishing accuracy and speed, so that she could prepare the successive and multiple versions of his manuscripts before he sent them to the publishers. Finally, she figured among only a handful of human beings who could easily read his microscopic and virtually illegible handwriting.

The casual visitor to Madame Maurois's library, which once overlooked the Bois de Boulogne, was immediately impressed by the luxurious bindings of the volumes that filled the shelves from floor to ceiling. Had this visitor wandered into an adjacent bathroom, he would have stumbled onto the overflow from this collection piled in the bathtub and all over the floor. Leafing through the shelves, he would have found the vast collection of André Maurois's complete works. On the title pages of these books he would quickly discern the essential facts revealing the true literary and personal relationship that held this couple together. Numerous interesting handwritten dedications by Maurois for his wife's personal copies underscore the fact that theirs was not merely a personal liaison, but also—and perhaps primarily!—a professional union of two people who needed each other for literary self-fulfillment. The bound edition of Maurois's *Mémoires* bears a handwritten *dédicace* sketching the period of their exile in America during the Second World War: "For Simone, in memory of those months of 1941 during which, in our unhappiness, we had the happiness of being together." Simone's volume of the novel *Bernard Quesnay*, published during the year of their marriage, bears an inscription in which Maurois calls her "a material and spiritual collaborator." In a more intimate vein, his volume concerning marital life, *Cours de bonheur conjugal (Course of Conjugal Bliss)*, bears the following inscription to Simone: "Why do I love my wife? . . . Well she has the same tastes as I. . . . My wife gives her life to my work, she is my social secretary; she works ten hours per day—and sometimes into the night— and always works well. . . ." The most tender dedication is in the form of a delightful jingle Maurois once wrote for Simone's copy of *Destins exemplaires (Exemplary Destinies)*: "The exemplary destiny/Is to be your spouse./This sentence is most clear;/let's not add anything at all (to it)."[35]

It is noteworthy that each of Maurois's novels following his earliest one, *Ni ange ni bête*, is officially dedicated "à Simone." The union between André Maurois and Simone de Caillavet Maurois lends itself to a fascinating bi-level study all by itself. Those interested in exploring the private crevices of their conjugal life may find much food for speculation in part 2 of *Climats*, *Terre promise*, *Cercle de famille*, and *Les Roses de septembre*. Most of Maurois's closest associates speculated privately about the extent to which his fiction coincided with his real existence. These speculations appear to be rather well founded, this despite Maurois's repeated insistence that fiction was fiction and life was life. One thing is certain: some of Maurois's personal life he has transformed with varying degrees of inventiveness into fictional themes; but in other instances he seems to have been unwilling or unable to convert some of the raw material of life into the ingredients of his novels.

Because the couple worked so closely, and because they quite obviously cared deeply for one another, the two relationships, personal and professional, were intertwined. In the essay "L'Art d'aimer" ("The Art of Loving") Maurois described the necessity of husbands and wives to cooperate fully in every aspect of their shared existence, even in the husband's business or profession. What he had to say in one of his aphorisms aptly sums up his own particular situation with his wife: "All work done with love is delightful, but love blended with work is what is the most delightful thing in the world. Thus are born these marvelous couples of scholars, artists, apostles, who are simultaneously a couple and a team."[36]

Out of his marriage with the former Simone de Caillavet grew Maurois's lifelong attachment to the Périgord region of France. Into her marriage Simone brought her huge estate, Essendiéras, with its impressive chateau and many hundreds of productive acres. The property, situated near the village of St. Médard d'Excideuil, in the northern tier of the modern department of Dordogne, became after their marriage a major center of intellectual and literary life. On intertwining his fortunes with those of the chatelaine from Périgord, Maurois the industrialist from Normandy duplicated the actions of the hero

Simone Arman de Caillavet, Maurois's second wife. (Courtesy, Estate of André Maurois.)

and heroine in his novel *L'Instinct du bonheur (The Instinct for Happiness)*, wherein a Norman husband establishes himself in his wife's Dordogne residence. Moreover, the Chateau d'Essendiéras is disguised under the name of Gandumas in *Climats* and appears in its own name in many of his essays and chronicles about chateau life. So faithful was Maurois to the Périgord area that he authored a lavishly illustrated guidebook entitled *Périgord*, issued in a special travel series by Hachette in 1955. For almost a half century Maurois spent most of his vacations in Essendiéras. Its patrician climates blended effortlessly with some of his most inspired pages of prose.

B. *The World of the New Marriage (1926–30)*

The new couple confronted some immediate practical problems. Their family now included four children: Maurois's own three by his first wife—his daughter, Michelle, and the two sons, Gérald and Olivier—and Simone's little daughter, Françoise, from her former annulled marriage to a Rumanian diplomat. The couple had first of all to resolve their housing problem.

If their housing needs had been settled with a minimum of difficulty, their

André and Simone Maurois with writer Robert de Flers, at the tomb of Simone's playwright father, Gaston Arman de Caillavet. In the parish cemetery of Saint Médard d'Excideuil. Photo taken on the day of Simone and André Maurois's marriage in 1926. *(Courtesy, Estate of André Maurois.)*

The Chateau d'Essendiéras in the Périgord (Dordogne) region of France. Photo by Combier IMP. Maçon [CIM]. Courtesy, Estate of André Maurois.)

psychological problems of adjustment were not so simple. Despite the excellent location of the rue Borghèse, despite the spaciousness of their new two-story arrangement, Simone Maurois never grew accustomed to the place. Her husband unwisely continued to display Janine's photographs everywhere. Wherever the second spouse turned, she encountered lingering scents and mementos from a former bliss. It was quite apparent to her—and all of their associates— that the writer's first marriage had been *the* romantic episode of his life. Though Simone bore her plight with stoicism, she continued to complain about the poor light in the apartment. She could never resign herself to the fact that the salons, her own office, and all the bedrooms faced a bleak garden with a northern exposure that never received sunshine. Discreetly she started to press for brighter, more attractive quarters.[37] Five years after the marriage, her husband finally yielded—as he had done earlier in the case of Janine: they purchased a truly splendid, sun-drenched apartment at 86 boulevard Maurice Barrès in Neuilly. The boulevard, one of the most stately in the Paris region, runs along the eastern edge of the heavily wooded Bois de Boulogne, the capital's largest and most fashionable park. Facing the park on the boulevard Maurice Barrès, elegant, multi-storied apartment buildings rise majestically out of a lushly verdant base of tree-lined sidewalks. The Maurois family installed themselves in these new quarters on Bastille Day of 1931.

The period of the second marriage was one of exceptional literary fertility for Maurois. During the first fifteen years of his union with Simone de Caillavet, he wrote some of his finest novels: *Climats, Le Cercle de famille, L'Instinct du bonheur;* six biographies: *Don Juan ou la Vie de Lord Byron, La Vie de Disraeli, Lyautey, Tourguéniev, La Vie d'Edouard VII,* and *René ou la Vie de Chateaubriand;* a thick volume of history, *L'Histoire d'Angleterre;* and several other assorted anthologies of essays and short fiction.

Prior to his second marriage, his taste seemed more geared to the airy, light, ethereal, almost unreal atmosphere found in the life of a Shelley. Quite clearly he was under the spell of the fanciful Janine. But the systematic Madame Maurois steered her husband toward heavy and highly erudite projects. The complex lives of Chateaubriand, Sand, and Hugo demanded enormous attentiveness to the preparation of successive manuscripts and to the analysis of correspondence and private papers. As Philippe Marcenat, the hero of *Climats,* was transformed by the two women in his life, so the very malleable Maurois bent first before the force of the personality of Janine, and later before that of Simone. Maurois's critics were often divided into two camps: those who preferred the charming flightiness of the works written during marriage number one and those attracted to the more ponderous, large-scaled biographies of the second era of his life. No work dramatizes more graphically than *Climats* the dichotomy of Maurois's literary and personal existence. Part One (Odile) contains the fictional transposition of the first state of his conjugal bliss and its subsequent anxieties; Part Two (Isabelle) depicts the hero's struggle to adjust to the more practical exigencies of life with a more realistic, unromantic wife.

Between *Climats* and the ensuing novel, *Le Cercle de famille*, *(The Family Circle)*, the novelist had undergone a virtual metamorphosis: he had been transformed from a relaxed and romantic writer into one who was more deliberate, structured, and, above all, more meticulously documented.

After 1931 Maurois divided most of his existence between the brilliant social and literary life of Paris, which radiated from the boulevard Maurice Barrès residence, and the more leisurely life of the rustic Chateau d'Essendiéras.[38] Even there, during vacations, however, he continued to write during much of the daylight hours, and his wife continued to type nightly.

As Maurois grew in stature, honors of all sorts were conferred upon him, one by one.[39] A fundamentally modest person, for whom nothing mattered outside of his ability to produce literary works, he accepted these honors both with a sense of mild satisfaction and also with irritation that these accolades often consumed too much of his valuable time. He wife, on the other hand, far more socially oriented, far more status-conscious, urged her husband ever onward, from prize to prize and honor to honor. Here are a few of the more noteworthy events of the period 1926–30 in which he received recognition for a job well done:

A. 1926: Maurois was named Chevalier de la Légion d'Honneur.
B. 1927: he was invited to deliver a series of lectures throughout the United States. From this date can be traced Maurois's ardent attachment to the people and land of America.
C. 1928: he delivered the Clark Lectures at Cambridge University in England. Succeeding E. M. Forster, who had spoken during the previous year on "Aspects of the Novel," Maurois treated an area in which he had developed quite a competence: "Aspects of Biography," the texts of which were later published in volume-form under the same title.
D. 1928 (June): he received his first doctorate honoris causa at the University of Edinburgh in Scotland.
E. Between 1928–30 he lectured on Lord Byron throughout the European continent: Vienna, Berlin, Bucharest, Istanbul, Athens, and Missolonghi, Greece. (Maurois was busy working on his biography of Byron at the time, a work that involved him in the essential research for this complex topic at the British Museum, in Italy, and Greece.)

A personal loss terminated this period of his life: his stepdaughter, Françoise-Georgina, suddenly died of cirrhosis of the liver during a vacation in the Alps. The child's mother, Simone Maurois, at the time physically incapacitated by major surgery, could not even attend the funeral rites and burial of her only offspring. The child was buried in the parish cemetery of St. Médard d'Excideuil near Essendiéras. Furthermore, as a result of her surgery, Madame

Maurois learned to her grief that she could never have other children. These unhappy occurrences affected André Maurois very deeply. His life illustrates his own thesis that human existences inevitably consist of a blend of happiness and sadness interwoven in a single tapestry.

H. The World of Old Nassau—1930

Maurois, who had already lectured to numerous American university audiences during his first trip to the New World, began increasingly to be pursued by learned societies and academic institutions inviting him to accept their many attractive propositions: speaking assignments, professorships, lecture tours. Among the academic acquaintances he had made earlier on the campus of Princeton University were the French professor Maurice Coindreau, Dean Christian Gauss, and University President Hibben. In 1930 the Pyne family, one of Princeton's most generous groups of benefactors, had established the Meredith Pyne Chair in French Literature. Maurois was invited to be the first to hold this title. After much soul-searching about his qualifications to teach as part of the faculty of a great university, he decided to accept, but only for one semester. He and his wife sailed to America in the fall of 1930. With them they took their two most faithful servants, Emilie and Gaston Wolff, a young Alsatian couple who later figured among their most untiring, supportive domestics.

The Princeton adventure proved to be a truly happy interlude in the life of the Maurois couple. Madame consider it a kind of honeymoon, four years after the fact. After all, they found themselves far from the old haunts that were so permeated with tensions and memories of the past. In Princeton she had her husband all to herself; her stepchildren had been left with their nannies and tutors in France.

Maurois gave a formal course on the French novel, from *La Princesse de Clèves* to Proust, also a series of public lectures designed principally for the broad Princeton community. Professor Coindreau, who could closely observe Maurois's performance as a professor of French literature, testified in the most glowing terms about the successful performance of the writer as a professor.[40] Most of his students agreed that his was one of the best-prepared, best-presented, and inspiring courses in their college careers.[41] So effective a teacher was the author of *Bramble* that he was invited to retain the Pyne Chair. It was true that he adored the idyllic charm of the then quaint college town of Princeton. He enjoyed too the spontaneity and original thinking of his American students. He had established close rapports with many of them by virtue of his participation in the Woodrow Wilson Preceptorial Program at Old Nassau. In fact, his novelette, *La Machine à lire les pensées*, really a curious combination of science fiction and fact, is imbued with the charm of the life-style of the Maurois couple during their Princeton venture. Furthermore, we may assume that virtually all of Maurois's short stories on American campus life are inspired directly by the things he personally saw during his tenure at Princeton.

Maurois the biographer-historian went to Princeton not only to teach in and to experience the delights of an ideal college community; he went there also to do the research needed for a projected biography of Woodrow Wilson, a figure who had fascinated him since the conclusion of the First World War. Once in Old Nassau, however, he discovered, much to his astonishment, that this president-statesman, so widely admired by the Europeans, was a most controversial figure in his own college town. So controversial was Wilson that Maurois could barely obtain unbiased opinions on the Princeton campus concerning the late president's presence from any of the living witnesses of the Wilsonian era there. The biographer prudently decided to postpone tentatively the pursuit of his project. This tentative postponement ended up by becoming definitive. Maurois never returned to his original plan, except in the chapter devoted to the Wilson presidency in his *History of the United States.*

When the fall term drew to a close, the Maurois couple decided, despite the invitation to remain, to return to their beloved shores of France. This they did with a keen sense of sadness, for they had developed a sincere affection for America and her people.

I. The World of the Thirties (1931–38)

Throughout the thirties the author's international reputation grew steadily. In America and elsewhere, generations of young men and women learned to read French in anthologies filled with his lucid prose. Honors continued to proliferate. He was elevated from Chevalier to Officier de la Légion d'Honneur on January 12, 1932; five years later, on July 29, 1937, he was promoted to the title of Commandeur de la Légion d'Honneur.

The five-year span of 1932–37 Maurois regarded as his least productive (hence, his least successful) period. At that time of life, he did spread his energies possibly a bit too widely: numerous lecture tours in France and abroad, two major lecture series in Paris, and so on. In three years, only one full-length book, *L'Histoire d'Angleterre, (The History of England)*, emerged from what Maurois lamentingly called "this scattering of my efforts."[42] Nonetheless, his self-denigration is partly ungrounded; his foreign and domestic adventures certainly did yield some interesting fruits. In his bibliography of the early thirties one notes various volumes on travel (America, Malta, etc.), a small-scaled but sprightly biography of Voltaire, impressive biographies of Tourguéniev and King Edward VII of Britain (both based on texts of lectures delivered in Paris). Two important novels, *L'Instinct du bonheur (The Instinct for Happiness)* and *Le Cercle de famille,* date from the first half of the decade. Maurois had also forgotten that during this period of travel and lecturing he composed several volumes of short fiction, essays of criticism, studies of moral conduct. That he could travel so extensively and still produce copiously proves his extraordinary vitality and physical energy.

André Maurois in his mid-forties, at the height of his productive years. (Courtesy, Estate of André Maurois.)

André Maurois and friends. *From left to right:* Maurois, the poet Valéry, and the novelist Paul Morand, at the Chateau de Montmirail (Marne), taken in July 1930. (Courtesy, Estate of André Maurois.)

Here is an accounting of some of the more significant trips he undertook between 1930 and 1935, always in the company of his wife. First, he spent three months as a visiting professor of French at the Lycée Français in Alexandria, Egypt. This was his first exposure of Near-Eastern culture. Then he spent an entire spring on the island of Malta, as a guest of the British Governor General of the Crown Colony. His particularly profound appreciation of Maltese history and life have been recaptured in his volume *Malta* (1935). Two summers he spent in the English countryside and at London's British Museum as he did research in preparation for his history of England.

Maurois spent much of the thirties in the close company of some of the leading French public figures of the era. *Choses nues (Bare Things)* and the *Mémoires* recount one of the least-known aspects of his career: the extent to which he mingled with the great men of state of his lifetime. Men like Mauriac and Malraux are well known for their closeness to major figures like Charles de Gaulle; but it is also a fact that few important events of state took place without Maurois being a participant in them. In 1932 he witnessed an unforgettable drama. One day, while only a few feet away from Paul Doumer, then president of the French Republic, the Russian madman Gorguloff rushed into the gilt chamber and fatally shot the president. Maurois was subsequently selected to serve with the president's closest associates and watch over his remains during the state funeral at the Elysée Palace.[43] With prophetic uneasiness Maurois noted the tragic advent of Hitler in Germany. He was among the first French men of letters publicly to deplore the appeasement policies of France and Britain. He complained that both countries sought to assuage the anger of this mad dictator by refusing to halt him before his power assumed frightful proportions.

Some of Maurois's less friendly critics occasionally blamed him for being uncommitted to human, national, and social causes. A close examination of his record fails to sustain their criticisms. During the thirties he spoke frequently before groups of workers and students, especially the Equipes Sociales (Social Teams) and the Union Chrétienne de Jeunes Gens (The Christian Union of Youth). He warned them against the divisive perils that fragmented France into all sorts of right-wing and left-wing political factions. In fervent pleas for national unity, he evoked with anxious foreboding the spector of Nazi Germany, which had just plunged with monolithic unity into feverish military preparations. Working closely with Pierre Brisson, the editor of the influential daily *Le Figaro*, as well as with Wladimer d'Ormesson, Lucien Romier, and Paul Morand, all concerned writers like him, he and they not only addressed groups but also editorialized, principally in *Le Figaro*, pleading for national solidarity.

Despite his national commitments, he found time to accept an additional string of honors. In 1933 he returned to America to receive an honorary doctorate from his former "employer," Princeton University. That same year he had a lengthy meeting at the White House with President Franklin Delano

Roosevelt, who sounded him out on the nature of public attitudes in France. Maurois and the President engaged in what the former described as a passionate discussion on the New Deal measures to bring economic relief to a depressed American populace. Soon afterward, the French author, who almost always transformed his personal adventures into literary form, wrote several books and articles on the New Deal and on the economic crisis in the New World, books and articles in which he expressed unconcealed admiration for President and Mrs. Roosevelt and for their efforts to alleviate the crippling conditions of the American Depression.

In 1934 Oxford bestowed upon this fervent anglophile her doctorate honoris causa. Not to be outdone, the distinguished Scottish University of Saint Andrews followed suit with a similar doctorate.

During the thirties Doctor André Maurois was so widely recognized as an ambassador of good will that there was scarcely an event involving France, England, and America to which he was not automatically invited. So it was that in February of 1936, upon the death of George V, he was asked to pronounce before the prestigious Franco-British Society of London the major funeral oration marking this sad event. On May 12, 1937, named by the British government to its highest honorary order, he received the title of knight Commander of the British Empire. That same year he eagerly accepted an invitation to attend the coronation festivities for King George VI and Queen Elizabeth in Westminster Abbey. This ceremony left on the French author an ineradicable mark of the richness of British history, while it profoundly impressed Madame Maurois, who took delight in mingling with the international society attending the event.

Maurois continued to scatter his energies. During the second half of the thirties he wrote weekly chronicles in several newspapers, especially in *Paris-Soir*, where he covered current events ranging from refugee and labor problems to the rise of fascism in Italy. In 1937 he became the film reviewer of *Cinémonde* magazine. He enjoyed going to movies, and it was not long before he was regarded not only as a successful novelist, biographer, historian, and lecturer, but also as an undisputed authority on the art of the cinema in France. Weekly he contributed his "La Semaine Théâtrale" column ("The Theater's Week" in the women's magazine *Marianne*. In addition to his work with periodicals, he gave generously of his time and money during 1937 to help make possible the emigration out of Nazi Germany of the eminent author Thomas Mann. One may also add that he found time to serve on the literary jury of the Prix Albert Ier of Belgium.

In 1938, following years of research, he published his first major biography in a long time, *René ou la Vie de Chateaubriand*, a work that must be regarded as one of his crowning achievements in a genre that became his specialty.

In sum, contrary to his own self-evaluation, the thirties were a decade during which he had demonstrated a remarkable physical endurance and literary fertility. His published articles, essays, and prefaces numbered in the hundreds. He

André Maurois wearing the academic robe of Oxford University on the occasion of his receiving the Doctorate Honoris Causa, June 1934. (Portrait by Philip de Laszlo.)

had produced at least twenty published volumes, all of which were instantly translated into many of the languages of the world. Maurois, at the prime of life, had reached the beginning of his fifth decade. The supreme recognition of a literary figure in France—l'Académie Française—lay ahead.

J. The World of the Academy (1938–39)

Maurois had for the first time sought admission to the Academy in 1936. He was rejected. But defeats were for him but temporary setbacks. He made himself available again as a candidate in 1938, when a vacancy developed after the death of René Doumic, the lifetime secretary of that company of writers. This time, on June 23, 1938, the Academicians voted for Maurois. André Chevrillon, a well-known anglophile, had been selected to deliver the traditional discourse to welcome another anglophile. The initiation ceremony for Maurois, scheduled on June 22, 1939, preceded the start of World War II by only three months and was actually the last such ceremony until after the liberation of France.

The pages of Maurois's *Choses nues*, otherwise barren of personal sentiment, betray the nervous tension experienced by him as he awaited the results of the Academy elections. If Maurois had by now understandably acquired an unusual degree of sang-froid, the Academy was something special. Perhaps it was the fact that the organization was the product of centuries of continuous French history. Perhaps too, few French writers could treat this institution with total disinterestedness. A few writers have considered it with derision; most, however, have coveted membership in it. Maurois clearly belonged to the second group. His notes of June 23, 1938, reveal his uneasiness as he speculates concerning his chances of being elected. This concern was dispelled when a journalist phoned Madame Maurois to announce the good news: Maurois had been elected on the first ballot by a majority of nineteen Immortals. The Immortal-to-be described his reaction like this: "With joy are mingled astonishment and a strange sensation of emptiness."[44]

Thus a new era started for Maurois. No longer could he sign his name as an independent man, free of labels. Henceforth, he would need to sign his books "André Maurois of the French Academy."

The slot he was to occupy had been nicknamed "the chair of longevity." Since 1635, when Cardinal Richelieu had founded the Academy, only ten men before him had held tenure in this slot. Maurois continued the tradition of longevity, occupying that chair for almost three decades. Ironically, the ultraliberal Maurois succeeded René Doumic, the ultraconservative editor of *La Revue des Deux Mondes.* Several years earlier Doumic had refused to accept for publication Maurois's *Le Cercle de famille,* mainly because in this novel Maurois depicted a six-year-old girl who, in one of the minor scenes, discovered her mother in the midst of an adulterous affair. The Academic Discourse of André Maurois disclosed no rancor whatsoever against Doumic.[45]

In the conclusion of his discourse Maurois referred to Doumic as a rock of Gilbraltar, a pillar of strength in his defense of the traditional French virtues of clarity and order, in his simple and modest life of work for the sake of work, and in his zeal to perform a job with perfection. With obvious delight André Chevrillon, the Academician selected to respond to Maurois, paid tribute to the creator of the Bramble-O'Grady cycle for his role in having cemented the Entente Cordiale between Britain and France. Chevrillon labored also to stress the traits common to Maurois and Doumic: " '(Doumic) told me: Maurois not only has talent, he has common sense.' " Chevrillon went on to define "common sense" as it applied to Maurois as "the ability to distinguish between the true and the false, a kind of faith in the principles of conduct and social life that guide healthy minds."[46]

During the decades of his membership in the Academy, Maurois developed "the optics" and "a way of seeing things from the viewpoint of the Academy and as an Academician," according to Maurice Genevoix, the postwar perpetual secretary. The latter opined that no one embodied the ideals of the Academy more than Maurois, and none was more prompt or more regular in his attendance at the weekly Thursday afternoon meetings. Seldom did he miss a working session when the company involved itself in the endless, thankless task of preparing a new dictionary of the French language. An independent writer and thinker, who boasted that he belonged to no school of authors, Maurois stressed the importance of his affiliation with the Academy. Unlike writers like Sartre and Henri Michaux, who, fearful that their freedom as creative artists might be compromised by the acceptance of literary prizes and by membership in academic and literary societies, Maurois had always been a "joiner." But he joined societies only when he believed in the values they represented. He played an especially active part in the committees for the annual Prix du Roman and in the one that selected the Grand Prix Littéraire de l'Académie Française. Indeed it was fitting that, when he died in 1967, his funeral service should have taken place in the presence of his Academic colleagues in the courtyard of the palace in which the Academy met.

Whenever Maurois was called upon to address the Academy, he stressed two points: first, the need for the Company to be liberal enough to make room for the most nonconformist literary innovators, even when the candidates led such nonconformist existences as did a Jean Cocteau, for example; also, he stressed the need for the individual members to continue to uphold the traditional virtues symbolized by the Academy during three centuries of French history. Turning to Cocteau, who once had poked fun at the stodginess of the society, Maurois reminded the new member, on the occasion of his initiation into the Academy, of the following facts:

People never tire of citing the several great men who failed to be admitted to the French Academy; they refrain from adding that her happy audacities were more numerous than her timidities. It received, at the time of their youth, Lamartine and Victor Hugo; it honored Valéry, when the public did not know him; it surrounded Bergson with admiration and respect; it would have welcomed Proust, if he had not died prematurely. Among the men of talent, there are some who keep their distance from it; there is no one from whom it wishes to keep its distance. The eager welcome which it had given to you proves that it does not fear bad disciples, provided that they are good writers.[47]

Since his own initiation in 1939, he extolled the role of the French Academy many times. In the preface to a guidebook on Paris he wrote: "You will hear young people make fun of it, but one makes fun only of those things which one respects.[48] In a *Holiday Magazine* article aimed at American audiences, he noted that France survived as a nation mainly through the unifying work of such tradition-bound organisms as the Academy, the University, the military, the Church, the primacy of Paris, this in spite of the turbulent political upheavals, invasions, and fragmented class system of the French people. Institutions like the Academy, he insisted, lent to the French nation a sense of unified purpose.[49]

Not only did the year 1939 mark his entry into the Academy, but it was the year of one of his most triumphant trips to the New World. For thirty days he and his wife traveled by train from coast to coast lecturing before audiences who heaped upon him endless bouquets of adulation. In Washington, D.C., he lunched with President Roosevelt. High American society feted the new Academician with testimonial banquets and dinner dances. In New York this ambassador of French culture was guest of honor at the formal dedication of the French Pavilion of the World's Fair in 1939. But the champagne that flowed at receptions in New York, San Francisco, and Paris abruptly halted: World War II burst forth in September of that same year.

K. The World of the American Exile (1940–46)

As Hitler's hordes overran Poland in September of 1939, Maurois, then fifty-four years old, immediately placed his pen and his person at the service of the French high command. With his customary lucidity he wrote articles designed to bolster the morale of the uncertain populace of France. Publishing articles like "What One Must Be at Times of War," urging inner tranquillity, confidence, and discretion. In "How War Is Triggered Off" he treated his readers to a historical account of the background of the war, pinning the blame squarely—and convincingly on the Germans.[50] Elsewhere, this anglophile reassured the French that they could rely unequivocally on the British to uphold their share of the war burden. In short, with the declaration of war, Maurois, who had been writing novels about the sometimes frivolous love affairs of the Paris demi-monde, transformed himself into a writer *committed* to supporting the policies of his country.

In June of 1940, with shocking rapidity the Nazi armies smashed through the French lines of defense on the eastern front. Paris seemed doomed. For months Maurois had feared privately that the joint Franco-British land and air units would be no match for the enemy's luftwaffe and panzer divisions. His premonitions of disaster gleam through the text of his *Mémoires,* especially in the chapter entitled "Blitzkrieg," a text in which he chronicled his impressions of the battle itself with the numerical and technical superiority of the Germans over the western Allies.

With the Germans virtually at the gates of Paris, Maurois, widely recognized for his staunch criticism of Hitler, realized that his very life would be endangered if he remained in the capital: "I knew, if I were captured, I would be lost; I had written violent articles against Hitler."[51] Nor could he forget the special significance the Nazis had been attaching to Jewish birth. The Paris high command ordered him to leave France. In fact, he received two conflicting sets of orders. The Ministry of the Army requested that he go to Britain, where he would expose over BBC and in the English press the seriousness of the French tragedy. The Ministry of Foreign Affairs, on the other hand, ordered him to render himself to Boston to deliver the Lowell Lectures, a program to which he had committed himself several months earlier. Apparently, it was felt by the latter Ministry that he could perform a more efficacious job on behalf of France in America rather than in Britain.

First he went to London, from which he broadcast with a trembling voice over BBC radio his version of the tragedy. Though France was collapsing so quickly, the Western world seemed to watch with utter impassiveness. Maurois made no attempt to conceal his bitter disappointment. At the request of Queen Elizabeth he translated into French the text of a speech she planned to deliver to console the grief-stricken women of France. Paris fell. He received no news in London from his wife, children, or mother, all of whom had remained behind in France.

The French mission in London asked Maurois to fulfill his obligation as a lecturer in America and to justify the cause of France before a seemingly complacent United States. Then suddenly a cable arrived from his wife, who had managed miraculously to escape to Montreal. She urged him to join her there. So Maurois flew first to Canada and then together with her he traveled to New York City, arriving in Manhattan with scarcely enough money to pay for his cab fare. He could not even count on his substantial American royalties that had been accumulating for him in various New York banks; earlier, out of a sense of patriotism he had authorized these monies to be repatriated into the national French treasury, so that his government could use his hard currencies to purchase war material.

Fortunately, he had many friends in America, all of whom used their influence to help him find a means of earning a livelihood. So influential were they that in reality he could have spent the war years living in the Ritz Towers. His extensive lecture circuits were paying off, for Maurois had established important contacts in most American cities and colleges. By now too he had acquired extensive experience in the art of negotiating contracts. Wherever he lectured, he attempted to remind American public opinion of the menace of Nazism. Everywhere he sought to document the true causes of the French humiliation, drawing from military statistics to support his contention that the French lost not because of moral decadence, political corruption, or cowardice, but purely because of military inadequacies. Many Americans refused to be convinced.

Those were grim days. Because he found himself relatively unoccupied, he utilized his years of exile in America to undertake the composition of several lengthy tomes: his two-volume *Mémoires*, the *History of the United States, The History of France*, a major novel *Terre promise (Promised Land)*, and a few lesser volumes. He also collaborated extensively in a French-language newspaper *Pour la Victoire (For Victory)*, which had been established on January 10, 1942. During 1944–45 Maurois's articles and editorials appeared there frequently. Most often he wrote in an unpolitical vein, stressing current events of a cultural and artistic nature. His most valuable contributions in *Pour la Victoire* seem to be the monthly critical reviews he wrote of current American books. His own books were published by a new French-language publishing house, the Editions de la Maison Française, which was established to serve the needs of French men of letters in exile in America during the occupation of their homeland. He reveals his feelings in a personal message, scrawled on the title page of his wife's own copy of *The History of the United States:* "In July 1940 there arrived in the United States the French writer André Maurois. Although he was very unhappy, having lost everything, his country, his house, his books, he was so courageously aided by his wife who became at the same time spouse, secretary, friend, collaborator, *housekeeper*, that he regained confidence rapidly and worked better than ever."[52]

Again he took to the pullman cars. His public appearances carried him to Boston, Harvard, Andover, Exeter, Groton, New York, Palm Beach, Atlanta, Los Angeles, Denver, Omaha, Saint Louis. During one month he held a special chair at Knox College in Galesburg, Illinois. In the spring term of 1941 he taught French literature at the University of Buffalo. Everywhere his audiences were large and enthusiastic. Everywhere he revealed his love of France, and appealed for the still "neutral" American people to recognize the fact that all of western civilization remained imperiled as long as France remained choked by the Nazi occupation. His lectures yielded generous honoraria, most of which he contributed to French war relief funds. His royalties from the sale of the book *Espoirs et souvenirs (Hopes and Memories)* (an anthology of some of his wartime lectures in America) he turned over in toto to French charities.

Vis-à-vis the disparate groups of French refugees in America Maurois played the role of a unifier. He refused to affiliate himself clearly with this or that French government. For a time he even appeared to flirt with the Vichy government of France. Soon he backed off from any clearcut position. Nor did he take strong stands in behalf of the factions supporting DeGaulle in London or those lined up with General Giraud in North Africa. Seemingly unable to decide which of these splinter groups represented *all* of France, he continued nevertheless in his public talks to call for the unity of all French factions. A few of his compatriots, especially in New York, where the passions seemed most ardent, condemned him for not lending his undivided allegiance to any of the groups they themselves favored so vehemently. Maurois was simply an unvehement man.

His public statements were almost identical to de Gaulle's most grandiose statements about French grandeur: "Tomorrow France will be as necessary to the world, as profoundly irreplaceable as she was yesterday; she is not and will never be a minor nation, but equal to the greatest and the most worthy of them. . . . French culture is one of the essential elements of western civilization."[53] At times Maurois advocated a position identical to that of the General two decades later: that is, Europe can never permit herself to be dominated by a non-European power. She must be free to resolve her own dilemmas, formulate her own destiny: "She [a free Europe] will never accept a European order founded on an outside domination."[54]

Despite the generally depressing news leaking out of occupied France, Maurois the social animal continued to function in New York in a most social manner. He continued to see many prominent friends, and his memoirs of the time read like a name-dropping social register. The following excerpt betrays the fact that there were some positive satisfactions in his New York exile to temper the many anxieties he felt at the thought of the Nazis occupying his homeland: "In New York, I saw above all Saint-Exupéry, Romains, Monica de la Salle, Rouchaud, Pierre Claudel, Robert Lacour-Gayer and numerous American friends. President Murray Butler of Columbia University often invited us to dinner, one evening with Mrs. Roosevelt who spoke to me of the positive effects of my lectures. Essentially she was in favor of the American intervention in Europe. My English friend, Granville Barker, brought us together with Sir Thomas Beecham. . . . We dined with our friend Coindreau at the home of the Casadesus couple, with the Girard couple (parents of Danièle Delorme). Then we went to spend Sundays at the home of Allen Tate, in a delightful Alpine landscape at the edge of a rushing stream. . . . In October I spent a few days on Long Island in a large house which had been rented by the Saint-Exupérys. Denis de Rougemont was there . . ." (*Mémoires*, pp. 343–351 *passim*).

The highlight of his American exile seems to coincide with his collaboration with two other creative artists from France, the painter Fernand Léger and the composer Darius Milhaud, in the academic program of the Maison Française at Mills College, Oakland, California. His name was included in the roster of the college faculty from 1940 until 1943. It is not often that three creative Frenchmen of this caliber have been assembled on the faculty of any college in America.

When the Allied military offensive extended its campaign into North Africa during 1943, Maurois joined his writer-associate Antoine de Saint-Exupéry to participate actively in the liberation of what had been occupied French soil in North Africa. While there he learned through clandestine sources that his elderly mother, who had miraculously been able to cling to life in occupied Paris, had just been arrested by the Gestapo. And when he and Saint-Exupéry landed in North Africa, instead of finding their countrymen united in jubilation at the arrival of Allied Forces of liberation, they encountered embittered French *colons* torn asunder by split loyalties. Maurois later accompanied the Free French armies in their return to another parcel of occupied France, Corsica.

A bitter attack against Maurois's integrity took place during the inflamed and inflammatory period of World War II. He was expected by his French compatriots in exile in New York to take sides, either in favor of or against one of the several political camps that had seemed spontaneously to burgeon forth during the chaotic days of the governmental vacuum after the fall of France in June of 1940. Because his stand was not at first decisive enough, because he refused to become entangled in the internecine rivalries of so many French groups that had been pullulating all over Manhattan, because he, like Saint-Exupéry—with whom he was most closely associated in those bitter moments—foolishly believed that fanatic rivals could all be united under a canopy of Mauroisean moderation, and because he refused to break off personal relationships with former friends merely because of their political passions, he suddenly found himself in an untenable centrist position. A vicious attack was mounted against him by a playwright "whom I do not wish to name because he has passed away." Throughout these bitter pages he steadfastly refused to name the writer Henry Bernstein who, according to Maurois, "pursued me for four years of ferocious hatred because once I had hurt his pride and gone counter to his ambitions." (Maurois refused to join a group of French Jewish intellectuals in exile with whom Bernstein had been affiliated.) This foe went as far as to threaten the author of *Climats* with total annihilation. "I shall pulverize you," Maurois quotes from a Bernstein threat: "I know how to hate. I shall ruin you. I shall isolate you. I will reduce you to a position of helplessness." (Maurois renders a decidedly subjective account of this incident in his *Mémoires*, published by Flammarion in 1970, pp. 335 ff.) Immediately Bernstein did launch a tirade of attacks in the French-language press of America and Canada and began to spread rumors that Maurois was an anti-Semitic Jew, that he was a sympathizer of Vichy, a fascist, a foe of the British, that he had impugned the integrity of some of his closest writer-friends. There were a few persons in America, Britain, and France who were truly persuaded of the authenticity of these incriminations. The principal French-language paper in America, *Pour la Victoire*, edited by Maurois's friends Geneviève Tabouis and Kerillis, despite their strongly Gaullist position, refused to print any of Bernstein's charges, believing them to be reckless and counterproductive. It was Bernstein's attacks in the Canadian paper *Le Jour* that finally inspired Maurois to issue a public denial of all the charges. This paper consented to print his statement of self-justification, and though Bernstein's stabs seemed finally to have lost their sting, the rumors bandied about by this playwright died a slow death.

When the Germans surrendered in 1945, he rejoined his wife in New York. He had a final fling at teaching on an American campus during the winter semester of 1945–46. Accepting a visiting professorship at the then municipal University of Kansas City, Missouri (today the University of Missouri at Kansas City), he taught the sons and daughters of the farmers of the American corn and wheat belt about the grandeur of Balzac and the subtleties of Proust. Struck by the gardenlike setting of the southern residential areas of Kansas City, and by its museums, he wrote appreciatively of the Hispano-Moorish Country Club Plaza—one of the first planned shopping centers in America—and of the genuine cultural interests of so many of his Mid-American hosts. In Maurois's *From My Journal: United States: 1946* he spared no superlatives about this mid-American city: "Who in Europe, or in America for that matter, knows that Kansas City is one of the loveliest cities on earth? And yet it is true."[55] Almost twenty years later, Henry Haskell, the well-known arts editor of the *Kansas City Star*, reminded his readers of Maurois's luminous aphorism about that city: "Better a garden in Kansas City than a park in Utopia."[56]

Meanwhile, his mother, who had stoically borne the brunt of her arrest by the Gestapo, died in Maurois's Neuilly apartment building, where she had been returned by the victorious Allies upon their entry into the City of Light. She had hoped to live long enough to see her son return to France. Thus, one of the reasons for Maurois to rush back to Paris had suddenly evaporated. Simone Maurois left for France to make arrangements for the restoration of their living quarters in Neuilly and Périgord. She wished to prepare her author-husband's home for him so that when he returned he could resume his creative work without being impeded by the vestiges of wartime destruction. Nervously Maurois awaited news from Paris. In his notes of May 14, 1946, he disclosed that "more than ever, since my exile began, I watch with piercing anguish for letters from France. Which of my friendships will be reknotted by a few lines of writing?"[57] Finally, there arrived a letter from Alain, who had managed to survive the ordeal. Over and over again Maurois read every precious line in this short missive.

One of Maurois's final acts of the American exile took place at the commencement ceremony of the University of Kansas City, June 2, 1946: clad in the traditional academic garb, the French writer delivered the commencement address to the graduates of that year; his theme, an appeal for confidence in the fledgling United Nations. At the same conclave he added another honorary doctorate to his collection of honors.

Eight days later Madame Maurois returned from France to join her husband in New York. She had completed the preliminary work needed to pave the way for her husband's return to Paris. On their final departure from a land that had bestowed upon them the warmest hospitality imaginable, Maurois knew that he could never forget the generosity of the American people. After all, thanks to America his very life had been spared. Several times during the early era of his sojourn in the New World, when the Nazis suspected him to be still in France, Essendiéras had been ransacked by the Gestapo, which kept searching for his whereabouts.

Nervously he set off for France. Had his compatriots forgotten him? Would the brilliant new generation of Existentialist writers, Sartre, Camus, and Malraux, eclipse the name of a more moderate writer who had been absent some six years and whose reputation seemed to be based mainly on a prewar literary taste? As a creative artist, he wondered aloud in his *Mémoires* about whether he still possessed the faculties and popular appeal to equal or surpass his former successes.

L. The World of the Postwar Years (1946–51)

Not only was Maurois not forgotten by the Parisians; he was welcomed back by a sympathetic public. To his regular French publishers he immediately submitted the titles he had written in America, all of which they readily accepted. Editors in Spain, Japan, Sweden, and England rushed to translate all of his works written to date. The heading "André Maurois de l'Académie Française" returned to its prominent place on the title page of some of the most popular books published in post-war France.

During the occupation, his apartment on the boulevard Maurice Barrès had been seized by the Nazis and turned over for occupancy to one of the highest officers in their military hierarchy, the nephew of the infamous Herman Goering. In this superbly furnished and bookish abode the Nazi captain enjoyed five supremely comfortable years. When the Germans retreated from Paris, Colonel Goering ordered all of Maurois's books removed or destroyed, the furniture mutilated, the Aubusson and oriental rugs torn, and the paintings carried off. This was the scene of devastation that greeted Simone Maurois upon her earlier return to France, a situation that she only partially remedied before her husband's arrival. More than anything else Maurois suffered from the demolished state of his library and the destruction of some of his rare papers. To his comrades, the books he loved, he addressed a plaintive apostrophe: "Oh my silent friends . . . I have no longer found any of you. The Gestapo has sent you off I know not where. The long bookshelves were nude, the library a desert. Sadly I sat down in my great chamber which had been yours."[58] In vain did he search for his Littré dictionary, one of the mainstays of his creative activity. Nor could he find his collection of original manuscripts, among which were Alain's *Propos.* Suddenly this library, which he had been building devotedly for some forty years, ceased to exist. Out of the ruins of the old existence he and his wife began to forge a new career, a new library. "My yellow leather armchair is still here," he gleefully noted. "Friendly hands [his wife's] prepared some paper for me there, the same type I used to use in formerdays. Let's get to work."[59]

With five years of indefatigable acquisitions of rare books and manuscripts, Maurois and his spouse succeeded in reconstituting their great library and in transforming their apartment into one that was at least as splendid as the prewar residence. He thrust himself into a period of immense productivity, which yielded considerable royalties. These royalties, coupled with the author's wise sense of investments and contractual negotiations, sustained the astronomical costs of rebuilding both home and library. By the time of his death Maurois was able to write his important postwar biographies in the sanctity of one of the really well-stocked private libraries of France and to receive his literary friends in one of the most magnificent settings enjoyed by any author in the world.

By 1946 Maurois had already embarked upon the sixth decade of his life. At an age when most men had already produced their finest works, this prolific author turned to a completely new phase in his career. The equivalent of his already published works would have sufficed to guarantee for Maurois a slot in the history of contemporary French letters. But for the author of *Climats*, his previous titles were merely a prelude to a rich array of titles he was only preparing to compose.

After years of absence from France, André Maurois experienced an unquenchable urge to devote himself to the biographies of some of the giants of French literature most closely attached to the history of France. Masterwork would follow masterwork. After three years of research and a lifetime of spiritual intimacy (through Simone) with the memories of Proust, he wrote one of his most universally esteemed biographical studies, *A la recherche de Marcel Proust (In Search of Marcel Proust)*. This opus was to be followed successively by massive volumes devoted to the lives of George Sand, Hugo, the three Dumas, Adrienne de La Fayette, and Balzac.

During the war years commercial air travel had developed so rapidly that long-distance trips no longer required week-long stints of transoceanic seasickness or tiring nights on the train. So, in 1947, Maurois permitted himself to be persuaded by a most persuasive Russian impresario, Alexander Rogednov, to make an extensive, continental lecturing tour throughout the length and breadth of South America. In Peru he was twice honored: first by way of an honorary doctorate honoris causa from the ancient University of San Marcos in Lima, and second by the highest honor of the Peruvian government, that of Knighthood in the Order of the Sun.

During April of 1949 Maurois delivered public lectures at the Ateneo of Madrid, on the topic "Memories of my Literary Life." He addressed other notable academic and social organizations on the Iberian peninsula. Anecdotally, he was pursued and lionized wherever he went in Spain by an attractive South-American actress, many years younger than he, whom he had met dur-

ing his Latin American tour two years earlier. This potentially scandalous
incident in his life seems at least partially to have served as the basis for the plot
in the novel *Les Roses de septembre (September Roses)*, a work that Maurois
insisted to the end was not an autobiographical account. Few who really knew
his life were convinced by his protestations. This tour marked the third time he
had gone to Spain to lecture.

That same year, 1949, Maurois—this time accompanied by Madame—went
to Milan and Turin to lecture on French literary life. During his Italian jaunt the
Jew from Elbeuf enjoyed a lengthy audience with Pope Pius XII in the Vatican.[60] The latter, who had always wished to meet the noted literary couple, had
transmitted an official invitation to Maurois through the Canon Fontenelle, a
mutual friend and Proustian authority. Maurois disclosed that his protracted
audience with the Pope included a discussion concerning the relative merits of
the Academy Dictionary of the French language and the Littré. The Pope and
Maurois also discussed the literary style of Bossuet's *Oraisons funèbres (Funeral Orations)*.

Of all of his 1949 lectures, the most personally gratifying was his commencement address delivered in July of that year to the graduating class of his old
Lycée Corneille in Rouen. His theme: a plea that young people avoid the

One of the last photographs of André Maurois. (Photo by Georgette Chadourne.
Courtesy, Estate of André Maurois.

excessive cynicism sweeping through the modern world and that they allow themselves to indulge occasionally in the luxury of old-fashioned sentimentality, even naïve emotion. Too many young people, the Rouen alumnus observed, idolized intellectualism for the sake of intellectualism.[61]

Maurois's journalistic productivity during the late forties was staggering. Every Wesnesday he published an article in *Opéra*, under the rubric of "Les Propos littéraires d'André Maurois" ("The Literary Words of André Maurois"). Some of these articles are really essays and not mere commentaries or literary criticism (see the issues of 1949–50). One of his most poignant studies, "Le Souvenir d'Edmond Jaloux" ("The Memory of Edmond Jaloux"), marks the death of his close friend; this literary critic had just passed away in Lutry, Switzerland. Maurois had remained closely attached to him over the years. This article confirms one of the pivotal traits in Maurois's character: his unswerving fidelity to his friends and associates. During 1949–50 Maurois engaged also in minor journalism by way of contributions to several provincial newspapers, all of which purchased the rights to a syndicated column he wrote. Maurois contributed regularly even to *Elle* magazine and to other equally popular magazines.

By 1950 the protean Maurois was known to the literary public as more than a mere novelist-biographer-historian-chronicler-critic-short-story-writer. He had gained the reputation of an authority on human sensibility and conjugal relationships; thus he was invited by the national network of Radiodiffusion Française to broadcast throughout Europe eight weekly "propos" (a title borrowed, of course, from Alain) devoted to the institution of marriage. The full text of this "course" on how to find happiness in marriage was happily published in 1951 by Hachette in book form *(Cours de bonheur conjugal* ("Course of Marital Happiness"). The work sold very well indeed.[62]

M. The World of the Fertile Fifties—Part 1 (1950–55)

Maurois had always dreamed of writing a work on his old teacher Alain. It is safe to say that no one had penetrated more deeply than the author of *Bramble* Alain's world of pithy thought and stark ideas. Virtually every morning and night Maurois would begin and end his days with the reading of several pages of the *Propos* by his master. And for decades he had reflected on how he could present Alain's complex aphorisms and teachings systematically. At last, in 1950, he felt ready for the job. His volume *Alain* contains what may well be the most incisive exposition of the principal lines of Alainean thought to date. "My mind was formed of this substance," Maurois confided, "and it is this philosophy which today I still assimilate most readily."[63] Alain lived just long enough to read his veteran pupil's book and was apparently most pleased by it. It is likely that Maurois's *Alain*, a best-seller that year, paved the way for Alain to be selected in 1951 as the laureate for the Grand Prix National des Lettres. In

June of that same year, Alain, after years of courageously living with the pain of crippling arthritis, quietly died in Le Vésinet, a suburb of Paris. To the surprise of no one Maurois had been selected "on behalf of the friends and former students of the master" to deliver the eulogy at Alain's funeral. In an emotional voice he acknowledged once again "all that I owe him."[64]

What, in effect, did Maurois inherit from his master-teacher, Alain? Much of his thought was shaped by Alain's thinking. Maurois learned never to be a determinist; that is, someone who relied upon destiny. Alain had taught him to become a master of willpower, to accomplish what he himself *decided* he would accomplish. Maurois learned never to permit anything to deter him from doing what he willed to do. He also learned to subscribe, as Alain had done, to the Cartesian method of solving problems. One had to think in an orderly, clear, logical way. Language had to be precise. Approximations and fuzziness, chaos and disorder were to be avoided at all costs. Alain had instilled in Maurois a horror of superstition, religious doctrines, fear of the unknown, and irrationality. Stylistically, the pupil learned from his teacher to be concise, direct, and economical in his literary means. Plunge right into the story, end with a punch-line, and avoid all but the most indispensable imagery! The rather stark literary

André Maurois in his library. (Photo by Georgette Chadourne. Courtesy, Estate of André Maurois.)

style of André Maurois did indeed elicit much admiration from his great professor. Finally, the author of *Climats* learned to prefer the conjunction "and" to "or." That is, he began to realize that things were not black *or* white, but black *and* white. Life was indeed a carnival of paradoxes and ironies.

The fact is that one ought never to study André Maurois without reference to his incalculable intellectual and moral debt to Alain. Nor should one really study the teacher without analyzing how his precepts were perpetuated by his avowed disciple.

The seemingly indestructible Maurois continued to produce book after book, lecture after lecture. Refusing to lose contact with the rapidly changing world, he followed with keen interest the most recent developments in the sciences and arts and diligently studied the recent trends of the new wave of the French cinema world. He was perceived by some of the leading cinematographic directors to be a veritable specialist of films (by Jean Renoir, for instance.) So he was elected in 1951 to serve as the presiding officer for the renowned Cannes International Film Festival. He returned to Cannes often to serve as a member of the Festival's administrative committee and board of judges.

During 1951 and 1952, Maurois's most sustained newspaper work featured his advice to the lovelorn; his column "Lettre à l'inconnue" ("Letter to an Unknown Woman") was printed every Wednesday in *Carrefour*. In 1953, perhaps tired of this kind of column, he transformed these weekly contributions into a "Journal" or autobiographical entry that represented the logical extension of his earliest *Mémoires*, already published in America.

Maurois continued to add to his honors. He was particularly moved (and so was his wife!) by his election to the Académie des Sciences, Belles-Lettres et Arts in the City of Bordeaux. This Academy had acquired considerable prestige among French learned bodies. Montesquieu had been one of its members in the eighteenth century. At the colorful initiation ceremony, held on May 18, 1953, in the Grand Théâtre de Bordeaux, Maurois delivered an address designed to flatter the local pride of his Bordelais audience. Following his praise of the town, he linked his career with that of his fellow author François Mauriac, who of course helped put Bordeaux back on the contemporary literary map: "Mauriac and I crossed the literary career side by side. Not at all rivals, for between two literary oeuvres there is no common measure, we have been emulators of each other's work and comrades."[65] Now that he had become an honorary civic leader of Bordeaux, Maurois and his wife visited that city frequently and each year attended the Bordeaux Festival of Arts and Music in the late spring season.

By this time Maurois was nearly a septuagenarian. Despite this, he enjoyed exceptionally robust health. When, on November 15, 1953, he was rushed to the American Hospital in Neuilly, it was not because of the usual geriatric degeneration but because of a perfunctory appendectomy. With Maurois now regarded as something of a national hero in France, the newspapers of the

On the terrace of the Chateau d'Essendiéras, 23 December 1964. *From left to right:* Jacques Suffel (former official at the Bibliotheque Nationale), André Maurois, and Jack Kolbert.

ensuing days, ignoring the routine nature of his illness, treated their readers to exceedingly detailed accounts of the recuperative progress of the Academician-Patient. In record time he was back at work at his writing-table.

On his sixty-ninth birthday (Monday, July 26, 1954), here is what he wrote in his diary: "My birthdate. I should be sad, having almost reached the age when most human existences terminate. But the sun is out, my work is coming along well. . . ."[66] Later that same summer the writer participated in the ninth annual "Rencontres Internationales" of intellectuals in Victoria Hall, Geneva, Switzerland. The conclave, which featured such internationally known authorities as George Boas of the U.S.A., the Italian poet Ungaretti, the Swiss critic Georges Poulet, the head of the International Red Cross and Swiss novelist Jacques Chenevière, and the French critic René Lalou, reached its climax as André Maurois rose to deliver the final summation on the theme of the "Rencontre": "The New World and Europe."[67]

Refusing to slacken the frenzied pace of his daily existence, Maurois ended the year 1954 with an extensive visit of the nooks and hidden corners of Holland. It was one of the rare times he was accompanied by one of his children, his older son, Gérald, a professional photographer, who had been preparing an art book of photography on the Netherlands. What turned out to be a fine pictural essay by Gérald Maurois was enhanced by a preface written by the photographer's famous father.

Maurois added one more link to his chain of laurels: he was promoted on February 2, 1955, to the rank of Grand Officer de la Légion d'Honneur. By then, no French writer had received more national and international decorations, more honorary doctorates.

N. The World of the Fertile Fifties—Part 2 (1955–60)

In 1955 Maurois fulfilled a long-standing dream. He had always wanted to write a play. That year he finally produced a one-act "proverbe," despite his conviction that he possessed few of the attributes of a dramatist. "Aux Innocents les mains pleines" elicited at the Comédie Française more than the perfunctory praise critics heap upon minor works of recognized authors. Yet it seems obvious that had Maurois not been a prominent member of the Academy his play would not have been accepted and performed so soon after its completion.[68]

In April of that year the Comédie Française took "Aux Innocents les mains pleines" on tour to Brussels, where the enthusiasm of the Belgians was impressive. Since then, this frail play has evaporated into the purgatory of so many charming but insignificant comedies. Now that Maurois had had his fling on the stage, he could return to more gratifying pastures of creativity, where he felt more at ease.

During that same year he had also published the following: *Portrait de la France et des Français (Portrait of France and the French)*, a penetrating study of socioeconomic conditions in France during the fifties; *Robert et Elizabeth Browning*, one of his lesser literary biographies; *Périgord*, an illustrated guidebook of his adopted province. Also, he put the finishing touches on what would be his final novel, *Les Roses de septembre*. He was deeply involved in the research for yet another mammoth biography, *Les Trois Dumas*. At the same time, he assumed the role of drama critic for the newspaper *Aux Ecoutes* and wrote weekly essays in a series entitled "La Chronique Théâtrale." Maurois continued to dabble in the field of conjugal advice; in 1958 he launched a new series of advice to the lovelorn for the women's magazine *Confidences*. In the late fifties he began also to collaborate with the well-known *Revue de Paris*, for which he wrote two or three major essays each year. At the same time, he affiliated himself with the prominent literary weekly, *Les Nouvelles Littéraires*, an affiliation that lasted from the time of his first series "Le Livre du Mois" ("The Book of the Month") on November 26, 1959, until his death almost a decade later.

O. The World of the Sixties

Maurois spent three delightful autumnal months in 1960 lecturing from coast to coast in America. Those who heard him recalled with much wonderment his still robust physical appearance, the youthfulness of his voice, the crisp liveliness of his mind. Never, it seemed, had he been in finer form. This was to be his final visit to America.

Only the year before he had completed the biography of Sir Alexander Fleming, the British scientist most directly responsible for the breakthrough in penicillin research. To accomplish his task he was forced first to take a special course on the fundamentals of bacteriology, then to watch an eminent scientist recapitulate each of the successive stages in the experimentation undertaken by Fleming. In the view of the scientific experts who reviewed Maurois's *Fleming*, his first and last biography of a scientist, this book matched the quality of his finest literary volumes devoted to the lives of Hugo, Sand, Proust, and Chateaubriand. Both the historical and scientific validity of the opus appeared to be impeccable.

By now Maurois was regarded as a kind of Prince of Biographers. Hence, during 1960, when the descendants of Gilbert de La Fayette, the hero of the French and American Revolutions, stumbled on a chest crammed with letters exchanged between the Marquis and his wife, which had been hidden in the attic of the cavernous Chateau de La Grange, they commissioned André Maurois to write the biography of their illustrious ancestor. They made available to him their mine of historical data. One year later Maurois completed the huge tome entitled *Adrienne ou la Vie de Madame de La Fayette (Adrienne or the Life of Madame de La Fayette)*. This work too was universally regarded by the critics as a genuine masterpiece.

Maurois wished to write still one more masterpiece, just one. At the age of seventy-six he was not sure that he would be granted sufficient time to do so. He had always wanted to do the life of Balzac. But he knew that this particular biography would be no puny project; the research alone would necessitate years of all-encompassing labor. Destiny—assisted by Maurois's indomitable will to live—permitted him the satisfaction of realizing his ambitious goal. In 1965, four years after starting his monumental work, he published *Prométhée ou la Vie de Balzac, (Prometheus or the Life of Balzac)*, a biography some regard as his most brilliant achievement. Again most of the critics applauded. Francis Steegmuller, who reviewed it for the *New York Times*, claimed that ". . . it shows once again that Maurois is the greatest living French literary biographer."[69]

On and on went this Old Man of the Pen. Then suddenly he collapsed with a serious illness. During his summer vacation of 1961, at the Chateau d'Essendiéras, he was felled by a case of double pneumonia. Again the press reported copiously on his daily condition. A few critics feared that the *Balzac* might never be completed. But this miraculous career had not yet seen the last of its miracles. The indestructible Academician recovered and returned to his writing table. During the same year and in the same chateau, on July 16, 1961, Madame Jeanne Pouquet, the legendary eighty-seven-year-old mother of Simone André Maurois quietly succumbed. With her passing it seemed that an era of literary life was vanishing into the winds of time. Her death was reported in the world's journals. Indeed, for decades now, the clan of André Maurois belonged to the world of international society. People seemed interested not only in reading what Maurois wrote, but also in reading about how he and his closest family lived.

At the same time Maurois accepted an invitation to serve as the principal speaker at the annual meeting of the World Congress of Writers and Authors in Rome. Speaking on the theme of the writer's obligation to seek truth, regardless of his own nationality, he made an eloquent plea for the right of dissent for the literary artist. Maurois's discourse, delivered in the historic Capitol of Rome, seemed to be aimed mainly at the Communist writers in the audience.[70]

On June 2, 1963, the University of Maryland's European Division conferred upon Maurois the degree of doctorate of letters, honoris causa. The rite took place in the Neue Aula on the campus of the University of Heidelberg. Presi-

André Maurois, Simone Maurois, and their Peugeot in front of the Chateau d'Essendiéras in the Dordogne country of France. One of the last photographs taken of André and Simone together. Inscription: *"Pour Jack Kolbert, amicalement, André Maurois, 23.12.63."* (Courtesy, Estate of André Maurois.)

dent Wilson H. Elkins of the University of Maryland presided over the ceremony and pronounced the following tribute to Maurois:

> In this ancient European seat of learning, this American university proclaims
> academic honors upon one of the most distinguished minds of France, upon
> a man similarly honored three decades ago by Princeton and Oxford and
> Edinburgh, upon a man of letters whose prodigious prestige has been con-
> stant in the eyes of three generations, upon a man who is a French immortal
> and a living classic, André Maurois.
>
> The genius of André Maurois, through scholarly synthesis, literary skill,
> superior gifts of analysis and intuition, has humanized and enkindled the
> lives of poets and politicians, novelists and men of action, and enriched our
> literature for all time with biographical masterpieces. . . .
>
> Twenty-five years ago, André Maurois's youthful and daring dream was
> fulfilled by his election to the French Academy. Today, as befits his time of
> life, he has tranquillity, respect, and honor worthy of a member of that
> exalted group. However, the rumble of destiny is not drowned out by
> tranquillity or exaltation; there is no indifference of soul because his fame is
> universal; there is no relaxing of work because his name is secure in immor-
> tality. There is still more truth and excellence to be brought forth by this
> great mind and pen, to be placed high in the annals of humanity.[71]

As Maurois bowed his silvery head, allowing the colorful hood to slip over it
onto his shoulders, he may have been meditating not about the pompous
proceedings but rather about the limited days ahead of him. He confessed that
he could hardly wait to return to Paris, where his unfinished *Balzac* was
awaiting him. Indeed, the near-octogenerian had reached that point in human
existence when it was perilous to allow oneself to fall prey to the luxuries of
ceremonies and leisure. He realized that his hand needed to keep holding the
pen; his words had to keep flowing; his mind needed to remain active. Otherwise the ravages of senility would surely debilitate his productivity. As he
addressed the commencement audience in Heidelberg, he emphasized the
theme of the unity of the disparate peoples of this planet and the necessity of
conciliating differences through mutual understanding. Gazing retrospectively
at his own nearly eight decades of experience, the biographer declared: "All my
life, I have thought that my mission as a writer should be that of an interpreter.
I know that the influence of one lonely man is infinitely small, but I did what
little was in my power. . . . I do not despair."[72]

P. The World of the Octogenarian

In his final years, Maurois continued to remain active in the literary,
academic, intellectual, and social events of his age. After 1960 he took few
lengthy trips outside of France. He did, however, travel extensively within

The French Government decorates André Maurois with the rank of "Grand Croix de la Légion d'Honneur." General Catroux, Grand Chancellor of the Legion of Honor, presents the decoration to Maurois at the Chateau d'Essendiéras on 4 August 1965. In the background *(left to right)*: Madame Jacques Suffel; Professor Grassé (biologist) from the Academy of Sciences, Mme Yves Guerra; Mr. Michel Droit, editor-in-chief of *Le Figaro Littéraire;* Edouard Feuillade; and Olivier Maurois, the author's youngest son. (Courtesy, Estate of André Maurois.)

France: for instance, to Monaco to take part in the annual selection of the literary prize of the Prince de Monaco; to Périgord and Gascony to attend the yearly festivals of theater at Sarlat and of music at Bordeaux; to Cannes for the film festival. As president of the binational society France-Etats-Unis in Paris, he seldom missed meetings of the organization and often addressed its membership. In 1963 he delivered an emotional memorial discourse on the assassination of President Kennedy, an event that had a profound effect on him. He served also as the President of the Association des Lauréats du Concours Général, a society of prizewinners in the national educational system, and of the Society of Friends of Alain.

During the final five years of Maurois's life, his visiting friends would find him working devotedly at his sunlit table either in the study of his Neuilly apartment or on the second floor of his Chateau d'Essendiéras. The Neuilly abode was elegant; the three front rooms—consisting of a well-appointed drawing-room and two library offices—that of the author on one end and that of Madame on the other—formed a most impressive interior. More than 10,000 lavishly bound volumes filled the libraries scattered throughout the apartment. On entering the lobby one confronted built-in bookcases lining every wall. In the rear of the apartment there was one entire chamber, stuffed from floor to ceiling with slender drawers containing Simone André Maurois's rich epistolary collection. This room served as a working and typing center for Maurois's aides, who did his correspondence there and classified his books and papers for him. The walls in the public room were graced with two masterpieces by Marquet and fine canvases by Kisling, Boudin, and Léger.

It was in this bookish setting that Maurois did his writing every morning except on Sundays when, during the early hours, he received phone calls and visits from guests from around the world. It was there that he spent most afternoons working with his secretary on his correspondence, keeping up with the contemporary literary scene by reading voraciously the works of other authors, and also scanning the metropolitan dailies of Paris, London, and New York.

Several times each week his secretary arrived to aid him in responding to his correspondence from around the world. Some of the special social or personal mail he would answer directly by hand. But in most cases he dictated his replies. So speedily could he dictate that in about thirty minutes each day he replied to a significant number of missives. Each week he would answer at least fifty pieces of correspondence. The largest portion of his overseas mail came from America and Britain, though he received a steady flow of letters from Latin America, Spain, and Italy.

Even his so-called vacations were periods of intense labor. His gracious Périgord estate beckoned guests irresistibly during the Christmas holiday season, again during a two-week period in May at the time of the Pentecostal break, and finally in July and August. Maurois went to Essendiéras not to escape from the labors of Paris, but rather to be able to devote himself more uninterruptedly to his literary efforts. In Paris he was too often the prey of invitations and official engagements. In Périgord, where the tranquillity of life was disrupted only by the chirping of crickets and birds and by the murmuring winds, he could work more productively: "I call 'vacation' that part of the year when I work hardest and best. . . . There in the chateau d'Essendiéras I find what Paris never gives me; long days without events, without visitors, without telephone calls." In the same passage he confessed that it was in that lovely countryside that he could approach nature most closely: "to take walks in these countrysides is a rewarding experience." Often his wife accompanied him through the thick forestland. Almost always their conversation dealt with his current literary projects: "As we walk we discuss the work, for my wife copies every day what I have written the night before. Musset, Chopin, Sandeau, Mérimée, Flaubert, Sainte-Beuve are infinite subjects of curiosity for us. We speak of them as of living friends, and what is even much better is the fact that we possess their letters."[73]

Here is a typical day at the chateau: He would arise at 6:45 in the morning. Thirty minutes later he would listen to the morning newscast on the radio. Immediately after a light breakfast he would proceed to his study, where he would write steadily between 8:00 A.M. and 12:30 P.M., a session during which no one whatsoever was permitted to disturb him. By 12:30 P.M. the clanging luncheon gong resounded throughout the spacious corridors, summoning everyone in the chateau—the Maurois couple and their often numerous house-guests—to the huge formal dining-room for lunch. By 2:00 P.M. Maurois would already be back in his study, poring over documents and manuscripts. Occasionally he would spent his afternoons in the country, visiting with friends in neighboring cheateaus and villages, or inspecting the work of his farmhands, who were raising apples on hundreds of acres of the domain. Around 5:00 P.M. the author would stroll through the gardens and woods around the chateau, hoping to stimulate an evening appetite. After a brief pre-dinner aperitif in the salon, he and his guests would customarily move to the dining room, where at about 7:00 P.M. they were regaled with a repast of superb Périgourdine cuisine, adorned with truffles, pâtés, magnificent sauces, meats, and rich cheeses. The chateau cook was a supreme artist of foods; moreover, that region of France was bountiful in some of the finest ingredients in the world. Following the dessert, Maurois generally spent an hour or more chatting with his guests and wife in the salon, or else he listened to records on his high fidelity set in the music room. When special documentary programs were presented on the na-tional television, he would forgo the music and the conversations to sit silently before the television screen. When he chose to listen to the phonograph, he arranged a formal program of recorded concert pieces that fit together as if they had been combined for a concert hall: he would assemble an overture, sym-phony, and concerto. His large record collection reflected his eclectic taste: Chopin waltzes, Stravinsky, Liszt, Borodin, De Falla, Beethoven, Wagner, not to mention numerous recordings of popular chansonniers.

From time to time, when the summer evenings were particularly balmy, he and his party of guests would retire to the marble terrace overlooking the gardens and a small pond. There, under the constellations, which, in Périgord's inky and clear sky, were especially luminous, Maurois engaged his houseguests in philosophical conversations concerning human existence; that is, the ques-tion of salvation and God, scientific progress, war and peace. These conversa-tions later found their way onto many of the pages of his books.

Maurois's virtues as a conversationalist par excellence were known only to the privileged few of his inner circle. He was better known to tens of thousands of others around the globe as a public speaker. Of the French authors of our century, Maurois was one of the best known lecture-hall personalities. His face, a familiar fixture on French television, made him instantaneously recog-nizable wherever he went, as if he were a famous film star. And his name sufficed to fill any large auditorium in Paris whenever he lectured. But it was at Essendiéras, not in the auditorium of Paris, that he probably felt happiest.

From Maurois's office in Périgord one enjoyed a sweeping view of the distant purple hills, the tiny village of Excideuil, and the ruins of the château de Talleyrand; his office communicated directly with the suite of his wife. This arrangement was particularly convenient, allowing for close collaboration and discussion over stylistic intricacies in his texts. The decor in the study featured three paintings by Jacques-Emile Blanche, a seaport watercolor by Carzou, and an oil by Edouard Dermit, Jean Cocteau's protégé. During the composition of *Prométhée ou la Vie de Balzac,* the biographer's tables were strewn with several editions of Balzac's complete words, as well as with numerous major secondary reference works devoted to *The Human Comedy.*

In one arena of life Maurois was most successful: financial affairs. He himself possessed an adequate degree of financial ease to circulate in the most fashionable circles and to go to elegant spas and resorts. He could afford to wear the appropriate wardrobes called for by this life-style. First, he did draw from a part of the profits from the Elbeuf mill, at least before the Second World War eroded its earning capacity. Second, his marriage with Simone de Caillavet was a financially attractive match. Not only did she inherit a magnificent chateau in Périgord, but her family owned major Paris property. She received occasional royalties from her literary father's plays (some of which had been set to operatic form, like the oft-presented *Merry Widow,* for instance). Then Maurois could almost always expect substantial royalties from his books, most of which sold extremely well. It was not rare for his books to sell between 50,000 and 200,000 copies in France alone. Nor were his foreign royalties insignificant. He wrote enormous quantities of articles for the newspapers and magazines, all of which yielded added income. Correspondence between him and various impresarios around the world indicates that lecture-series were accompanied by generous honoraria. Because he had been accustomed to a life of great and costly aplomb, he found it necessary to assume weighty burdens of writing for periodicals and news syndicates as well as of undertaking personal lecture junkets. His fees and royalties he negotiated personally, generally without the intermediary of an agent. The shrewd ex-industrialist from Elbeuf had read his Balzac well and learned many entrepreneurial skills from the latter's mistakes in the business world. Not only did Maurois negotiate contracts well; he knew also how to invest wisely.

If Maurois did not have to struggle to exist, the truth is that he was less affluent than people realized. Nevertheless, he was certainly far more comfortably situated than most of his literary colleagues. By juggling well the time needed for work and socializing, he could at once share the pleasures of people in the loftiest social register and still produce copious numbers of books.

The chateau d'Essendiéras, itself a kind of minor museum, was cluttered with rare Chinese objets d'art, finely carved old French furniture, ancient Oriental carpets, and a library containing bound collections of journals and deluxe editions of books. Those guests who climbed into one of the third-floor turret-towers stumbled upon still more books. At least two entire rooms there were stacked high with recent volumes in the process of being catalogued by the wife of an official of the Bibliothèque Nationale. Everywhere the brightly painted walls (Madame Maurois had a definite penchant for lively yellow) were covered with paintings, mainly portraits of members of the family, and several canvases by eighteenth- and nineteenth-century French and English artists, and by several fine tapestries.

Life in this literary and artistic chateau was not always one of solitude and isolation. At Christmas and during the Sarlat summer theater festival, various social events punctuated the tranquillity that usually prevailed there. As Madame Maurois once confessed, there seemed to be no point in maintaining an entirely livable (even by the most exiguous modern standards) residence of more than thirty rooms unless guests could grace its many attractively furnished suites. Even when filled with visitors, however, the house was so large, and the guests so mindful of the author-host's need for silence, that the place was relatively quiet.

One of the highlights in the social calendar of Essendiéras was the annual Christmas party scheduled by Madame Maurois around the great Christmas tree. The elderly author played the role of a congenial Père Noël for a least a hundred and twenty children plus their parents, the prefect of the Département of Dordogne and other major officials, all of whom filed past him to pick up their annual Christmas present.

In addition to Christmas, the other major fête of the year was July 26. Here is how Maurois himself described one of these dates:

> Sunday, July 26, 1964.—My birthday. Today I am seventy-nine years old. That seems frightening. . . . The sky is ablaze, a sky of a pure blue, immutable, without a threat. The house is full of friends: Jean and Camille Dutourd, Henri Sauguet, Jacques Dupont. Each one offers me the fruits of his industry. Dutourd, a writer, had composed a little poem; Sauguet, a composer, a cantilena of seventy-nine notes; Dupont, a painter, has sketched a lovely decor which is that of Essendiéras: the mass of trees, the line of cypress and the distances of gentle hills. Telegrams rush in, sent by my children, by my faithful friends and also by people I do not know. My wife has made a holiday cake, planted with seven large candles and nine little ones. I must, with one breath, extinguish this long past. Then, we go out on the terrace, where we find an admirable evening under the stars. Suddenly, one of these attracts our attention by its speed in moving about among the constellations. Having left the bunch of central trees, it rapidly heads for the linden trees. It is *Telstar* and I remember the American professor from Harvard who was the first to show me this golden voyage in the skies which he himself had launched into the field of stars.[74]

If Maurois's pattern of life in Périgord was for the most part placid and encouraged him to be productive in his creative work, his existence in Paris was punctuated, on an almost daily basis, with a myriad of social and literary obligations. A random page from his pocket-calendar (the date was December 10, 1958, when he was in his mid-seventies) divulges the following frantic schedule:

Between 8 A.M. and 1 P.M., writing the biography of Sir Alexander Fleming.
1 P.M. Lunch with Julliard, the publisher.
5 P.M. Reception for the Chambrun marriage.
6:30 P.M. Reception at the Embassy of West Germany.
7:30 P.M. Rushing home to change into formal clothes.
8:30 P.M. Dinner-Banquet "en smoking" at the Swiss Embassy.

The entry of Thursday, June 13, 1957, reads as follows:

8A.M. until 1 P.M., working on the biography *Les Trois Dumas.*
1 P.M. At his own home he received the Comte and Comtesse de Paris (the heirs
    to the throne of France) for a private luncheon.
6 P.M. Reception for the laureate of the Grand Prix du Prince de Monaco, given
    by the publisher Bernard Grasset for Hervé Bazin at the Hôtel Lutétia.
6:30 P.M. Reception at the Paris home of the pianist Artur Rubenstein, Avenue
    Foch.
8:45 P.M. Opera, *Adrienne Lecouvreur* presented by La Scala of Milan at the
    Casino d'Enghien, outside of Paris.

Despite the above pattern—more the rule than the exception—the following
day, at precisely 8 A.M., he was back at his writing table hale and fresh, working
on his manuscript of the moment.

With each succeeding birthday Maurois became more and more conscious of
the importance of time. Having completed *Prométhée ou la Vie de Balzac,*
which he publicly announced as his final biography, Maurois decided not to
embark again on any other vast projects requiring years to complete. Preferring
to undertake smaller-scaled works, he began to write short stories in which he
carried the lives of some of his earlier fictional heroes forward into the era of
the nineteen-sixties. He wrote also some occasional articles of criticism mainly
for *Les Nouvelles Littéraires* and *La Revue de Paris.* Above all, he began to redo
his earlier two-volume *Mémoires* of 1942, for he desired to bring this work up
to date, adding to it his experiences of the final three decades. The newly
revised and expanded edition of his *Mémoires* would eventually appear nearly
three years following his death. In his final years of life he understandably
became more and more retrospective about the role he had played in the
twentieth century. An isolated entry in his memoirs, dated June 7, 1964, betrays a mixture of mild anxiety and his more usual tranquillity of mind. A
propos of human salvation, he wrote:

What throws me into a long rêverie on this Sunday evening is this question: And I, what have I done to promote the idea for which I was born?
And what was and what is this idea? I believe that I was born to explain, to
conciliate. When I was very young, I used to like to comprehend people,
what triggered them off and, if they were not monsters, I used to like to find

excuses [for their actions]. This is what threw me into biography. . . . And it is also what threw me into history, for peoples, like individuals, have memories, weaknesses, greatnesses that we must understand.

Have I succeeded? Sometimes. . . . Should I have gotten more involved in action? I directed a factory; took part in two wars; but I did not, like Barrès, choose political action. Was I wrong? It seems to me that I would not have been happy there. Political action requires trenchant choices, even injustices. . . . My nuanced views, my indulgences would have badly accommodated themselves to these necessary rigors. And then, [consider] the writer, who so easily must escape from reality as he transposes it, can such a man really be a man of action?[75]

On April 1, 1965, the French Academy gathered to greet a new member, Jacques Rueff, the world-famous economist and Chancellor of the Institut de France. The latter had been elected to fill the vacancy caused by the death of Jean Cocteau. Since Maurois had sponsored and received Cocteau (and he had pronounced the principal eulogy at Cocteau's burial), it seemed logical for the Company to ask him to pronounce the welcoming discourse for this poet's successor. His voice scarcely differed from the one that had delivered his own initiation address twenty-seven years earlier. Certainly his mind was as acute as ever. And his language was as limpid and as decoratively simple as that with which he wrote *Climats* and *La Vie de Disraeli* decades earlier.

An eightieth birthday is a very special event. Thus on June 2, 1965, Maurois was roundly congratulated on his own eightieth birthday party at a mammoth garden-party given by Jean Mistler, one of the directors of the Hachette Publishing Company. Two thousand notables of the cream of Paris society attended. A photograph in *Le Figaro* (June 3, 1965) depicts the silvery-haired author stooping over a five-layered cake, extinguishing the candles symbolizing the eight decades of his life.

The French government marked Maurois's eightieth birthday in its own fashion: the government had just promoted him to the highest level of the Légion d'Honneur. General Catroux, the Grand Chancellor of the Legion of Honor, traveled to Essendiéras expressly to place across the author's chest the wide diagonal ribbon of the Grand Croix de la Légion d'Honneur, an honor reserved for only a chosen few. That same week, on July 22, 1965, *Les Nouvelles Littéraires,* the important literary weekly with which Maurois was becoming increasingly affiliated, published a special commemorative issue entitled "Homage à André Maurois."

He planned one more trip to America: he would be the first nonscientist to deliver a series of lectures in November of 1967 before a conclave of scientists at the Brookhaven National Laboratory on Long Island, New York. Always deeply interested in the theme of creativity in the world of scientific research, André Maurois elected for his topic the provocative title of "The Illusions." He planned to compare artists with scientists as two groups of creative people confronting Truth in its purest form. He now realized that man would never succeed totally in eradicating illusory distortions, caricatures, and façades of reality. Therefore the human race must learn to utilize illusions as a positive force leading toward the ultimate Truth. Besides, was art not in fact an illusion of reality? And would it not even be possible to go one step further and designate reality as an illusion of art? Maurois never delivered these paradoxical lectures. They were published posthumously.[76]

Because the details of Maurois's death have been inaccurately reported in the press, it is appropriate here to state exactly what did occur. In September of 1967, following recurrent pain, he consulted first with the local village doctor in Excideuil, and again on September 15 with a gastroenterologist in Périgueux. The latter, on discovering a polyp in the lower intestinal tract, advised emergency surgery at once. From outward appearance Maurois seemed to outsiders to be in perfect health and of robust physical stamina. However, the urgency with which the specialist recommended surgery overwhelmed the heretofore controlled Maurois to such an extent that the very next day, September 16, he even invited his notary and a friendly priest (Abbé Pomarède) to have private consultations with him. No one knows for certain what was discussed in either session. We may surmise that with the former he discussed certain questions related to financial affairs, while whenever he was with the latter he usually discussed questions concerning Scriptures. One thing is absolutely sure: the Jewish-born, nonpracticing, even skeptical Maurois never underwent any kind of religious conversion to Christianity.

The Maurois couple departed for Paris on September 19. Immediately. upon returning to the Capital, he was examined by a renowned gastroenterologist, Dr. Varay, and by the renowned surgeon, Professor Lortat-Jacob, who had been selected to perform the operation. Maurois's entry in his *Mémoires* of September 20, 1967, reads like this: "And now it is up to God. Written prior to visiting the surgeon." Unquestionably this unfailing optimist was having some qualms about surgery at his advanced age. Also he may have been reexamining his thoughts about the meaning of "God." In earlier decades the problem of deity seldom concerned him—at least overtly.

A nonmalignant polyp was indeed removed at a private clinic in Neuilly on September 26. The surgeon believed that the patient might pull off one of his many miraculous recoveries. This optimism was justified during four days. Then, on September 30, the patient developed complications: a pulmonary congestion speedily set in and, despite massive doses of antibiotics, despite Maurois's strong constitution, he succumbed on October 8, 1967, at the age of eighty-two. Ironically, not unlike his hero and fictional alter ego, Philippe Marcenat in *Climats*, whose last words were "J'étouffe" (I am choking for air), Maurois too suffocated.

The state funeral took place on October 12 in the monumental courtyard of the French Academy. It was the first time in the history of the ancient Company that a funeral had been held there. High officials of the French state, virtually every member of the Academy itself, and distinguished leaders from the literary, diplomatic, academic, and industrial worlds came to honor the late man of letters. Many thousands of others—students, teachers, housewives, young writers, workers, businessmen, were also there. Over the black-draped coffin were arranged his academic paraphernalia—the legendary green outfit, the two-cornered hat, the sword, and his Grand Cross of the Legion of Honor. Most of the Academicians wore their uniforms. This finery was fitting for Maurois's funeral, for he had much loved pomp and ceremony. For the Academy Jacques Chastenet stepped forward to pronounce the official funeral oration. Then the audience listened to the words of Alain Peyrefitte, Minister of Education, who had been charged by President Charles de Gaulle to speak for the French State. As Maurois's remains were carried into the outer court-yard, the military band of the Republican Guard solemnly interpreted the funeral march from Beethoven's Eroica Symphony. Other tens of thousands of Parisians lined the Quai Conti as André Maurois, this time transported in a bier, passed along the banks of the Seine for a final time. He was laid to rest in the old cemetary of Neuilly, not far from the house in which his pen had once sketched the climates that live on in his books.

Maurois's death was given worldwide attention in the press and media. *Le Figaro* of Paris (October 13, 1967) featured on the front page a huge photograph of the funeral service in the Academy courtyard and a banner headline. Full texts of the various eulogies and reactions by prominent Academicians filled subsequent pages of this issue. The *New York Times* (October 10, 1967) also accorded the event a front-page story. The leading socialist paper, *Combat* (October 10, 1967), compared Maurois's orderly life and his distinguished literary career to " a French-styled formal garden," while *Le Monde* featured a first-page headline entitled in its usual understated language "André Maurois n'est plus" ("André Maurois Is No Longer") (October 10, 1967). *Les Nouvelles Littéraires* (October 12, 1967), devoted most of its first page to three essays of farewell, printed under the sentimental banner "Adieu à André Maurois" and authored by the paper's director, André Gillon, and by the well-known Academicans Henry de Montherlant and Jules Romains. On subsequent pages there appeared other necrological articles by Jacques Suffel, Jean Dutourd, Pierre de Boisdeffre, and P. Sipriot. *Paris-Match* devoted to this late author sixteen full pages, replete with pictures of Maurois's major events of life, from his infancy to the final days. Perhaps it was the lengthy headline in the *Philadelphia Inquirer* (October 10, 1967) that summed up most succinctly the stature of the man: "André Maurois, whose humor and humanism distinguished him as a giant of modern French literature, died Monday at 82." *Le Figaro Littéraire* (October 16–22, 1967) issued what was by far the slickest coverage of the Maurois death: a large colored cover portrait of the latter, one of the best he had ever taken, while within the magazine virtually the entire issue was given to nine lengthy articles by Jacques de Lacretelle, André Chamson, Maurice Druon, Jean Dutourd, J-J Gautier, Robert Kanters, John Lehmann, Jacques Suffel, and Michel Droit, whose offerings were divided into three categories: the man, the writer, and the friend. But the most moving words in this magazine were probably those written by Maurois's fellow octogenarian François Mauriac, in his "Bloc-Notes" of that week's *Figaro Littéraire*, who wrote simply "André Maurois: he died this morning. . . . He was my friend, my oldest life companion."[77] In the same magazine of the following week Mauriac devoted virtually his entire "Bloc-Notes" to his reflections about the many years during which he and Maurois had shared so much in common. He noted that the similarity of the names Mauriac and Maurois often confused readers of literature around the world. Radio Copenhagen in fact, in its announcement of Maurois's death confused the two men, insisting it was Mauriac who had died and calling Maurois a profound Catholic writer.

Post-Scriptum

His faithful widow-collaborator no longer had anyone with whom to collaborate. Simone Maurois would live only fourteen months longer. Even before her husband's death she confided to close friends of the family that her eyesight was failing rapidly. Before his death Maurois had been especially concerned with her drastic loss of appetite and rapid decline of weight. With her husband gone, she seemed to do little but wait for death. This woman, who once had adored the social and literary life of Paris, who had loved to reign over a chateau filled with witty guests, became a recluse who ceased to answer mail or to attend public functions. On December 26, 1968, she was found by her servant in her bathrobe, lying lifelessly on the floor, her head leaning against the radiator in the bedroom of her apartment on the boulevard Maurice Barrès. Her funeral took place in the Saint-Pierre de Neuilly church, with Abbé Pomarède officiating. Simone André-Maurois (she had stubbornly insisted on hyphenating her husband's first name onto her married name) was laid to rest alongside her husband in the Neuilly cemetery.[78]

The Chateau d'Essendiéras passed on by agreement to a certain Madame Créange, the daughter of one of the leading industrialists of France, Monsieur Sylvain Floirat, with whom the Maurois couple had been jointly engaged in an apple-growing venture. The property had in fact become one of the leading apple-producing centers in France, with Floirat financing a large portion of the venture. Some compared Essendiéras as a provincial literary center to George Sand's estate in Nohant, near Chateauroux. But this modern "Nohant" was destined not to enjoy the same kind of peaceful second life. During 1968, not long before Simone's death, a violent tornado savagely attacked Essendiéras, ripping off the great roof, causing enormous damage, and uprooting countless trees. It was almost as if Nature would not allow this literary chateau to remain unscathed, now that the literary people were gone. As for the apartment at 86, boulevard Maurice Barrès in Neuilly, it passed on to Maurois's children to be disposed of as they saw fit.

Maurois's seat at the French Academy was filled on April 24, 1969, by Marcel Arland, the co-editor of *La Nouvelle Revue Française.* To the surprise of many of the Academicians present and the newspapers reporting the event, Arland's initiation address went beyond the bounds of traditional Academic protocol: in lieu of praise of Maurois, he expressed certain personal reservations about the latter's true stature in the hierarchy of French letters. Even his tone shocked some by its irreverence. For the Academy, Jean Mistler responded in a welcoming address that left no doubt that Maurois's colleagues had always held their late associate in the highest personal and professional esteem. Academician Jean Delay, on leaving the room, remarked that "André Maurois had many friends among us. These believe that he merited a warmer discourse."[79]

A portrait of a man is really never complete without some understanding about how he feels with regard to matters of faith and the spiritual side of man, the existence or nonexistence of deity, the relations between the human being and the cosmos, salvation or the lack thereof. The religious attitudes of Maurois, despite his usual lucidity, defy easy definition and labels. Let me try to untangle some of the knots.

We must recall that he was born a Jew and that on two occasions married Catholic women. His second wife was, in fact, uncompromising and vocal in her observance of the rituals of Catholicism. In the eyes of the literary and social worlds of Paris, Maurois, despite these two marriages, belonged to a Jewish milieu in its broadest and nonsectarian scope. And in the eyes of the Nazis he was always regarded as a Jew. Nevertheless, by his own admission, his training in Judaism during childhood was minimal. There was not even a large enough Jewish community in Elbeuf for his family to belong to a congregation of his co-religionists. In contrast with most Jewish boys of thirteen, he did not have a bar mitzvah ceremony that would have introduced him formally to the rites of Jewish manhood.

During adulthood Maurois did not practice Judaism at all. He adhered to the rites or dogmas of no established religious sect. Nor did he actively oppose rites, dogmas, and sects, either. He did contribute his services as a lecturer to a variety of widely differing religious groups. Often he would appear as a speaker in fund-raising programs for Catholic charities. Occasionally he participated in Protestant and Jewish functions. He was especially active in the society known as France-Israel. His acquaintances included leading clergymen from all segments of the Christian and non-Christian worlds. For the most part he was an assimilated Jew who behaved more like a secular Frenchman than a sectarian Jew.

In his credos of life, in books like *Ce que je crois* for instance, he makes scant mention of the religious question and scarcely quotes from the Scriptures. His whole art of living seemed to revolve around the idea of a finite life here and now on this planet. As for an afterlife, Maurois always maintained an ambiguous position that derived from his blend of skepticism, agnosticism, and smiling pessimism. To those who sought to persuade him that one must at least hope for eternal salvation, he would often reply, not with vigorous counter-arguments but rather with polite, evasive assurances that *perhaps* (an oft-used term in his letters and conversations) one day he might be willing to consider adopting a less agnostic stance: "Perhaps, one day, after interrogating this apparently indifferent universe piously with the ardent desire to comprehend its sense, I shall see the rising up and eventual dissipation of the wall of haze that prevents my eyes from seeing the promised land" (from a private conversation with him).

Thanks to his second wife's constant contact with Catholic churchmen, the author had more personal relations with the latter group than with those of any other faith. In fact, Simone Maurois never abandoned hope that her husband would someday convert to her faith. She is guilty of having translated some of her wishful thinking into rumors that too easily spread throughout the high society of Paris. Some of Maurois's closest friends even thought he had once converted to Catholicism. Nothing was farther from the truth, as the final *Mémoires* of 1970 so strongly confirm. If anything, these *Mémoires* reveal a distinct reidentification with the faith of his parents as he grew older. One of his closest friends was the Canon Mugnier—who had performed the wedding ceremony in the small church at St. Médard d'Excideuil (to make Simone happy Maurois was ever willing to make concessions like a church wedding). Moreover, just prior to departing for the hospital for what was to be his ultimate operation, Maurois did hold a lengthy private conversation with the local priest from Excideuil, Father Pomarède, as already noted. Maurois did manifest a very real appreciation, even admiration for some of the precepts of Christianity. Nevertheless, despite these numerous, brief, and friendly flirtations with Catholic churchmen and laymen (let us not forget his audience with the Pope), André Maurois, né Emile Herzog, never forgot his birthright and did not consent to convert to the Catholic faith of his wives.

Nothing is more significant than the kind of funeral he had had: a public, even civil, ceremony in the courtyard of the French Academy at which a brief prayer by Father Pomarède was only one of several discourses presented by representatives of the government and the Academy. Maurois's true religion was after all that of literature, French culture and civilization, and the mundane world in which he played such a prominent role.

Part II
The World of Biographies

2
André Maurois in Search of a Genre—Biography

Biography—it is a beautiful genre.
Maurois, 1964 Lecture

It is dangerous to call a modern artist the greatest exponent and practitioner of his genre. Who would be bold enough to single out with impunity the greatest modern poet or novelist? But in the genre of biography few would refuse André Maurois the title of the greatest biographer of our time. This universal esteem is a fact. Pierre de Boisdeffre bestowed upon him the honorary title, "the Prince of Biographies."[1] The German magazine *Das Schönste* bravely referred to him as "the Master of the Biographical Romance,"[2] while in America the *Chicago Sunday Tribune Magazine* called him "France's greatest biographer of men and women."[3] Cyrill Connolly of the *London Times* had no qualms about writing that "M. André Maurois is the greatest living biographer. He is objective, subtle, truthful, painstaking, and he has the flair of a true biographer."[4] Michel Droit was once asked to predict Maurois's role with posterity. With no hesitation whatsoever he replied that "the biographical work will remain for all time. What people will know about Disraeli, Proust, Dumas they will learn from André Maurois."[5] In his sensitive book devoted to André Maurois, M. Jacques Suffel, a former high official at the Bibliothèque Nationale, called him "the greatest biographer of our time." In his chapter on Maurois's art of biography Suffel summarized the place this biographer holds in the history of the genre: "M. André Maurois is truly the renovator of a genre which before him Saint-Beuve and Taine had brought to a high point of perfection."[6]

A. Biography as a Genre

The ancient genre of biography goes back to the epoch when men started to trace verbal portraits of others. As an art-form the history of this genre could easily fill several volumes. Biography is a mixed literary type, containing elements of history, literary criticism, the essay, fiction, and epic poetry (like an epic poet the biographer should be able to relate his story with vigor as well as with accuracy), the literary portrait à la Plutarch and La Bruyère, and even dramatic art. For the great biographer is he who can reincarnate some of the stirring dramatic scenes from the lives of his subjects. The risks in such a heterogeneous genre are formidable. The biographer must be extremely skillful in blending these disparate elements. His concern for historical accuracy must not be excessively apparent, or he will bury his hero under a heap of dusty documents. The life of his subject should not be engulfed by an infinite series of critical analyses of texts. The biographer must avoid the dryness of a too abstract essay. But in his zeal to excite his readers he must not tell his story so well that its veracity suffers.

The biographer's *métier* can be a thankless one. The man who related the life of a Flaubert or a Vigny can lose himself in the glow of his brilliant subject. But he must avoid inserting his own personality too obtrusively into the text, for he could eclipse his subject with his own witticisms, which would be contrary to his goals as a biographer. On the other hand, it is not possible nor desirable for the biographer to efface himself entirely from his created work; all artistic works must bear the stamp of the artist who engendered them.

Few biographers have been able successfully to contend with the many hazards of their art. Of these few André Maurois seems to have been the master. Of course, Maurois did not begin in a vacuum. In the early years of his career and indeed throughout the decades of his life he could study the biographies written by others and emulate this genre as he read from such proven English biographers as Harold Nicolson and Desmond MacCarthy, from whom he must have learned much. Following a lifetime of incessant searching for the correct formula, he helped establish this important genre on a lofty plane. Jean Dutourd stated that "he had made of biography a major genre of literature."[7] Let me now trace the stages of Maurois as a biographer, from his earliest work, *Shelley*, to his last published, *Balzac*.

B. The Preparation of the Biographies

The total repertory of Maurois's lives of British, French, and Russian poets, politicians, explorers, novelists, scientists, and monarchs is impressive if for no other reason than that a single biographer proved himself equal to painting the portraits of so many different kinds of men and women. Maintaining a steadfast faith in the philosophy of action and will, no subject matter became an obstacle for him. In his volume on Alain he wrote: "One becomes an artist by making oneself what one wishes to see or to hear. There is only one way of making a bison or a hut appear, and that is to create it."[8] Once he selected his biographical subject, Maurois gave to it his unrestricted devotion, time, and energy. Any activity in his life unrelated to the project of the moment he relegated to secondary importance. From such an existence emerged an anormous list of biographies, of which André Billy wrote: "His faculty of work is prodigious. Undoubtedly he is of all today's writers the most fecund, without haste and fatigue ever being felt in what he writes."[9] No matter how large the biographical project or how complex the subject, Maurois seemed always to emerge from the travail victoriously.

Each of the biographies represented the culmination of a lifetime of slow maturation and reflection. Once he made the decision to do a biography, he needed an average time-span of three years for the actual research and composition. The journals and memoirs all attest to his lifelong interest in certain subjects long before his biographies on them had been undertaken. How many times did he visit or pass Nohant, en route to his chateau in Dordogne, before embarking upon his life of George Sand? The specter of Shelley had haunted him for many years before his biography of the poet was even begun. In fact, his first novel, *Ni ange ni bête* was really an attempt by a frustrated biographer to write a life of a Shelleyan hero without having at his disposal the necessary documents. What biographer could live in the intimacy of such numerous and fascinating documents as those available to him in the priceless epistolary collection of Simone Maurois without being tempted to make use of them? Long before he sent his manuscripts to his publishers Maurois devoted whole lecture series and weekly *feuilletons* to Hugo, Tourguéniev, Proust, the three Dumas, Adrienne de La Fayette, Edward VII, so that in reality his biographical volumes grew out of fragments and bits he had been writing on the same subjects. In short, he first nurtured his subject matters within the incubator of his mind long before he ever put pen to paper to deal with them for the first time.

While actively engaged in the composition of his biographies Maurois lived "in symbiosis" with his subject, to quote from Marcel Thiébaut.[10] He identified himself totally and emotionally with his heroes. Those who observed him during the preparation of his *Balzac* could corroborate the totality with which he actually lived with his subject. Every third sentence he uttered in casual conversation seemed to refer to some portion of *La Comédie humaine.* During their most ebullient conversations with him, his interlocutors sensed how often his attention darted from the subject under discussion toward some mysterious aspect in the life of Balzac on which he had been meditating.

The years of composition of a biography were a peripatetic period in Maurois's life. The pursuit of the requisite documents and facts about the worlds in which his heroes lived carried him to the superb Spoelberch de Louvenjoul Collection at Chantilly, needed for so many of his Romantic lives, to the British Museum for Disraeli and Edward VII, to Lorraine for the life of Lyautey, to Pisa, Venice, and Viareggio for the lives of Shelley and Byron, to the Chateau de La Grange for the lives of Gilbert and Adrienne de La Fayette, to the farthest reaches of Britanny for the world of Chateaubriand, to London's St. Mary's Hospital where Fleming did his research, to the home of Victor Hugo in Brussels, to Missolonghi, Greece, where Byron died. He also visited the cemeteries and burial places of his heroes. It was essential that he know from intimate experience the exact "climates" in which his subjects lived. After visiting Byron's haunt at Newstead Abbey in 1928, he wrote: "Rarely did I better comprehend the necessity for the biographer to see with his own eyes, the places where his heroes have lived."[11]

The preparation of a great biography undividedly engaged not only Maurois but also his wife. The role played by Mme Maurois in the preparation of all of his lives, since *Shelley* and *Disraeli,* could form the basis for several large chapters. With charm and candor she described this role in a lecture she presented in 1956, published by Les Annales of Paris under the title "The Writer's Wife."[12] Endowed with an unusual flair for tracking down, classifying, and cataloguing rare documents, she aided her husband, as noted earlier, not only as a historian and researcher but also as a secretary: she typed and proofread the several versions of each of the biographical manuscripts and prepared single-handedly the useful indexes of names and works cited and the monumental bibliographies that appear at the end of his biographies.[13] The "note liminaire" of every one of her spouse's biographies contains some acknowledgment of Mme Maurois's important role in his work. In *Les Trois Dumas* and again in *Adrienne,* Maurois describes his wife as "another myself." In *Olympio:* "This work—the most vast and difficult that I have yet undertaken, never would have been realized without her." In *Lélia:* "Never has my debt toward her been greater than at this time. She has gone through and classified mountains of letters, archives and documents. She has copied this long manuscript five times, in successive versions." It is primarily in the composition of the biographies that the florescent collaboration between husband and wife attained its most successful fulfillment.

In every one of his great biographies, since *Ariel ou la Vie de Shelley,* André Maurois had been deeply concerned with his need to feel secure in his erudition. He struggled to sketch with exactness his subject's tormented face. In his search for documentary accuracy he consulted police records, archives of births and deaths, scribblings, sketches, manuscripts, unpublished speeches. Nothing seemed too sacred or too trivial. In *Olympio* he quotes from bills sent by the Laiterie Suisse to Mme Adèle Hugo for creamery products delivered to her and from Juliette Drouet's weekly accountings of her domestic expenditures down to the last sou. In *Les Trois Dumas* he analyzes the terms of the mortgage of Dumas père's chateau at Port-Marly. In *Adrienne* he lists the exact costs of refurnishing and remodeling the Chateau de La Grange. The quaintest fact, he reasoned, sometimes throws more light on a subject than the most polished epistle.

Immense collections of documents can be dangerous. The historian runs the risk of being devoured by sheer quantities of facts. Maurois the artist always rescued Maurois the historian from this danger of excessive data. In the final composition, the author of *Climats* came to the rescue of the author of the lives of Fleming and Edward VII by selecting only the essential items and eliminating the overly weighty or superfluous ones. "But once the research has been done with the greatest care possible, then the work of the artist begins," he wrote. Of the biographer, he continued: "His duty is to know everything, not to utilize everything."[14]

C. A Parade of Varieties

André Maurois's career as biographer started in 1923, with *Ariel ou la Vie de Shelley;* his Balzac appeared in 1965. He published fourteen large-scaled biographies and several volumes of shorter lives and portraits. Collectively, this production forms an imposing group of titles which, when seen from a distance, appears as a relatively unified block. In *Portrait d'un ami qui s'appelait moi (Portrait of a Friend Whose Name is Me)* Maurois emphasized with surprising objectivity those elements which unify his volumes (see especially pages 45–52). Nevertheless, within the sum total of these biographies one finds also an impressive variety of types, traits, and subjects.

The biographies can be classified into various groups of subjects, which we may call galaxies or clusters. The first galaxy is that of the British world. There one finds *Shelley* and *Byron.* Nurtured by their poetry, another hero, *Disraeli,* extends the British web into politics. This web includes *Edward VII et son temps* and the shorter biography of Sir Cecil Rhodes.

The second and largest galaxy consists of what Maurois described as his "romantic gallery."[15] In this latter category figure George Sand, Dumas père and fils, Hugo, Tourguéniev, the aging Chateaubriand, Balzac—not to mention such accessory persons as Pauline Viardot, Liszt, Chopin, Musset, Vigny, Marie Dorval, Mme Récamier, Sainte-Beuve, all of whose portraits appear in the longer works. Chronologically this Romantic world starts with the childhood of Chateaubriand and ends with the death of Dumas fils. A third, but closely related galaxy, is that which surrounds the French Revolution. In *Adrienne* and *René* the reader is witness to the similar effects of the terror upon two different families. Maurois's *Voltaire* forms the prelude to this group of biographies.

If his largest galaxies were centered in the eighteenth and nineteenth centuries, he did not neglect his own epoch. The most interesting chapters of *Edward VII* deal with the decade preceding the First World War. The life of Fleming is a twentieth-century drama. Marshal Lyautey belongs to our century. The biography he wrote "with the greatest love," in fact, is that of a twentieth-century figure, Marcel Proust.[16] His anthologies are rich in shorter lives of contemporary figures. All of the portraits in *Etudes littéraires* and *De Proust à Camus,* a large proportion of those in *Etudes Anglaises* and *Destins exemplaires,* and a few of those in *De La Bruyère à Proust* are of figures of the present century.

The biographies vary in form. Most are massive in size and serious in tone. A few seem less ponderous, more informal; these latter ones had originally been lectures delivered by Maurois under the auspices of the Société des Conférences or the Université des Annales. Such are the life of Dickens (which occupies at least half of the *Etudes Anglaises* and which he refused to describe as anything more than an "esquisse") and *Tourguéniev,* a collection of five complementary discourses. In the latter volume the style is direct, uncluttered by footnotes and documented quotations and dates, all of which would have made it tedious for the auditor of a lecture to follow.[17] The shorter biographical essays contained in *Etudes Littéraires* are reprints of lectures presented in America during the Second World War, Maurois's "biography" of biography, *Aspects de la Biographie,* was, in fact, the text of four lectures delivered at Cambridge University in 1928. *Edouard VII et son temps* had also originally been a series of lectures, but it was so substantially revised and expanded that it belongs with the group of large-scale biographies.

The most important set of biographies, from the point of view of scholars, is probably the series that started with *René ou la Vie de Chateaubriand* (1938) and extended through *Prométhée ou la Vie de Balzac.* This group stands out by virtue of the enormous emphasis given by the biographer to scholarly documentation. These are large volumes, in which the text seems to be consubstantial with the sources and footnotes. Such scrupulous attention was given here to the question of documentation and completeness that the block of lives devoted to Chateaubriand, Hugo, Sand, the three Dumas, Balzac, Fleming, Mme de La Fayette, and Proust, cannot fail to be considered as one of the most comprehensive monuments of research erected by a nonscholar literary artist.

Maurois's biographies vary according to the types of lives his heroes led. In the main his subjects were selected because of the spectacular nature of their existences. With the important exception of Proust, most of his heroes lived rich external lives. They dreamed great dreams, enjoyed and suffered from turbulent love affairs, wrote herculean quantities, and involved themselves in the tempestuous politics and violent wars of their times. For Byron, George Sand, Victor Hugo, Dumas père, "the most beautiful drama was their life . . . the epic melodrama."[18] These titanic figures altered the character of art and politics in the western world. Most were people who had to conquer formidable obstacles. Like Maurois himself, who once as a scrawny adolescent succeeded by sheer dint of will in winning the highest medal in gymnastics, Byron, Disraeli, Hugo, and Voltaire all overcame similar weaknesses or afflctions. George Sand had to struggle to exert herself as a woman in a world where only men were taken seriously. Voltaire, of common birth, campaigned against a society where only aristocratic birth counted. Dumas père had to cope with prejudice against those with mixed racial blood, while his son had the problem of a similar prejudice against those of illegitimate birth. The child Chateaubriand had the psychological struggle of feeling himself the least loved of his sisters and brothers. Even Edward VII, as a child, could barely satisfy Queen Victoria's and Prince Albert's ambitious hopes for their heir apparent. Among the many other striking coincidences between Maurois the biographer and his many models, one notes that Maurois and Lyautey both had to overcome physical weaknesses caused by defective vertebral formations. Also, let us remember that no one better than this Jewish-born biographer could more poignantly describe the inner conflicts sustained by the half-Jewish children, Disraeli and Proust, in predominantly gentile communities.

In the following passage, the biographer justifies his preference for heroes who led stormy lives and reveals some of his reasons for writing their biographies:

> At any time in history, a small group of privileged souls seems entrusted to live, by proxy, as it were, passionate lives for the account and the pleasure of those of us, an innumerable mass, who will know only mediocre and dull existences. Some thirty intrepid men and women, freed by birth, power or genius, take immense risks, yield to their desires, and console, both by their triumphs and their failures, those to whom circumstances did not allow the same courage. In the seventeenth century, the august troupe that played, before the French public, the dramas of life, was composed of royal personages and mistresses of the kings; in the eighteenth century, this troupe still existed, but to it are already added the *philosophes* and their lady friends; in the nineteenth century, the bourgeois monarchy no longer fed the appetites for the romantic ("appétit de romanesque") which time has never alleviated. The thirty persons who make love for the entire world from 1820 to 1850 are artistic types.[19]

His thousands of readers scattered around the world still persist in sharing an "appétit de romanesque." For them his biographies offer rich satisfaction.

D. *From Ariel to Prometheus*

The evolutionary path of Maurois's art of biography is an interesting one to follow. From *Ariel,* once accused somewhat unjustly of being only "une vie romancée," to *Adrienne* and *Balzac,* with their hundreds of notes, long lists of references, and thousands of quotations, his art underwent a massive transformation. Each successive work marked increased concern for accuracy and erudition. The importance attached by this biographer to scholarly documentation was appreciated by the scholarly René Lalou: "He who will consult these notes will only appreciate all the more the suppleness of the narrator, who has arranged his abundant information and dominates it without any apparent effort."[20]

Ariel ou la Vie de Shelley must be considered as the debut of this biographer. In his preface to later editions of the work, Maurois revealed slight uneasiness about his first attempt at biography and implied that he wished that *Ariel* "were separated from my other biographies." Written as a kind of "personal confession" of his own adolescent faults and not mainly out of concern for documentary accuracy, *Shelley* is indeed unique among his biographies. He admits that "I conceived badly what a work of research might and ought to be."[21] Whenever documents were unavailable, Maurois the novelist accentuated the rapid flow of the poet's life or filled in with his imagination some of the gaps of information. Detractors immediately charged that this was "a romanticized biography" or "a novelized biography," a charge that failed to disturb the author. He candidly retorted: "Let's say it then, if you wish, that *Ariel* is a novel."[22] Unfortunately, even competent critics occasionally remain fixed in their earliest judgment of a writer, though that writer has since changed drastically. So nowadays one occasionally finds readers who, without having truly analyzed the subsequent biographies, persist in referring to Maurois's lives of Chateaubriand or Hugo as "fictional biographies." Nothing can be farther from the truth.

Soon after the appearance of his *Ariel,* a vicious campaign was launched against Maurois in which he was accused of plagiarism. With three seemingly facile succeses to his credit—*The Silences of Colonel Bramble, The Discourses of Doctor O'Grady,* and *Ariel or the Life of Shelley*—several writers sought to disparage the apparently too effortless ascendancy of a newcomer from the provinces. The publisher Bernard Grasset had already warned Maurois to expect a Machiavellian attack to be launched against him by those who envied his easy achievements. Several professional writers had felt that the *Shelley* read too much like a novel; it flowed too effortlessly. Besides, hadn't Maurois acknowledged his reliance on a number of books that had already appeared on the English poet? Maurois refers to his attackers as the "Team from the *Mercure de France*," which included Louis Dumur, Valette, and especially Paul Léautaud. After trying in vain to obtain some distinguished anglicist to substantiate their charges that Maurois had plagiarized other source books, this "Team" finally located a foolish young critic, Auriant, whom they persuaded to write two accusatory articles during 1928 in the *Mercure de France.* In Maurois's words: "The attack was brutal, but totally ineffective." The assault continued until it encompassed even Maurois's newly published *Life of Disraeli.* His enemies had gone too far. If Maurois acknowledged freely that the *Ariel* was "a novelized biography" ("une biographie romancée,") he knew that the *Disraeli* could stand on its own feet as a genuine piece of literary art and of biographical soundness. Unable to ignore his assailants any longer, Maurois was granted "equal time" and replied in the *Mercure de France,* effectively obliterating his critics, including the British writer Frank Harris, who had belatedly joined Auriant, Léautaud, and company. Later on in his life, Léautaud regretted his anti-Maurois assault and, à propos of the latter's novel *Climats* he wrote: "He has written a beautiful novel. We were wrong in attacking him." (Maurois gives the complete account of this incident in his *Mémoires* (Paris: Flammarion, 1970, pp. 193–95). Following this painful episode,

Maurois went to great lengths to protect himself from further public abuse by relying increasingly on documentation and by regularly stating his attributions.

In fact, even *Ariel* can be defended as a more or less exact reproduction of the English poet's life. Who can deny that Maurois's airy version of Shelley is consistent with the impression of him one gets when reading his poetry? Louis Chaigne is right in calling Maurois's art of making each page live with Shelley's poetic presence "a new formula in biography."[23] The essential parts of *Ariel* are based on documentation. But the story is recounted with such charm that the reader believes he is reading fiction. On a few minor points the biographer, for want of key documents, did err. In his second preface he admits his mistakes. Taking into account certain shortcomings, *Ariel* nonetheless is significant because it marks the beginning of an important biographer's career and because it is a fascinating life of an attractive literary figure. André Chevrillon summed up the quality of this work:

> The life of Shelley, which was so brief, was so great; such dramas traversed it, that you were able to detach it from his work and to present it like a novel. But your entire book is based on documents. At times you make one of his texts enter into the free flow of the tale, at times you draw out of it the elements of a scene, of a dialogue.[24]

Almost the entire emphasis is on Shelley's life rather than upon the relationships between the poetry and life of this writer. Some of Maurois's detractors have raised this point as a criticism. But the title, *Ariel or The Life of Shelley* adequately invalidates this objection.

La Vie de Disraeli is Maurois's most celebrated and most read biography. Translated into all of the major languages of the world, it and the novel *Climats* made of the former Emile Herzog a writer of best-sellers.[25] *Disraeli,* his second biography, represents a noteworthy step forward in his career. In terms of rigorous documentation, it is an improvement over *Ariel.* Every paragraph is solidly buttressed by such sources as Disraeli's own writings and by quotations from or references to some seventy-five works concerning him. With extraordinary finesse Maurois blends quoted sources with his own text into a coherent fabric. Stylistically, this work must rank with Maurois's finest. He achieves here a perfect balance between a narrative presentation that reads like a novel and one that is solid in erudition. The book is further enhanced because the hero, Benjamin Disraeli, is both irresistible and unforgettable. Some of Maurois's most colorful sentences and felicitous images grace this impeccable book. Identifying himself more closely with Disraeli than with any of his other heroes, Maurois confided that "never did I write a book with greater pleasure."[26] This is obvious to anyone reading the book. For many Frenchmen, Disraeli is Maurois's most distinguished creation. François Mauriac, who followed his contemporary's works closely and systematically, summarized the reactions of so many others when he stated that "*Disraeli* is, in my opinion, his masterpiece."[27]

More than the life of a hero, *Disraeli* is the history of an era. Demonstrating his competence as a historian, Maurois has painted here a portrait of a heroic figure who stands out against the background of a reverberating historical fresco (a rolling carpet, "un tapis roulant," as Maurois himself calls it.)[28] The biographer-historian succeeds here in relating the personal life of a great man, while at the same time depicting the main internal and international developments of the British Empire. Later, in *Edouard VII et son temps*, he would not only relate the life of a king but his book would become "the crossroads at which we ought to place ourselves in order to comprehend the Europe of 1900."[29] His other biographies concerning men of letters also unfold against the setting of eternally shifting history. As the author of three large histories (*England, The United States,* and *France*) Maurois manifested a predilection for subjects who had involved themselves in the historical currents of their times: Byron, Voltaire, Chateaubriand, George Sand, Hugo. His life of Dumas père reverberates with the political changes in post-Napoleonic France. That of Tourguéniev does not properly begin until after a long historical section devoted to the political and social conditions in Tzarist Russia. In all of the great lives the reader is constantly reminded of "this initial canvas" against which background his heroes and heroines live.[30] The life of Adrienne de La Fayette is more than the history of her sentimental and personal relations with her husband; it is an attempt by the author to make us "relive the most interesting period of France (and of the United States), through private existences, which are so rich and so mingled with the life of the two nations."[31]

In *Shelley* we find no notes. References to sources there are so subtle as to be almost indiscernible. *Disraeli*, on the other hand, is a more open attempt to reconcile scholarly accuracy with novelistic art. It opens with several pages of acknowledgments and lists of sources. However, it contains no notes at the bottom of the pages or at the end.

Maurois's third biography, *Don Juan ou la Vie de Byron*, represents a more advanced stage in his search for the ideal biographical formula. The pendulum has swung from one extreme to another. *Byron*, constructed of two volumes that total more than five-hundred pages, is almost oppressively laden with sources, quotations, facts, and dates. One senses here that the biographer was determined this time not to lay himself open to possible charges that his latest work was a "fictionalized biography." Every paragraph seems to contain some specific facts. Every event is accompanied by an exact date. Maurois's *Byron* can be criticized precisely because its documentation seems too apparent, even too self-conscious, and sometimes impedes the reading of the text. It lacks the airiness of *Shelley* and *Disraeli* and reads much more ponderously. Instead of notes at the bottom of each page, the author lists his references at the end of each volume, chapter by chapter. The two volumes contain some eighteen pages of densely printed notes and an eight-page chronological summary of events covered in the biography. Though less exciting to read, the *Byron* offers those who reach the terminal point in this great life story an inevitable sense of intellectual enrichment. One feels a real pleasure in studying a portrait that has been so meticulously constructed. The distinguished British biographer and critic, Desmond MacCarthy was quoted by Michel Droit on the subject of Maurois's *Byron:* "One must not forget that it is the most serious and the most complete book which we possess on Byron."[32] The British do not easily extend such compliments to foreign writers who write monographs about their own national heroes.

The year following *Byron* there appeared the life of Lyautey. This biography may still be considered the most authoritative study of this dashing military and administrative hero. After several successful reprints, the same publisher (Plon) reissued the *Lyautey* in 1964, this time in a bound edition. *Lyautey* is the first biography by André Maurois to contain footnotes (though not many). Its documentation is solid and evident. Maurois quotes generously from hitherto classified ministerial reports, telegrams, military dispatches. But here the most important document is the Marshal himself, whom the biographer knew intimately for many years. In fact, Lyautey was the only model Maurois actually observed personally during the composition of a biography. In the final pages, the Marshal even injects himself directly into the scene. One has the feeling of seeing a movie in which the director becomes an actor and allows the camera to capture his gestures. The warm affiliation between the portraitist and his subject is reflected in each page, which breathes with the latter's presence. In his relations with his biographer, the marshal was astonishingly uninhibited. Lyautey wrote in a letter to Maurois: "With you, who are on the best terms with me, I pour forth my heart."[33] Lyautey remains a valuable work for those who wish to understand the historical background of events in North Africa and Madagascar today.

Following the first four lives, *Voltaire,* published in 1932, is indeed the allegro movement in Maurois's symphony of biographies. A small-scaled, quickly paced volume, its exciting chapters are easily traversed by the breathless reader in a few short hours. But the book is not devoid of serious documentation; at the outset, the biographer lists his sources—Voltaire's works and correspondence and such books as the memoirs of Longchamps and Wagnière, the letters of Mme de Graffigny, the monographs of Argentol, Lanson, Brunetière, and others. Because of its minuscule proportions and the speed with which he wrote it, the author refused to consider this biography among his more important achievements. It had always been a source of wonderment to him that Alain, whose judgment he esteemed more highly than that of anyone else, should have been so favorably impressed with the work. In pencil Maurois has scribbled this note on the frontispiece of his wife's personal copy of *Voltaire:* "Here is a too brief book, written as the pen flows and without research, but Alain liked it. He judged it Voltairean by this very rapidity and this allegretto movement. Alain was a good judge and I endorse my professor."[34] The book resembles *Candide* in size, tempo, and spirit, and deserves serious attention as a minor masterpiece that combines the competence of an eminent biographer with the compactness of a modern essay. It really constitutes a pastiche of the style of Voltaire himself.

Edouard VII et son temps is the biography of an important king and the history of a dramatic moment in European affairs. Graphically, Maurois depicts the epoch starting with the waning years of Queen Victoria's reign until the epochal funeral of Edward VII, an event that many consider the threshhold of World War I. The biographer patiently and lucidly synthesized piles of sources: wires, bulletins from the British War Office and the Quai d'Orsay, memoirs and correspondence, agenda and minutes, newspaper editorials and even cartoons in French and German humor magazines. Those who knew the inner world described by Maurois with such drama attested to the accuracy of his version. For example, King Albert I of Belgium wrote in a letter to Maurois: "This book is a masterpiece. It adds a documentation of the highest order and some original insights to contemporary history, which is still the least known."[35] In this biographer's career, *Edouard VII et son temps* represents a vital link between two genres that consumed so much of his creative energy: history (his *Histoire d'Angleterre* appeared four years later) and biography. With this work we have the impression that the biographer has established a comfortable reconciliation between the art of narrating a story well and the art of portraying a model precisely.

After years of research and composition, he published in 1938 the first portrait in his gallery of French Romantic writers, *René ou la Vie de Chateaubriand*. André Maurois seemed to have attained in this work his final formula for biography. The *René*, in fact, is a premonition of the postwar biographies, in its tone, unimpeachable scholarship, and size. (It ends with ten pages of carefully prepared notes.)

The composition of a life of Chateaubriand proved a real challenge. The character of this figure contained frightfully drastic contradictions. Maurois's problem was this: how could a biographer give cohesiveness to the portrait of such a man? "A disciple of Rousseau and an enemy of Robespierre, an admirer of Bonaparte and an enemy of Napoleon, a monarchist and rebel for his kings, a liberal and an ultra, a reasonable man and a visionary, Chateaubriand had been for forty years a cruelly divided man. . . ."[36] But Maurois succeeded in his unifying task, just as the painter succeeds in creating out of a combination of clashing colors a harmoniously organized painting. The lesson the biographer learned in arranging an orderly biography out of "the boiling mélange of his passions"[37] served him well when after the Second World War he wrote the lives of such complex souls as Proust, Hugo, and Sand. In his *Chateaubriand* the biographer demonstrated that he could smile at some of the humorous defects in the character of a hero despite his admiration of the subject. Like Stendhal, who smiled at some of the foibles of his hero Julien Sorel, Maurois painted Chateaubriand's obsession "of sculpturing for posterity a statue of himself which would fix him for eternity in the pose which pleased him."[38] Maurois's veneration of Hugo, Chateaubriand, George Sand, Dumas père, and others combined, in fact, a delicate blend of sympathetic admiration and candor as he described both their virtues and defects.

The closing sentence of *René* is a tour de force. In a dozen lines Maurois sums up his biography. His final words can readily stand as the coda for all of his biographies: "Such was *approximately* [italics mine] the story of François-René de Chateaubriand."[39] The final sentence of *René* ranks also with some of Maurois's other superb sentences that sum up entire volumes, among them, the twenty-eight-line sentence at the end of *Adrienne,* the thirty-line sentence that begins and sums up the life of *Lélia,* the eighteen-line sentence that opens his *Proust* and describes the latter's life in one vast Proustian curve. Specialists of stylistics would find the study of Maurois's first and last sentences to be most rewarding research projects for at least a minor research article.

From *René* to *A la recherche de Marcel Proust* there was an interim of eleven years. The Second World War and the intervening years spent in America delayed his creation of new biographies. The first postwar biography on Proust demonstrates that while Maurois produced no lives during more than a decade, he spent this period reflecting on ways of refining the art of biography even further. His *Proust* contains one singular innovation: all of the copius notes appear at the bottom of the pages, an innovation that he would repeat in all of the subsequent biographies. He seemed happy about this development: "For a long time I feared notes at the bottom of the pages. I have come to require them."[40] The documentation is, furthermore, inextricably integrated with the text of the biography. Almost invariably the biographical works that follow *A la recherche de Marcel Proust* are considered by the critics reviewing them as among the definitive biographies of these subjects.[41]

It is possible that no one before Maurois had written a finer work on Marcel Proust that includes both a biography and an incisive analysis of the Proustian writings. The spirit of this author haunted Maurois for many years preceding his composition of Proust's life. His essays and discourses on him were scattered throughout his career. In 1932 Maurois wrote a curious little volume, *Le Côté de Chelsea,* as a surprisingly authentic pastiche of Proust's style. Also, when Maurois married the former Simone de Caillavet, he began almost literally to bathe in the luminous atmosphere of Proust. We know that she served as the main prototype for Proust's Mlle de Saint-Loup. Also she could relate many true anecdotes about this writer. Proust had been closely associated with her father, the playwright Gaston de Caillavet, and with Robert de Flers, her legal guardian following her father's death. Finally Proust frequented the salons of Mme Maurois's grandmother, Mme Arman de Caillavet, and her mother, Mme Jeanne Pouquet. These salons are depicted in his great novel. Maurois's career had been so tightly linked with Proust that in France he was regarded as one of the truly eminent authorities on this subject.

Much of the importance of Maurois's *Proust* stems from the fact that Mme

Gérard Mante-Proust, the famous author's niece and heiress, permitted him for the first time to quote from Proust's unpublished and previously confidential *carnets* and *cahiers* and from the correspondence beween Marcel and his parents. Thus this biography was more than a life of Proust; it was important as a work of major scholarly value; in it new light was thrown upon the personality and the work of the protagonist. Thanks to previously unpublished documents André Maurois unraveled some of the mysterious aspects in the Proustian personality. Although the biographer devoted entire chapters to thematic and stylistic analysis, his particular art of story-telling made the volume interesting for the specialist and layman alike. Because of the consubstantial relationship between Proust's life and *A la recherche du temps perdu*, this biography is unique among Maurois's collection. Emile Henriot, in his review of the biography, pointed this out: "You can't disassociate in Proust the man from the writer, which are only one."[42] As the biographer told the life of his hero, he indulged simultaneously in a kind of genetic criticism, demonstrating how the book was gradually engendered, bit by bit and character by character. Robert de Montesquiou gradually was transformed into parts of Charlus, Céleste into Françoise, Cabourg into Balbec, Illiers into Combray:

> At the beginning there was Illiers, a hamlet of two thousand inhabitants, but in the end there was Combray, the spiritual fatherland of millions of readers, dispersed today on all of the continents and who tomorrow will line themselves up along the centuries—in time.[43]

Structurally the *Proust* is different from the others. After the first chapters, concerning the gradual impregnation of Proust's existence by his work (and vice-versa), there comes a crucial middle section of three chapters in which the novel assumed complete mastery over Proust's life (and also over Maurois's story of that life). In these three chapters, the biographer, undergoing a kind of Proustian reincarnation, emerged as a literary critic who devoted the core of his volume to a series of investigations into Proust's themes, characterizations, poetic imagery, temporal and spatial relationships, varieties of love, and sense of humor. On the last of these, Maurois's chapter may well be the best essay yet written. In the final chapters the life of Proust glides smoothly to its ultimate conclusion.

Following *A la recherche de Marcel Proust*, master biography followed master biography. Three years afterward, *Lélia ou la Vie de George Sand* appeared. "Friendships of the mind," wrote Maurois, "are formed by chains and encounters, like friendships of the heart."[44] Through his attachment to Proust, who was nurtured on George Sand, and his loyalty to the tastes of Alain, who warmly admired her work, Maurois was irresistibly drawn into the little circle of "friendships of spirit" that included George Sand. Simone Maurois possessed impressive collections of correspondence by Sand. André Maurois knew Nohant intimately. From his special affinities and resources, and after years of research at Chantilly and the Bibliothèque Nationale manuscript department, he recreated the biography of one of the most fascinating figures in French literary history. Of this biography Robert Kemp boldly wrote: "And there you have, I do not fear the term, an authentic masterpiece."[45]

Maurois consulted an unimaginable mass of conflicting documents, all of which thrust him into the inner folds of the lives of Musset, Chopin, Jules Sandeau, Liszt, Dr. Pagello, and a great many other Romantic figures. Out of this mass he succeeded in creating an entirely fresh (and quite probably authentic) portrait of a much-abused, much-misunderstood heroine. His George Sand was no licentious ogress, who unscrupulously tormented the souls of gullible men. An exceedingly complex personality, she thirsted for absolute happiness through a wide variety of amorous relationships. The bibliography for *Lélia* is immense; thousands of references and footnotes abound. The index of names cited in the text is twenty pages long and includes approximately a thousand different persons from the worlds of politics, music, journalism, science, letters, sculpture, painting, and the military.[46] *Lélia* evolves against the background of two empires and two republics.

By now Maurois's hand as a biographer was strong and steady. No obstacle seemed insurmountable. It was time to attempt the life of the most Olympian figure of an Olympian age, that of Victor Hugo. The careers of Chateaubriand and George Sand seemed logically to lead to that of France's greatest poet.[47] Maurois's largest biography, *Olympio ou la Vie de Victor Hugo* is an enormous volume of over six hundred pages. Perhaps posterity will even regard it as his most important biography. Again the documentation is impressive. At least twelve hundred persons figure in this dense volume. The author of *Aspects de la biographie* synthesizes all of the aspects of Hugo's many earlier biographies, so that we observe the poet not only through the eyes of André Maurois but also as Balzac, Sainte-Beuve, Théophile Gautier, Flaubert, and the Goncourt brothers saw him. Previously most biographies painted Hugo as he related to a particular subject: Hugo and Mme Biard, Hugo and Juliette Drouet, Hugo and politics, Hugo and the two Napoleons, Hugo and Romanticism, and so on. In Maurois's book all of these topics have been woven into one unified tapestry. In contrast with *Lélia*, where the life of George Sand is more interesting to posterity than her published volumes, *Olympio* contains many probing analyses of Hugo's greatest works arranged in the order in which he produced them.[48] Here it is apparent that Hugo's poetry, plays, and novels count more than his life and are at least as interesting as the tale of his existence.

After the research for *Lélia* and *Olympio*, Maurois's romantic itinerary led him to recapture the amazing careers of Dumas père and fils. Again Mme Maurois's collection of letters proved extremely useful. *Les Trois Dumas* is as rich in erudition as the other great biographies. Myriads of notes adorn the bottoms of the pages. Some thousand names traverse the careers of the three protagonists. Quoted documents are integrated with the descriptive text. Critical analyses alternate with biographical passages. The lives of Dumas père and fils, in particular, seem as melodramatic as some of the fictional lives created by them. This biography is equally valuable to the scholar of literature and the amateur of fiction. What is innovative here is Maurois's successful treatment of grandfather, father, and son in one smoothly flowing and unified sweep. Convincingly he demonstrated how qualities and defects were transferred from generation to generation.

At the midway point in the twentieth century the reputation of André Maurois as one of the world's two or three leading biographers was undisputed. Lady Fleming, the wife of the celebrated British scientist, considering him "the best biographer there is,"[49] actively solicited the cooperation of the only man she deemed qualified to render justice to her scientist-husband. Maurois's initial reaction to her proposal was understandably negative. In the preface to *La Vie de Sir Alexander Fleming* he candidly describes his earliest trepidations about doing the life of a pure scientist. But finally he accepted. His real reason for doing a project for which he doubted his qualifications was that "difficulty is itself a challenge."[50] As a matter of fact, he thrived on difficult challenges. To tell the truth, the life of Fleming was not entirely a novel experience for him. In his lives of Shelley, Byron, Disraeli, and Edward VII, he had already established a fundamental knowledge of the English (and Scottish) people and customs. Once again he visited England, studied the facilities in Fleming's laboratories, consulted with his old friend, Dr. G. W. B. James (the principal model for Dr. O'Grady), who had known Fleming, and had conferences with other scientists associated with Fleming in the penicillin research. The three-year process of Maurois's composition of his *Fleming* is described in an article by Dr. Albert Delaunay, the then director of pathological research at the Garches Annex of the Institut Pasteur. Early in his scientific career, as a kind of intellectual escape from the rigors of pure scientific research, Delaunay formed the hobby of collecting every single item ever published by Maurois or ever written by others about him. Later in his life, one complete room in his then Vaucresson villa (in the eastern suburbs of Paris) was laden with a voluminous collection of Mauroisean archives. Delaunay even ends letters with the bizarre salutation, "Mauroisionnement vôtre." The biographer took a complete course in bacteriology and even carefully retraced Dr. Fleming's research, step by step, as demonstrated in the laboratory by Dr. Delaunay. Because of the technical nature of this subject Maurois asked Dr. Delaunay to read his manuscript before he submitted it to the publisher. One of France's leading pathologists, Dr. Delaunay described his reactions to the manuscript as follows: "Who knows, Maurois as a microbiologist might have perhaps brought to his country the glory he gives her as a writer. . . . Maurois showed me his first manuscript. I read, I read avidly. There wasn't a single scientific error in it. . . . I remained confounded before this *tour de force*."[51] And when the manuscript did finally appear in published form, the critics were ecstatic in their praise. Here was a biography equal in documented excellence and artistic quality to Maurois's best. The eminent British biographer Harold Nicholson summed up these reactions: "M. Maurois, with the aid of experts, has described the scientific aspect of these researches in language which even I can understand. He has with his accustomed skill mingled the private and the public life into a consistent pattern, describing as all good biographers ought to describe, the impact of character on circumstance."[52] The book reads easily, and the nonexpert reader has the double pleasure of learning a great deal about bacteriology and about the life of a very likable human being, whose destiny is as engaging as that of Sand or Byron.

La Vie de Sir Alexander Fleming and *Adrienne de La Fayette* stand apart from the other biographies because of the circumstantial reasons for their composition. In the one case Lady Fleming proved persuasive and the challenge irresistible. In the second case, the descendants of La Fayette had accidentally discovered in one of the hidden corners of the Chateau de La Grange, in the Brie country, the correspondence between Gilbert and Adrienne de La Fayette, believed lost and preserved almost miraculously. Maurois, by then the foremost biographer of the time, was invited to use these incredibly rich archives and to write the first "official" biography of La Fayette. Again an irresistible challenge! Interestingly he elected to tell the story from the point of view of the wife of the great La Fayette. A significant international hero lives through the eyes of his spouse, and her nobility of character creates the tone for the volume. The biographical focal point shifts from husband to wife and vice versa, but above all the domestic life of the La Fayette couple is skillfully intertwined with the history of their epoch. Approximately six hundred figures stalk across some five hundred fifty pages.[53] Each of Maurois's biographies has had its adherents who regarded it as his finest work. Among the admirers of *Adrienne* was Pierre Audiat: "With a sureness of infallible judgment, Monsieur André Maurois drew from this treasure intimate unpublished letters which allowed him to trace of Adrienne de La Fayette a portrait that was more precise and nuanced than the image which her contemporaries had formed of her."[54] According to Audiat, this work was Maurois's masterpiece.

After *Adrienne*, Maurois had time to produce only one additional biography, *Prométhée ou la Vie de Balzac*, which appeared in 1965. Alain nurtured in him the requisite admiration for *La Comédie humaine*, an admiration that he described in his penetrating essay on Balzac in *Destins exemplaires*. Maurois had always dreamed of doing a biography of Balzac. In his early science-fiction tale, *La Machine à lire les pensées*, *(The Machine for Reading Thoughts)*, the protagonist (quite obviously Maurois himself) is a professor (Maurois the biographer had often confessed his frustration at not having been a professor) who has written a brilliant thesis on Balzac and who goes to America to teach a course on this novelist. (In 1946 André Maurois also gave a course at the University of Kansas City that covered Balzac.) Like the professor's thesis in the short story, his biography of Balzac turned out to be a brilliant work.

According to the preface to *Prométhée ou la Vie de Balzac*, the indefatigable writer was concerned at the outset with the indomitable realities of his eighty

5 Avril 1965

Mon cher ami

Merci pour les articles. Vous faites du bon travail. Le <u>Balzac</u> marche très bien. Tous les critiques sont délicieux. Je vais vous l'envoyer. (J'ai épuisé mes exemplaires et j'en demande à Hachette. Vous trouvez ci-joint le questionnaire Kraus avec mes réponses. Isabelle s'est établie libraire! J'espère que cela ne durera pas et qu'elle nous reviendra. En ce moment elle ne peut travailler pour nous ni pour vous.

Mille amitiés à tous deux

André Maurois

Personal letter from André Maurois to Jack Kolbert. Jack Kolbert Archives. (Courtesy, Estate of André Maurois.)

years of age: "My age will no longer permit me henceforth either vast projects or infinite research. This biography will be the last that I shall write. It pleases me that *Balzac* should be its hero." As a work of scholarly solidity, the *Balzac* compares with the best of Maurois's biographies. Charged with at least two thousand carefully prepared notes, four appendixes, unpublished materials, and a twenty-page index containing approximately a thousand names that figure in the text, this biography contains a complex apparatus of documentation that could not possibly fail to satisfy the most demanding scholar. At the same time Maurois, the unembarrassed hero-worshiper, does not make the slightest effort to conceal his unabashed admiration of his hero. Exalted praises—"Balzac was the greatest novelist of his century, if not of all time"— interchange freely with anecdotal truths that reduce Balzac to human proportions. Indeed, Balzac in Maurois's eyes was at once a god, a magician, and a human fool.

The masterful work represents the culmination of a career in which Maurois devoured all of the Balzacian correspondence, studied regularly at the Spoelberch de Louvenjoul archives in Chantilly as well as at the Bibliothèque Nationale, visited the numerous locales in the life of his Promethean hero— Paris, Tours, Saint-Cyr-sur-Loire, Villeparisis, Les Jardies, Italy. Balzac in Maurois's version was much more than the sensitive observer of the reality of his epoch. He was also a great *voyant*, a visionary and a powerful creator who could transfigure the reality of his times into a literary fantasy that would endure for all times. Here is not only a life *of* Balzac but also a work *by* André Maurois, for we have here a product created by an octogenarian artist who pours into it all of his slowly accumulated talents as a stylist, moralist, critic, and biographer. Critical reaction to Maurois's final achievement as a biographer was once again uniformly enthusiastic. A typical reaction is the *London Times Literary Supplement* (March 3, 1966). While complaining a bit unjustly, since the complaint is based on the English-language translation containing a few truncations, *The Times* asserts that Maurois "affects an uneasy compromise" between critical analyses of Balzac's texts and purely biographical discussions. But the paper acknowledges that "in *Prométhée* the author's uncanny skill has made possible what seems to have defied his predecessors—a picture of the novelist in all the toils of his family and personal relationships, pathetic and truculent. . . . As a purely biographical study it stands on the highest level." Indeed, no one dared seriously to challenge Maurois's position "at the highest level" of his genre par excellence—biography.

E. The Formula for the Genre is Found

As in the case of all of André Maurois's manuscripts, that of *Balzac* is written in his microscopic, instantly recognizable handwriting, which is not always readable. All sorts of corrections, changes, insertions, erasures, and grammatical variations decorate the pages. Though his completed pages can be negotiated with grace and ease, each represents the result of intense effort to produce a refined finished product. Certain distinguishing traits set his art apart from the works of others. The loyal reader, familiar with several of these biographies, recognizes a particularly effective use of large numbers of adjectives in unusual combinations. The sentences are interesting in themselves; some are series of tiny fragments or groups of staccatolike short sentences, while others are infinitely long and sinuous. Musical metaphors abound, and certain themes recur in each of the biographies like leitmotifs. Transitions from section to section are brisk and sudden. The maxims of a genuine moralist are found everywhere. The paragraphs twinkle with clever wordplay. We have in Maurois's biographies not only interesting substantive material, but also stylistic texture of high quality.

Above all, the biographies live! "I wish to write a book that before all else is alive," wrote Maurois.[55] He did succeed in his aim. Marcel Thiébaut called his art that "of keeping his reader constantly breathless."[56] The figures in the biographies live with such vividness that the reader cannot help but feel grief at the inevitable death of the hero. It is true that Maurois, better than anyone else, successfully developed the formula of making the greatest possible use of minute documents while at the same time telling his story with the dexterity of a great novelist. In a personal letter to Maurois, Henri Bergson seemed to have had this point in mind: "I must tell you the pleasure and interest with which I have just read *Edouard VII et son temps*. It is a real *tour de force* to have made such an instructive book so engaging. How do you manage to bestow upon a very exact history the charm of a novel—the charm of one of your novels?"[57] One of the answers to Bergson's question stems from Maurois's incessant search for lucidity, even when analyzing the most complex questions. The eminent scientist Jean Rostand summed up the clarity of this writer's art in an unpublished letter: "Once again, through this delightful book, you give a lesson to those who do not know that depth can be transparent and that something serious can be smiling."[58]

The reader of these biographies will not easily forget them. Replete with memorable scenes, they contain all the pathos and drama that we find in great plays and novels. Who can forget the scene in which Disraeli presented his first speech before the British Parliament? Or one of Dumas père's masked balls? Or the descriptions of the quaint laboratory in which Fleming discovered his "mould juice"? Or the agony of the dying Byron while outside there raged a violent storm? Or Lyautey personally escorting Maurois around "his" city of Casablanca? Or the cruel death of Adrienne de La Fayette's mother at the guillotine? Or the burial scene of George Sand at Nohant or that of Juliette Drouet at Saint-Mandé? Or the elderly Chateaubriand dictating his *Mémoires d'outretombe* to his pale secretary, Danielo? These scenes and dialogues read like fiction, but in this case they are "true fiction." The secret of André Maurois's art as a biographer is that he narrated true lives as though they were as exciting as fiction. In reality, the heroes and heroines of his biographies really did live lives that were even richer than those of fiction. And the reader has the satisfaction of knowing that these lives were real.

When Maurois graduated from the Lycée he wished to become a writer like Balzac. After his novel *Climats*, Alain issued a challenge: "And now you must animate a world." But Maurois poignantly admitted: "In fact, I was not adequately armed for such a great combat."[59] He was the first to confess that as a novelist he failed to be a Balzacian demiurge. In spite of his many qualities as a novelist, the characters he invented for his books lack the variety of types and the vigor found in *La Comédie humaine*. But as a biographer he *did* most certainly activate an entire world and did create a powerful human comedy. Robert Kemp aptly described André Maurois's Comédie Humaine: "We will tell him that his biographies are fragments of a Human Comedy and that to recreate the characters of history is as worthy a task as to create imaginary ones. His comedy extends far beyond the present; it goes from Byron to Edward VII; from Sand to Proust; and around each character he groups a crowd of associates, all of them characteristic of the times and alive. Each of them acts in a political, sentimental, and social landscape."[60]

Maurois, in his lifelong search for the formula for great biography, created that genre in the fullest sense of the term *create*. In a moment of truth—in his *Mémoires* (p. 44)—he described the art of biography as having been an imperfect, unfulfilled literary genre, prior to his own entry into that field: "There were several illustrious books: the *Charles XII* of Voltaire (which I scarcely like), the *Life of Rancé* by Chateaubriand (which is a confession), the very summary lives written by Stendhal, the flat lives of Victor Cousin, the biographies of scattered unknown people of Sainte-Beuve, the heroic lives of Romain Rolland. Each of these works had its merits; none was a biography according to my heart or taste. In short, nothing in France could attract me into these unusual paths." It was through his discovery of the English heroes, like Shelley, Byron, and Disraeli, of course, that Maurois began his long uphill ascent that finally culminated in such admirable achievements as the great lives of Hugo, Sand, Proust, and Balzac. To combine in one unified genre impeccable scholarship, the art of a fine story-teller, and the ability to reproduce history with vividness—to do all this is no minor feat. In the realm of biographical creativity at least, Maurois the disciple was worthy of Balzac, his model!

3

André Maurois's Aesthetics of Biography

> There is an incompatibility between ethics and aesthetics.
>
> Maurois, 1964 Interview

Out of his long career as a biographer André Maurois slowly forged a philosophy of biography. While grappling to achieve his ideal formula, he developed and followed a core-cluster of flexible guidelines. From the very outset, he faced the necessity of defining the nature of biography as a literary genre. Maligned and praised for his earliest attempt, *Ariel ou la Vie de Shelley*, which at first glance resembles a novel more than a biography, he was also maligned and praised for his *Don Juan ou la Vie de Byron*, which at first glance resembles a well documented treatise more than a biography.

He had first to resolve a pressing question: how could he reconcile the biographer's concern for scholarly veracity with the personal point of view of the artist who writes the biography? An accomplished creator of novels and short stories, André Maurois did not wish to suppress his natural tendency as a creative artist to express himself in a style uniquely his own and to impregnate his text with his personal view of life. But as a scholar his freedom of movement was severely compromised by the need to adhere to the conventions and requirements of documentation. Yet, he refused to believe a reconciliation between art and erudition to be impossible. In fact, he defined a great biography as a work where "the two enemy sisters Erudition and Poetry are united in order to create the image."[1] In the case of certain lives, which stand out all by themselves owing to their dramatic intensity, and which required little embelishment, he believed that the more strictly the biographer adhered to precise and adequate documentation, the more readable would be his biographies. According to Michel Droit, however, Maurois's kind of documentation did not necessarily stamp out art: "His documentation is scrupulous and all of the traits are verified. There is in effect a romantic element in most existences, and the biographer can satisfy his need for the romantic element—and ours—if he retains in his tableaux the profound effect of reality."[2]

Over the years one could easily discern the continual growth of Maurois's reputation as a distinguished authority in this field. He not only wrote biographies; he had the uncanny ability to explain, even to teach the art of biography to others. With objectivity he also explicated and evaluated his own created works. His chapter "Caractéristiques du Style," in *Portrait d'un ami qui s'appelait moi,* is an astonishingly lucid explanation of his own style. We may read other important self-studies of biography by Maurois under the guise of an "inédit" in Michel Droit's monograph, *André Maurois,* and as a response to Jacques Suffel's essay on Maurois's biographies in Suffel's work, *André Maurois—Portrait—Dialogue.* From time to time Maurois published articles on his art in various journals, above all in *Les Nouvelles Littéraires.* He also explained his views in lectures and courses, especially at Cambridge University where, under the auspices of the Clark Foundation, in 1928 he delivered six lectures on "Aspects de la Biographie." As sources for these Cambridge lectures he referred to two English works, Waldo Dunn's *English Biography* and Harold Nicolson's *Developments of English Biography.* But by far the most significant and original theories on biography were his own reflections, which formed the substance for his early volume *Aspects de la Biographie.* In 1946 he gave a course in sixty lessons on "L'Art de la Biographie" at the University of Kansas City, a course he described in his *Journal-Etats-Unis* (especially pages 58–59). Other shorter pronouncements and brief statements on the subject of biography are sprinkled throughout the biographies themselves.

He had steadfastly contended that theories can be formulated only after they have emerged from the tests of application and not vice versa. This disciple of Alain believed no intellectual activity more hollow than theories and meditations created in the vacuum of abstract thought that are not tied directly to action. Therefore if, in the case of André Maurois, we can speak of an aesthetic theory of biography, this theory is intimately interwoven with this author's formulation of the biographies themselves.

A. Biography and Its Related Fields

Certain questions dealing with the nature of biography must be discussed. What is biography? What is its relationship to literary criticism? How does it depend upon the other social sciences? Is not biography also related to the science of psychology? In the final analysis, can we claim that biography is a legitimate art-form, like the novel or the poem?

Biography is both a relevant and irrelevant part of literary criticism. But the rapports between the two fields depend upon the definition one attributes to criticism. Critics differ sharply among themselves on the nature of their craft. Naturally, the literary critic with an exclusively textual point of view tends to disparage the role of the biographer in the field of criticism. But the literary critic who stresses the importance of a work's genesis and its historical background must unavoidably indulge in biographical activity. Most critics combine the textual and genetic approaches. Maurois's views accord with those moderates who, in order fully to comprehend the significance of an artist, study both the works and the life of the author. He acknowledged that criticism was, above all, the study of texts: "It is entirely true that literary criticism consists in studying a work, and not the life or the character of its author."³ He concedes further that a creative artist proves interesting to the critic only to the extent that the work he has produced is interesting and not necessarily because of the dramatic life he had led: "It is a mistake to measure a great man by the acts and the words coming from him which are handed down to us or even which we witnessed. The real measure of a writer is his work."⁴ Nevertheless, Maurois held that there was no conceivable reason why certain extremist critics should feel compelled to disassociate entirely the artist from his work simply because they wished to concentrate on the text, or why other equally extremist critics should speak exclusively of the life of a man and neglect his work. Maurois's position was that much could be learned through a patient, deliberate study of the documents bearing upon a man's life and character. But, in his view, much could also be learned about the personal traits of the man through a scrupulous investigation of his produced works. Thus we get a literary criticism that in its fullest development is what the modern critic Edmond Jaloux described as "a progressive illumination of the work by the man and of the man by his writings."⁵

In reality, Maurois the biographer confronted his subjects primarily because of the lives they led; but he made use of both their confessional works (memoirs, personal calendars, diaries, correspondence) and their nonconfessional (in appearance) works (novels, plays, poetry, essays) to reconstruct their lives. Sometimes an author's life stood out in greater relief thanks to Maurois's analysis of a minor work. Sometimes an apparently uninteresting life became more dynamic after Maurois approached it in relationship to certain exciting works written by the author. As a novel, Sand's *Lélia* was a minor work, but it threw unquestioned light on the life of this author. Published works, according to Maurois, clarify the lives of authors long deceased. We know relatively little about their personal existences except through glimmers released by their texts. His essay on Shakespeare in *Destins exemplaires* illustrates this point. In the final analysis, a creative artist should be studied from both angles, life and work: ". . . it becomes easy to justify the work of the biographer, for, if the work is interesting in itself, this is no reason for the life and the person of the extraordinary man who engendered this work to be without interest."⁶ Maurois sums up by stating that the biographer must inevitably involve himself in criticism, although the critic may, if he prefers, avoid becoming involved in biography: "If the literary critic has the right to neglect the life, the biographer, for his part, has no right to neglect the work. It is part of the life. . . ."⁷

A sympathetic admirer of Marcel Proust, he took issue with the latter's position (as expounded in *Contre Sainte-Beuve*) on the relations between criticism and biography. He insisted that biography as a genre must maintain close bonds with criticism; after all, the biographer of the artist studies inevitably how creative genius awakens and develops. The data yielded by a biographical study can be extremely useful to the critic. In *Choses nues* Maurois explains this view to several interlocutors, among whom are André Billy, Emile Henriot, and Robert Kemp:

> I reply that the thesis of Proust seems false to me. He claims that the man who has written a masterpiece is not the one who puts on his bedroom slippers, or lives an amorous adventure. Why yes! He *is* the same man; and the entire interest of a biography is to show how genius can be born out of very ordinary elements. Proust showed it while speaking of Bergotte and furthermore has recourse, in order to demolish Sainte-Beuve, to the kind of facts which he condemns. The life does not *explain* genius; it nourishes it.[8]

His biography of Tourguéniev consists largely of a concentrated demonstration of how the personality of the Russian writer was inextricably bound to the nature of his fictional characters, and how these, in turn, contained elements of the writer's character:

> The truth is, I believe, that a writer, no matter how objective he wishes to be, can never prevent his personality from appearing through his work. A man is marked by a certain number of preoccupations. They manifest themselves in spite of him. . . . One can cut the umbilical cord between characters who have nourished them; one cannot prevent them from having a natural resemblance to their creator or from resembling each other.[9]

André Maurois had consistently refused to cut the umbilical cord between the artist and his work. In *Lélia* he illustrated how Musset used letters from George Sand and certain romantic experiences with her as the basis for the personalities and situations in *On ne badine pas avec l'amour (One Doesn't Trifle with Love)*. In the same biography he noted that some of Chopin's finest sonatas reflect moods and moments spent by the Polish musician at Nohant. Maurois's *Balzac* underscores the close interplay between Balzac's personal experiences in ruinous business ventures and *La Comédie humaine*. The two volumes on Byron's life illuminate the interrelationships between the poet's published works and his personal adventures. For example, in the case of *Manfred:*

> A work always is born out of a shock that fertilizes a favorable terrain. In Byron's case, the terrain was ready; it consisted of this boiling mass of inexplicable feelings, horror, love, desire, regrets, a lava which once again threatened to engulf everything. Out of the shock produced by his reading of *Faust* and out of the landscapes of the Alps, there arose a great dramatic poem: *Manfred.*[10]

One of Maurois's favorite theories was that the literary public appreciated a work more when convinced that the text reflected the true experiences of the author. Consequently, the literary critic makes literature more meaningful for the public when he draws its attention to the combined arena of life and work.

"A work of art," Maurois wrote, "must suggest the reality of the feelings which it expresses; but how much stronger is the suggestion, how much more natural it is, if the public, incorrectly or correctly, believes that these feelings are those of the author."[11]

Despite all of the foregoing reservations, for André Maurois the genre of biography existed independently of literary criticism. Neither was a branch of the other. However, as a genre, biography did contain in it elements of criticism. This was unavoidable; one cannot discuss the life of a creative artist without relating him to the work he has engendered. Maurois's conception of biography hinges on this elemental fact. Luc Estang claimed that the crowning achievement of André Maurois as a biographer was "to make meaningful for us this narrow interdependence of the man and the writer.[12]

Maurois was very familiar with the history of the development of literary criticism in France. He was himself at once a somewhat disabused and a loyal disciple of that branch of criticism which stemmed from Sainte-Beuve and Taine: recognizing the dangers inherent in this approach, he wrote in *Lélia* that "It is always dangerous to explain a character by heredity."[13] But in virtually all of his biographies he started out by tracing the heredity, background, and milieu of his hero. In *René* he pointed to the qualities that Chateaubriand inherited from his father: "Before becoming castellan of Combourg, the Count of Chateaubriand, his father, had shown himself to be a skillful man of business; the son received from the old corsair and slave trader not only the taste for adventure, but also the taste for precise forms of action."[14]

Before commencing the formal part of Byron's life he first discussed the various aspects of the poet's maternal and paternal heredity, then went back three centuries before Byron's birth to describe the founding of Newstead Abbey, where the latter was born, painted the haunting atmosphere of the surrounding countryside, and subsequently recounted the true and untrue legends about the strange Byron and Gordon clans. After such a lengthy introduction—filled with "race, moment, and milieu"—he finally turned to the birth and childhood development of Lord Byron. In the biography of Lyautey, the story starts two generations before the Marshal's birth, and depicts with considerable detail the Alsatian environment in which the latter spent his childhood. The earliest pages in the life of Fleming feature the racial and environmental differences between the Scots and the English. *Adrienne* opens with a long section called "Les Grandes Familles" (the Daguesseaux, Noailles, Ayens, Polignacs, and La Fayettes) and ends with five family tables that follow the development of the ancestors of these families. Sentences like the following (taken from *Adrienne*) illustrate the influence of Tainean ideas on Maurois: "The scruples, the indecision and the excess of reason were hereditary evils which Henriette got from the Chancellor."[15] The life of Proust does not start until after Maurois has first devoted a lengthy portion to the Prousts of Illiers and the Weils of Paris and Auteuil. Whether consciously or not, he subscribed to a large degree to the theories of Sainte-Beuve and Taine, and in actual practice his thinking often coincided with theirs. However, one major difference separated Maurois from Taine: Maurois explains only part of the genius of his subjects through deterministic factors. His heroes appear to evolve with a great deal of freedom and are not molded by the rigorous laws that characterize Taine's philosophy.

André Maurois's conception of biography also calls for guidance received from history. His lives of Lyautey, Disraeli, and Edward VII are almost pure history. Whole chapters of biographies like those of Victor Hugo and Chateaubriand present these men in the light of their political and sociological ideologies. They behave like historical (as opposed to literary) figures.

For at least three reasons a great biographer should be well versed in historical methodology. First, most biographies deal with figures of the past. Biographers generally prefer not to select living subjects. André Maurois wrote only one biography of a living figure, Lyautey. Second, both the biographer and historian collect and study the same kinds of documents: letters, journals, unpublished papers of all sorts. Third, both must adhere closely to the chronological order of events. Maurois described his methods of research as if they were those of a historian:

> I have developed, for my own use, a technique of research and construction which is adapted to this kind of work in biography. An extensive research which explores all of the veins and even those which, at first glance, seem poor or exhausted; a research that is avid for testimonies, letters, journals. A research on *all* of the secondary characters who were mixed into the life of the hero. Research on the period, which constitutes the backdrop. Then an organization of innumerable documents which I have gathered, while at the same time respecting the chronological order and introducing events and beings only at the moment when the hero could conceivably know them.[16]

The life of a George Sand, a Voltaire, or a Lord Byron is more than a recapitulation of the events in the private career of a heroic figure; it contains also the impact of dramatic events of public, national, or social history on the heroic individual. Maurois the biographer occasionally halts the plots of his biographies in order to bring his readers up to date on the historical data of the period. Passages like the following illustrate the prominent role history plays in his biographies:

> A revolution divides the inhabitants of a country into three groups: those who can only be revolutionaries, those who can only be hostile to the revolution, and those who are divided or torn apart because, even though they remain linked to the threatened class, they also have certain griefs against this class. It was to this third party that Mme Dupin de Francueil belonged. (*Lélia*, p. 22)

It is impossible to comprehend the problems that General Lyautey was going to have to resolve without studying, at least briefly, the situation in Morocco in 1903. (*Lyautey*, p. 77)

Between Maurois's *Byron* and his *Histoire d'Angleterre,* and between his *Olympio ou la Vie de Victor Hugo* and his *Histoire de la France,* the resemblances and interrelationships are multitudinous. Maurois the historian served well the cause of Maurois the biographer, and vice versa.[17]

But we must not overstate the interplay between biography and history. If biography is to be considered a full-fledged genre, it must be allowed to exist independently of history. Maurois did emphasize this point: "I believe that biography is a literary genre that is important, beautiful, difficult, entirely distinct from history and the novel."[18] In his early book *Aspects de la biographie,* written when his only biographical works had consisted of *Ariel* and *Disraeli,* he regarded the role of history as little more than a background or a fresco against which there unfurled the life of the hero. The biographer must take care *not* to permit history to dominate the flow of the subject's life. He must reduce the importance of the historical context so that the dramatic force of these events does not stand out too garishly: "Biography is the history of the evolution of a human soul; history must be in this case of biography what the background is for the painter of portraits, the background against which he [the biographer] places his model."[1] The latter, more often than the historian, selects a single individual as a focal point and arranges the structure and the stream of events of his book in such a way that the reader never loses sight of the evolving nature of the hero's personality, character, and career:

> Biography places a man (or a woman) at the center of the tableau and arranges the events in relation to this hero. History, even in the case of individuals who have exerted an immense influence on their times, for instance Caesar and Napoleon, must bear collective currents in mind. . . . But the biographer takes an individual as his center, makes all the events that must revolve around him begin and end with him.[20]

In a sense, history is the biography of a collective group—a nation, a society, a political party, a social class; biography is the history of an individual—a king, a writer, a general, a politician, a scientist.

The biographies of André Maurois contain a profusion of the elements of the various social sciences that relate to history. One cannot treat Lyautey, La Fayette, even Marcel Proust without understanding the sociological, economic, and political forces that activated the period during which these persons lived. George Sand, Tourguéniev, and Voltaire not only painted these forces at work in their literary works, but their patterns of thought and personal conduct were shaped by them. George Sand's career as a writer and as a human being was tightly bound to the new socialism that evolved during the nineteenth century.

Dumas fils' plays reflect the tensions within the social structure of his day. Proust's novels are not so self-contained as some have claimed; they mirror the economic and sociological habits of a certain kind of populace that gathered in the salons of Mme Strauss and Mme de Caillavet and resided near the affluent quarter of the Parc Monceau. How can one write a life of Balzac unless the social and economic framework of the Restoration and the era of Louis-Philippe have been treated in great detail? In any resurrection of the personage of Shelley one must also explain the social philosophy of Godwin. The biographer does not successfully relate the life of Disraeli without also discussing the economic crises and depressions in Ireland. Whole parts of Maurois's biographies deal then with questions of fiscal policy, the changing social order, the science of party politics. Having spent many years at the helm of his family's wool mills in Elbeuf, he acquired through contact with economic and industrial life a solid competence concerning labor-management relations, economic recessions, depressions, and inflations, the role of minorities and their relations with religious and ethnic majorities. This competence sustains the infrastructure of all of his biographies.

But the biographer must be more than a historian and social scientist. He must be a master of human psychology. He must comprehend how exceptional human beings react to various external stimuli, how they behave under the impact of success and failure, how they alternate between moments of elation and moments of despondency, how they love and how they hate. The biographer must comprehend the factors that impel the artist to create and those which deaden his creative powers. As long as biography is what Michel Droit called "a patient pursuit of the inner reality of the model,"[21] the biographer necessarily indulges in penetrating psychological studies of his subjects. Documents concerning the subject must be studied with the precision, systematic thoroughness, and objectivity of the scientist. No conclusions should be reached until all the facts have properly been considered. Maurois acknowledged that his favorite genre had been invaded by "the habits of the scientist."[22] Like the scientist the modern biographer embarked upon his project free of preconceived notions. As a human being and an artist Maurois had certain personal opinions of his heroes before commencing his research of their lives. Subsequently, however, during the stages of his "experimental research" his earlier prejudices almost always underwent modification. Like the scientist too, the biographer is haunted by the desire to achieve "verity." His job is not done until he feels that he has painted his portrait as authentically as possible.

So the biographer is a multiple artist: an artist-historian, artist-critic, artist-sociologist, artist-psychologist; but before and after all else he is an artist. If biography can claim a place among the legitimate genres of literature, this claim must be based on its integrity as art. We expect each work of art to have a style that sets it apart from other works. Its content must reflect with fidelity the state of mind and/or feelings of the creative human being who has engendered it and given it form. The elements in the style of expression and in the content have been carefully chosen, arranged, and combined by an accomplished artist. In this connection Maurois once wrote: "A great scientific book, if it is perfectly successful is a work of art. A fine portrait is, at the same time, a portrait that resembles and transposes reality artistically."[23] Biography is closer to the art of portraiture than to the art of candid photography. And the portrait is a view of a subject as seen through the eyes of a specific individual. The portraitist selects and organizes his colors, lines, details, and forms. He makes the essential traits stand out sharply and softens the less significant details. "The biographer must, like the portraitist and the landscaper, isolate what is essential in the considered whole."[24]

Perhaps more than in any other genre the biographer must exercise the most stringent controls in selecting his ingredients if he is to distinguish the important from the paltry. The preparatory research for a biography inevitably involves the study of multitudinous heaps of often contradictory documents, some of which must be retained while more often much must be discarded. Details should be chosen for their pertinence to the central theme of the biography and not merely because they excite the biographer. Often minuscule facts are more revealing than massive ones: "In this elimination of the useless, the biographer must not lose from sight the fact that the tiniest details are often the most interesting ones."[25] Once he has completed the agonizing job of selection, the biographer charts his structure, his course of action. The whole work must be carefully arranged and put into a proper order. Finally, during the composition of the work itself the biographer should express himself in a style that adds to the readability of his biography and resurrects the central figure with vividness. All of these stages of composition necessarily figure in the formulation of biography as they do in the formulation of other valid forms of literary art.

The biographies of André Maurois not only rank among some of the relatively significant products of French literary art in our times, but also contain many interesting statements by the artist on his own philosophy of art. In *Les Trois Dumas* he summarizes his notions on the relation between art and reality: [art] is a transformation, or a deformation of reality, destined to provoke certain emotions for which the spectator is searching."[26] On the question of the choice of elements in a work of art, the following statement, taken from Tourguéniev, reveals Maurois's own aesthetic philosophy: "But if Tourguéniev is a realist by the truth of the details, it is by the choice [of these details] that he is a great artist."[27]

In the final analysis great biography is a legitimate art form because it introduces the experience of the artist-biographer into the lives of his readers and permits them to identify themselves both with him and with his subject. The biography becomes a meeting place where creator and audience share a pervading sense of common association. Maurois confesses that "I have especially written in order to give myself—and if possible to my readers, some of these moments of pure, musical emotion, where it seems that suddenly life stops in an enchanted bubble and remains suspended with one foot in the air, like certain phrases of Chopin."[28] The great biographies of André Maurois are, as a matter of fact, attractive bubbles into whose crystalline universes the reader penetrates effortlessly. There one relives all the pathos and joys of great human figures whose careers are recreated by the consummate artistry of a self-confident biographer.

B. *The Affinities between the Biographer and His Model*

As an artist forges his work bit by bit, he establishes close association with it. The work begins to occupy a certain place in his daily existence. Maurois never started to compose a biography until after he assured himself of being able to devote almost his entire being to its realization. No artist more than he plunged more thoroughly into his work at hand, for he believed that "mastery belongs to the one who belongs only to his art."[29] A biography, he knew, could germinate only after a long period of incubation. During this time the biographer gathered his materials, read, and reread them, mulled over them at length, sifted them, worked out his outline, and wrote several increasingly refined versions of the manuscript. In short, the preparation of a biography required what Alain, referring to Maurois, called "an almost violent attention."[30] But how else could one compose the biography of a Chateaubriand or a Balzac?

Maurois's basic attitude toward his subjects was invariably warmly sympathetic. He could not write the biography of someone toward whom his sentiments were antipathetic. Paraphrasing Alain, he wrote that "there is no knowledge without some effort towards sympathy."[31] Generally, he selected subjects for which he had already entertained a strong positive bias. Occasionally, circumstances caused him to embark upon a project concerning which he had few defined pre-attitudes (Fleming, Adrienne de La Fayette). In the latter cases, he made such concerted efforts to appreciate the positive qualities of his subjects that in the end he acquired a warm sense of sympathy for them. As we read *Byron, Les Trois Dumas, Voltaire,* and *René ou la Vie de Chateaubriand* we get the impression that the more Maurois studied these figures the more he learned to admire them. This positive approach formed an important principle in Maurois's aesthetics of biography. Alain, on reading his disciple-biographer's monograph on him, paid tribute to his ability to coincide sympathetically with his model:

> Each time I understood better my own thought. . . . Really I instructed myself on my own self while reading your *Alain.* Gabrielle [Alain's wife] said without hesitation, "That is written with love." I also discover this point of doctrine, it is that one cannot comprehend what one does not love. Ah well! I admit it. I am putting myself in school, I in turn am taking lessons. My fellow man certainly owed me that. What does it mean to think? It means to

think like the other fellow. Well, I have succeeded in that; I shall no longer allow myself to be displaced. *I shall be human.* It is a great drama that I have played with you, my Hamlet, it is not insignificant. . . . What I find admirable, it is that you have given this pupil, who teaches, a serious authority, one that is not without a light touch. You have even grasped my style; it is marvelous. In short, never was an author read as I was read by you, my only friend.[32]

Maurois osmotically imbued himself with the essence of his subject. He learned to feel the way his hero felt and to think the way he thought, even to write the way he wrote.

It is one thing for the biographer to confront his subject with sympathy and another to permit his positive attitude to degenerate into adulation. Adulation distorts one's objective vision. The writer must never permit himself to admire with such ardor that he becomes insensitive to the faults of his hero. In the opinion of André Maurois, one might simultaneously hold a cult for a great figure and recognize that this figure possessed many disparate elements, including both defects and good qualities. One critic of *Lélia ou la Vie de George Sand* rightfully observed that although in Maurois's "note liminaire" he admitted that "I have the good fortune—or the weakness—of loving her," he nonetheless portrayed George Sand with discernible objectivity: "The tenderness of Maurois for his model does not blind him for a single moment. He does not seek to hide her weakness, to dissimulate what for the reader might be tiring, I mean her need for the absolute, her taste for the sublime, the bad faith with which she justified her infidelities. . . ."[33] Nor did Maurois in his other sympathetic biographies conceal the defects of an excessively idealistic Shelley, an inconsistent Chateaubriand, an insatiable Dumas père, or an overly egocentric Victor Hugo.

At all times this biographer manifested a genuine concern for intellectual honesty. Often owing to a paucity of documentation, he readily admitted that he did not possess all of the requisite facts concerning a given issue in the life of his subject. Rather than trying to supply a neat answer for every uncertainty, so that no hiatus interrupted the flow of his story, he candidly disclosed his lack of information. Sometimes he speculated on why his hero behaved in one way or the other, but he left it up to the reader to solve the riddle. Occasionally he posed several rhetorical questions, and again it was up to the reader to formulate the most satisfactory or plausible reply. In the following passage he is not sure whether Dumas père's grandmother ever legally married her husband: "Was the slave later promoted to the rank of a spouse? Her grandson says so. The mores of the time make marriage seem hardly likely; no document proves this fact; none permits us to deny it."[34] Occasionally Maurois, the specialist of human nature, posed certain questions first and then attempted to answer them according to what seemed in his judgment to be the most logical way a typical human being might react to a similar situation. In *Byron,* for example: "Byron had stopped over at the Albergo Imperiale, which had nothing imperial but its name. Would he stay a day, a week, a year? He wasn't sure. Destiny would take care of regulating his life. He had come because a woman had called him. He would leave if his departure became desirable."[35] As a biographer he made no claim to omniscience. When dealing with the life of another human being, especially one who had long since departed from the scene, it was inevitable that some secrets would defy even the most skillful and erudite biographer.

André Maurois knew his heroes and heroines well. He not only had been reading their works since childhood, but he incorporated both their lives and their works into his own existence. He found this easier to do in the case of writers with whom he had many personal affinities. He chose to write the lives of figures with whom he had much in common; consequently, when he described their ideas and their temperaments he described to a certain degree his own ideas and temperament. With him biography became a medium that enabled the author to express himself almost as fully as if he were writing a novel or a poem. René Lalou quoted Maurois on this subject:

> Biography considered as a means of expression, is the one genre whose subject has been chosen by the author to respond to a secret need in his nature. It will be written with a more natural emotion than another subject because through the feelings and adventures of the character the feelings of the biographer will express themselves: to a certain degree, it will be an autobiography disguised as a biography.[36]

We know, by Maurois's admission, that *Ariel ou la Vie de Shelley* was a personal confession by the author. If this first work went too far in the direction of confessional literature, all of his subsequent biographies nonetheless contained a personal element, but on these subsequent occasions he held them in check, "to a certain degree." The lives of Chateaubriand, Victor Hugo, and others reveal many aspects of Maurois's own personal nature, but they do so unobtrusively and incidentally. What really counts before all else is the life of the hero, not that of the biographer. In fact, André Chevrillon is only partially correct in claiming that "biography is for you [Maurois] a means of personal expression."[37]

Let us examine a few of the many affinities between André Maurois and his heroes. Like Maurois, many of his heroes came into the world with some kind of weakness, which they later overcame. Earlier I mentioned that Maurois had vanquished a physical weakness accruing from a spinal defect, and that not only had he won a gymnastics prize but he had also been proficient in equestrian activities. Sentences like the following taken at random from the biographies contain more than a trace of autobiographical substance:

> He admired the little crippled Lord Byron who tried with so much courage to follow the strongest boys in the school in their athletic exercises. (*Byron*, 1:47)

He had the taste for games and the desire to shine in spite of his physical inferiority. (Ibid., p. 53).

In his need to dominate, to be everywhere first and the leader, there will enter to some extent his memory of childhood weakness. (*Lyautey*, p. 3)

Furthermore, the uniform attracted the young man; for a long time he had been infirm; he was happy to be able to show that he was not so any longer, as he manipulated the weapons, the foil, as he climbed on the horse. (Ibid., p. 14)

Victor remained frail and sad. He had an enormous head, too large for his body, which made him look like a deformed dwarf. . . . One can imagine what went on in the heart of this motherless boy, the weak companion of his two older and vigorous brothers. (*Olympio*, p. 22) But Victor Hugo overcame this weakness. . . . No trace remained of his fragile childhood. . . . A strength of a great and wild beast. (Ibid., p. 159)

Maurois also paints the young Voltaire and Disraeli as emerging all the stronger from similar struggles.

Another link between the biographer and at least two of his subjects, Proust and Disraeli, stems from the fact that he could, from personal experience, analyze with sensitive understanding the question of their being born a Jew in a predominantly non-Jewish community. The following passage from *Disraeli* seems to come straight out of his own *Mémoires:* ". . . but there in this school, they made him feel as though he were not like the other boys. He was a Jew and his comrades, except for one, were not Jewish" (p. 17). In *A la recherche de Marcel Proust* Maurois pursues this theme, insisting upon Proust's Jewishness as one of the sources of his greatness; he adds that Proust's combination of French-Christian and French-Jewish qualities is a healthy state of being: "In literature, as in genetics, a crossing is healthy."[38] One can draw an analogy between Maurois, who had a sincere appreciation of the beauty of Christian churches and services, and Proust, who manifested a similar appreciation: "But if Proust was not one of those who, as Mauriac says, know that there is truth, he showed since childhood a very vivid sense of the beauty of churches and the poetry of religious ceremonies."[39]

The affinities between Maurois and his models could be enumerated almost endlessly. He revealed his predilection for political figures, who, like himself, were moderate and liberal, who respected the great traditions of the past while advocating reform and improvement. Maurois fundamentally opposed change through violent revolution, change that sought to destroy the heritage of the past while erecting a brand new system. But he also opposed those reactionaries who believed that present-day abuses could be corrected only by turning back the clock to the "good old days." His biography of Disraeli revealed not only the Prime Minister's political development but also his own political philosophy. He admitted Disraeli's influence on him: ". . . through him I could express a political doctrine which was precisely the one that I was seeking, I mean popular conservatism, the mélange of a great respect for tradition, for what has been acquired in the past by humanity, with a concern for the happiness of everyone and a desire of reforms in the midst of order."[40] *Lélia* is a life in which the heroine sympathizes with neither the right-wing faction of Gambetta nor the left wing of the Commune. In *Olympio* the biographer goes to great pains to illustrate Victor Hugo's refusal to become linked with the rising movement of Communism while at the same time favoring some of the goals of the Commune. In *Adrienne,* Gilbert and Adrienne de La Fayette, in their advocacy of human liberty, were opposed both to the uncontrolled anarchy of the Terror and to the uncontrolled despotism of an absolute monarchy. In *La Vie de Cecil Rhodes,* the protagonist is a moderate who believes that the only possible political solution in South Africa must derive from a compromise between the views of the Boers and those of the British. Maurois emphasized, in *René,* that Chateaubriand was an outright legitimist who nevertheless favored certain basic social and political reforms.

One can point also to artistic affinities between Maurois and some of his subjects. For instance, like Tourguéniev, he could depict in his novels only the world he knew personally. He could not invent characters and situations fashioned by unbridled imagination alone. The following citation describes not only the literary position of the Russian, but also that of the Frenchman: "But Tourguéniev more than any other writer needed to model a sketch precisely. An honest, precise artist, he could not paint anything except what he knew perfectly" (*Tourguéniev,* p. 93). In Tourguéniev's novels and stories the decors were limited to those the Russian author lived in. But this is true also for Maurois, who, despite his extensive travel and periods of residence abroad, placed his novels mainly in the three regions of France most familiar to him: Normandy (Pont de l'Eure), Paris, and Dordogne. After reading two novels by Tourguéniev we visualize his personal settings. But this is true for Maurois too:

> After two novels we know the decor of Tourguéniev . . . The truth seems to me to be, on the contrary, that it is often excellent for an artist to know how to limit the field of his studies. One cannot know everything well, and a small painting done with exactness teaches us more about humanity than a "great inexact fresco." (*Tourguéniev,* pp. 189–97 *passim*)

Throughout the other biographies Maurois reveals and explains his own philosophy of art. But he does not halt the flow of these works to digress on art. Instead, to develop his own ideas, he takes advantage of the coincidences between his views and those of his subjects and expounds his own theories through his elucidations of those of his subject. The defense of Dickens's themes gives him the opportunity of exposing his own favorite theories: that if the novelist is to write powerful and stirring novels, he must himself first live a rich, active life. Maurois placed little confidence in the novelist-aesthete who withdrew from humanity to ponder various technical and stylistic questions. For inspiration the novelist must rely upon the raw materials of daily existence.[41] The latter should transpose the real world rather than search for new styles of presenting his subject. This is the theme that Maurois develops in his biographies of Byron and Balzac. In *Les Trois Dumas,* he emphasized that Dumas fils wrote his best plays when he based them directly on his experiences, and his worst when he invented their plots: "The author of *La Princesse de Bagdad* imagined. But imagination sustains itself badly in a vacuum."[42] He uses the same work to expound again his contention that an author must limit himself to the depiction of those types of people who populated his own universe, a contention that I shall discuss more fully when treating Maurois's novels:

> Love, the relations between man and woman, those of the couple with the child, there you have his immutable themes. How could he paint with realism workers, peasants, little businessmen? He lived in the most modern of the elegant districts (the Monceau plain), among well-padded furniture, statues, green houseplants. That is his world; that is his decor; those are his limits. (*Les Trois Dumas,* p. 399)

In the above quotation, if we substitute Neuilly and Dordogne for "La Plaine Monceau," we have a perfect description of Maurois's own fictional limits and strengths.

There are many striking resemblances between this biographer's own daily mode of existence and that of many of his heroes. The recipient of many budding writers' requests for prefaces and various other kinds of support, Maurois admitted on several occasions his own overly generous responses to these demands on his time. The following passage, ostensibly referring to Tourguéniev, might also relate to the Russian's biographer: "He received them with a delicate courtesy, one that was generous, too generous, for he was incapable of refusing a preface, of admitting that a manuscript was bad, and sometimes he compromised his judgment in strange adventures" (*Tourguéniev,* p. 134). Maurois describes the daily work schedule of Dumas fils. Except for the fact that the former did not himself have to light his fire and warm his breakfast, the similarities with the latter are striking: "Dumas gets up early and goes to bed early. In the morning, he lights his fire himself and heats up the soup, which he prefers, for breakfast, to coffee and tea. Then he sits down at his table, on which he finds some paper, a blue satin-type, a bundle of pens (goose feathers) and works until noon. At lunch he joins again his wife and his two daughters (*Les Trois Dumas,* p. 398). Another curious coincidence: Maurois suspended the publication of his first volume, an anthology of short stories written in Elbeuf, while the book was still being printed. He sensed his inadequacies and preferred to wait until he could mature before making his literary debut. This incident is identical to a similar sacrifice made by Lord Byron and described by Maurois in terms that leave no doubt that the portrait-ist understood all too well the way his model must have felt: "All of the copies were burned, except the one which had already been sent to John Pigot, who was then a student at Edinburgh, and one (this was rather comical) of Becher. *It is hard for a young author to abandon his first book.* Byron had made the sacrifice heroically." (*Byron*, 1 : 92–93. Italics mine.)

The biographies of André Maurois represent an unusual blend of objective reporting about the life of a great figure and of the subjective presence of the biographer himself. This presence manifests itself mainly through the biog-rapher's own personal style and through the multiple affinities between him and his subjects. Occasionally, however, his presence is discernible through the use of a single word that discloses his own approbation or disapproval of the actions of these subjects. Note how he deftly insinuates himself into the text through a word like *legitimately:* "This time, Proust was deeply and legiti-mately hurt. . . ."[43] At times Maurois even makes a direct first-person appear-ance on the stage of his biography. *Olympio* terminates with a description of his own visit to the cemetery in which Hugo's wife, Adèle, and his daughter, Leopoldine, lie buried. In *Lélia* there is a detailed account of one of his per-sonal pilgrimages made to Nohant. In *Lyautey* a long chapter is devoted to a visit he himself once made to the city of Casablanca, with the marshal person-ally escorting him about the town. In *A la recherche de Marcel Proust*, Maurois abruptly halts his third-person account of Proust's last days and switches to the first person: "I recall having read this page publicly, some months ago, and of having been struck by the silence, which is heavy with emotion, that arises around works of genius" (p. 329).

The general impression one gets after reading Maurois's biographies is that they constitute unique works of art in which an objective subject is presented in a manner that is at once objective and subjective. The copious and painstaking documentation and supporting citations lend a tone of objectivity to the biog-raphies. But on virtually every page a curious affinity between the biographer and his model seems to assert itself, sometimes coming in the form of a spar-kling little maxim, an elusive verbal gesture, or a brief editorial comment. Biography here does indeed approach becoming autobiography in masquerade.

C. *The Structure of the Biographies*

Part of the success of these works stems from the great care with which Maurois selected the subjects most appropriately suited to his own talent. An artist creates his finest works when he has selected his theme well, when this theme lends itself to his peculiar capacities and to the genre in which he works best. In the genre of biography certain lives are more easily recaptured than others. These are the most exciting, more eventful, and richer ones. Most biographers prefer not to try to resurrect the career of someone who has led a colorless, bland, and monotonous life. The greatest biographies usually concern exceptional persons, who soared above humanity not only because of their unusual prowess as writers and statesmen, but also because their daily existences were dramatic and their personalities dynamic. Before embarking upon his biographical projects, Maurois assured himself that the careers he would seek to recapture were "naturally beautiful,"[44] that is, they were careers animated by heroes who could fascinate his readers. Who can dispute the fact that figures like George Sand, Lord Byron, or Dumas père were, as Chevrillon states, "outside of common?"[45] Maurois hesitated before commencing his life of Fleming; the scientist did not seem to possess a sufficiently active life. Once he investigated carefully into the hidden corners of this existence, however, he saw in it real promise for a great biography: "I very soon realized that there was no lack of human drama in an existence which on the surface appeared to be remarkably uniform."[46]

After assuring himself that his subject was a suitable vehicle for a biography, André Maurois charted out the stages of composition for the new project. Generally these included three overlapping periods: the period of research, when he accumulated and studied the documents; the period of writing the manuscript; and the final period during which the text of the manuscript was corrected, refined, and cast into its publishable form.

The period of research for Maurois was long, all-encompassing, and difficult. Usually he spent at least a full year reading an enormous mass of the most diversified data. He left no stone unturned to secure every single available item in the great libraries and private collections. He read every pertinent work published or unpublished on his subject. During his readings he took voluminous notes. In the case of prolific authors like Dumas père or George Sand, the array of documents was appalling. In the life of the less loquacious Alexander Fleming, he had the reverse difficulty of insufficient autobiographical revelations by the scientist himself. Usually the quantity of documents was so staggering in size and variety that, at first glance, they seemed to lead nowhere and everywhere at the same time. But with untiring patience he eventually succeeded in transforming chaos into order and in establishing a logical and cohesive organization of all materials. Michel Droit described this stage as a "struggle." "Sometimes he must struggle against a too great richness, sometimes against an excessive paucity [of documents and events]."[47] Out of the lifeless mountains of paper Maurois sought to create the warm breath of a departed hero. He searched for certain unifying themes and recurring rhythms. These could serve as skeletal pillars on which the fabric of the biography could readily be draped.

In his attempt to retrace the geographical movements of his subjects, he visited their places of birth, their various town and country residences, their schools and colleges, their studios and offices, and finally their burial places.

Thus he could recapture not only the spark of their presence as human beings but also the ambiance in which they evolved. In his final *Mémoires* he revealed that his greatest influence as a biographer emanated from his ability "to give the reader that feeling of the discovery of the world through a hero" (p. 154). He had in mind not only the world, in its largest sense, but also the world in which the hero himself had lived his own life.

Once all of the notes were gathered, studied, evaluated, and sifted, Maurois launched the second stage of his task: the actual formulation of the earliest version of the manuscript. First, he had to establish a coherent architectural structure to guide him from chapter to chapter. This architecture he made so fluid and subtle that, to the reader, it is hardly discernible. His aim was to make the story move along at an orderly pace, as gently and swiftly as possible, with almost no diversionary digressions. Yet he hoped to make the reader aware of the gradual flow of time, from day to day, week to week, and year to year. He described the effects upon the hero of temporal transitions and of spatial displacements. Once he arranged his basic outline he did all he could to conceal it from his readers. He did not wish to give them the impression that the biographies were forced or manipulated, or that the events in them were too artificially propelled by the biographer. Unlike marionettes, the figures must appear to the reader as living actors who act out their own destiny freely. Maurois describes this concern in the following metaphor: ". . . but once his scaffolding is established and his house constructed, he [the biographer] demolishes the scaffolding and tries to present to the reader only a solid house that stands on its own."[48] The hand of this biographer was exceedingly deft, light, and virtually unobtrusive.

As one can establish a kind of posthumous order in the ex-lives of all human beings, there must be an order in the biographies that concern the lives of these same human beings. Above all, the order of chronology must be observed scrupulously. The biography should go back to the period preceding the hero's birth, so that the terrain is prepared for his entrance into the arena. Then we reach the birth of the hero and trace his childhood, family life, and schooling. The heart of the book revolves around the crucial middle years and period of maturity, when the hero produces his finest work. The concluding chapters deal with the years preceding the subject's ultimate end. Generally the last pages contain stirring renditions of the funeral scene. Occasionally they are followed by a short epilogue in which the biographer traces the destinies of those who survived beyond the hero's death: his heirs, spouse, children, and friends. Maurois tells his story in such a way that we cannot help but attach ourselves intimately to the destiny of the hero, and by the time the final pages are reached, inevitably we feel a sense of commiseration for all those who grieve at the funeral of the protagonist. The reader has the impression that he has just lost a dear friend. Actually, most of Maurois's biographies were written so that we never lost sight of the documentation supporting every event in the tale. At the conclusion we seem really to have undergone the same experience as if we had traversed the pages of a great novel. We feel as sad at the passing of George Sand as at the death of Anna Karenina. We have relived the heroic adventures of Victor Hugo and Lord Byron in the same way that we relive the heroic lives of Julien Sorel and Jean-Christophe.

This artist-biographer once defined a work of art like this: "The material of art is the image of reality that is sufficiently removed from us so that we are delivered from the desire to act, and, at the same time given an orderly structure by a human mind."[49] As we read from page to page and chapter to chapter in the biographies of Maurois we do not easily perceive the framework that holds the work together. Yet, this framework does exist, and it is very discreetly "given an orderly structure" by the biographer. Without such a framework, a complex life like that of Chateaubriand would have fallen apart. Not only is there an orderly quality about the way Maurois has arranged the flow of the chapters, but there even seems to be what he called "that mysterious symmetry" in each of the lives he depicts. The symmetry stems from the chronological arrangement of the events, from certain themes that are repeated throughout each work (e.g., Shelley and the sea, Byron's abnormal gait, George Sand's search for the absolute experience, Fleming's taciturn nature, Disraeli's love of flowers, Adrienne's fierce loyalty to her husband, etc.). The symmetry stems also from the way in which Maurois has placed his hero at the center of the stage. All else he relegates to secondary stature. As the latter develops associations with other persons, the biographer paints brief portraits of them, but he is careful to do so at the moment when these characters directly affect the life of the hero. As the subject moves from one site to another, Maurois paints the new setting, but only when this setting is pertinent. All of the characters in the life of the hero are described only insofar as they affect that life. No matter how interesting Chopin and Musset are in their own right, in *Lélia* they play supporting roles. Gautier and Nerval become secondary figures in the Olympian panorama of Victor Hugo's existence. Clémenceau is treated as a background figure in the biography of Lyautey, and Queen Victoria, majestic as she was, is made to lurk in the shadows of Prime Minister Disraeli. In the biography of Shelley, Lord Byron plays a supporting role, and in the life of Byron it is Shelley who is eclipsed by the creator of *Don Juan*.

Maurois allowed little to interrupt the movement of the biographies. Even when he analyzed the literary works of his protagonists he integrated these textual analyses so skillfully that we are hardly conscious that they exist. The reader generally does not sense that the flow of the biography has thus been halted.[50] These biographies seldom develop into essays of literary criticism. If Maurois analyzed the works of his heroes, it was because these works were related to certain phases of their lives. (In the case of Balzac, as in the case of Proust, the situation was somewhat different. For Balzac and Proust the greatest events of their lives were their literary works.)

D. The Biographies as Lessons for Humanity

These biographies were written by a distinguished moralist. The author of *Un Art de vivre (An Art of Living)* had only one way of treating a subject: he came to grips with an individual's life as a specialist of human nature studies the behavior of a given personality. This approach was indispensable for someone whose task it was to study the amorous escapades of a Byron, the paternal instincts of Dumas père, the brother-sister relationship between René and Lucile de Chateaubriand, and the sexual proclivities of Marcel Proust. His subjects were exceptional human beings, but they were human beings all the same, endowed with most of the same underlying instincts that are shared by ordinary people. Only they were less restrained by social conventions than most of us and gave fuller vent to their particular human drives. In a commencement address, André Maurois insisted on the common nature of human passions: "We get the same impression, not only in Space, but also in Time, when we read great books. Open Homer or Plato, Goethe or Dickens, Tolstoy or Balzac, and you will realize that human sentiments, fundamental passions and feelings, changed very little in the course of three thousand years."[51] As a biographer he tried to demonstrate how the moral behavior of his models typified that of other human beings and in which ways they were at the same time similar to and different from ordinary people.

The laws and reflections of a moralist have value only when they are pertinent to the human race as a whole. If the reader can associate his own feelings with a Fleming or a Madame de La Fayette, he takes greater interest in their exploits. Similarly, as the biographer prepares his manuscript, he becomes more interested in his topic if he can link his own emotional and intellectual reactions to those of his model. As he imagines himself in his hero's footsteps he gains clearer insight into his own nature. What Maurois wrote of the novelist in the following paragraph certainly applies to the biographer:

> To become a great novelist, it is necessary to be capable of comprehending the souls of others, and since, if we consider only appearances, it is impossible to exit from one's own soul, you need an act of faith; you have to believe that the human feelings and passions are approximately the same in all beings; you have to try to understand others through yourself.[52]

The biographer identifies himself with his subject, and the reader in turn identifies himself with the same subject through the personality of the biographer.

The spectator, according to Maurois, when brought into contact with a distinguished figure, has much to learn from him. An exemplary life can serve as an inspiring lesson for others. If the biographer selects his subjects with this in mind and if they are worthy of admiration, he can offer his public a valuable series of lessons on human conduct. Maurois considered biography a genre that conveys to a large number of readers some of the loftiest examples of human achievement, examples that, he hoped, would inspire others to live better lives. Here indeed is the ultimate mission of the biographer: ". . . it is exalting and healthy for the reader to find in a being whom he admires some of the passions which are those of total humanity. It is a noble spectacle to observe the struggle of the hero to surmount his weaknesses and to draw out of himself something which within himself is greater than he is."[53]

Temperamentally, André Maurois was the kind of person who was susceptible of being molded and influenced by great masters. (Cf. his lifelong reactions to the dynamic personality of Alain.) In reality, he was not so different in this respect from most of us. We tend to be strongly influenced by those with whom we come into close contact in our personal, professional, and social lives. But few of us consciously realize the extent to which we are capable of undergoing such influences. Fewer still are the creative artists who overtly reveal the names of those who helped influence their formation; the creative artist too often fears compromising his claim to originality by disclosing the names of his masters. Among the leading writers of his age, Maurois was one who repeatedly and unabashedly conceded that certain great figures influenced him immensely. His *Mémoires* and *Portrait d'un ami qui s'appelait moi* contain many admissions of indebtedness. His greatest guide, Alain, he called "the one who directed my life and inspired all my work."[54] From Descartes he learned to have faith in free will. From Balzac he learned that men are basically "immutable," that they should, therefore, not try too hard to transform their fundamental natures. Stendhal taught him to scorn the whims and snobbishness of public opinion, and to admire things and people because he himself was pleased by them and not because it was fashionable to like or dislike them. Lyautey taught him "la morale de l'action."[55] Just as he had learned from the exemplary lives of others, Maurois hoped that his readers would learn much from his biographies.

In1949 André Maurois contributed regularly to *Les Nouvelles Littéraires* a series of short biographical portraits entitled *Destins exemplaires (Exemplary Destinies)*. He later gathered many of these articles and in 1952 published them in a little volume of the same title. The term *destins exemplaires* not only summarizes the themes in this particular volume but really describes all of his biographies. Each in its own way is a vivid demonstration of an exemplary human life.

Not that all of Maurois's heroes lived such impeccable lives that they should be imitated in every phase of their careers. On the contrary, these great men and women possessed many undeniable weaknesses and committed many blunders, all of which their biographer candidly described. But the reader has the prerogative of emulating the virtues and avoiding the defects. In a sense, Maurois's biographies follow the strategy of Molière's comedies: in pointing out some of the human foibles and the effects of bad judgment of a Chateaubriand or a George Sand, Maurois expected that his readers would convert a negative example into a constructive lesson.

The author of *Ariel* and *Olympio* insisted that a great creative genius must not be judged according to the conventional standards of right and wrong or good and bad. The life of the genius is often richer, denser, and more turbulent than most other lives. The genius thrives on complex, extraordinary experiences, which he incorporates artistically into his created work. The life of George Sand is filled with many shocking experiences, which, by normal standards of morality, should be abhorred. But how necessary these experiences were for the works that resulted from them!

> But one must not weigh on the same scales the actions of the artist and those of other men. Every artist is a sublime actor who needs, and he knows it, to go beyond the tolerable emotions in order for his thought to transform itself into something rich and strange. A moralist has the right to judge that Sand and Musset might have been able to live more wisely. But the particular works of art which were born out of their errors and their sufferings would not then have been possible. Musset knew desire before he met George Sand; he did not know passion; he could write *La Ballade à la lune*, not the dialogue between Camille and Perdican.[56]

Taken as a whole, the rich human existence lived by George Sand forms an admirable example of a great human character, who, in spite of many defects and errors, was propelled by an insatiable desire to do everything possible to attain perfect happiness, a goal not unworthy of all human beings. Similarly, taken in their entirety, Maurois's lives of Byron, Chateaubriand, the three Dumas, and others form tapestries in which the reader is ultimately more impressed by the heroic accomplishments and sympathetic characteristics of these figures than by some of their defects, which resemble only minor discords drowned out by the harmony of the whole.

Actually Maurois opposed the use of biography—or any other work of art—as a means to preach overtly. Nothing was more antithetical to his conception of art than preaching: "Yes, every moral preoccupation in a work of art, whether it concerns a novel or a biography, kills the work of art. As soon as one wishes to prove something, one proves nothing. This does not prevent great moral themes from being able to impregnate the work."[57] Maurois believed that teaching through implication was a more eloquent way of teaching than through outright sermonizing. This he learned from his parents: "The best moral teaching, the only efficient one, is example. [My parents] feared grandiloquence and never spoke of such subjects. . . ."[58] Never once did he yield on this point. Never did he dogmatize in his biographies: "A great biography is a lesson, not because the biographer dramatizes, but because a great life is beautiful."[59]

When he wrote "a great life is beautiful," he did not necessarily signify that a great life was beautiful because it contained only good deeds and great acts of mercy and charity. Beautiful lives also contain blemishes. A distinguished administrator and military hero may also be a very egotistical man, but his life stands out because he is above all a man of great courage and vision (Lyautey). A man may be a fumbling stammerer in elegant social gatherings, but in the privacy of his laboratory he is endowed with the qualities needed to become a world-famous scientist (Fleming). A poet may be petty in dealing with his immediate family in private life, but through his stirring public proclamations he may be capable of inspiring whole generations of men and women to work toward exalted human ideals (Hugo). If these exemplary heroes had been too perfect, we, as readers, would find it difficult to identify ourselves with them. Their lives assume greater authenticity for us mainly because their frailties make it seem as if their feet are on the ground. We sympathize more readily with heroes scaled down to our dimensions than with infallible demigods.

The biographies of André Maurois contain a two-pronged lesson. First, they teach that the examples of the lives of immortal men and women are worthy of being studied. Second, because even these immortal men and women are not indefectible, we are consoled with respect to our own lives. If the most successful men and women have erred and suffered profoundly, what more can ordinary human beings expect from their own existences? But, as was the case of a Disraeli, a Victor Hugo, or a Mme de La Fayette, we must not allow early defeats and disappointments to vanquish our will to improve our ultimate destinies. Nothing was more alien to Maurois's philosophy than submissive resignation. In a sharply honed maxim inserted in his biography of Voltaire, Maurois declared: "We must act. Everything is not well, but everything can be made better."[60]

Biography as a genre permitted Maurois to study human life itself more closely through the exegesis of the careers of certain great figures from the past. It enabled him also to expound his own personal philosophy of life and to fulfill his mission as an artist. For he believed that the artist was he who must serve humanity. For a long time he held the conviction that art must never be allowed to sever itself from the raw material of life itself. This is why he once expressed a preference for biography over the "fantastic short story." "But this genre [the short story] had, in my opinion, the defect of keeping me too distant from real humanity. Biography gave me the same distance but at the same time maintained me better within life itself."[61] André Maurois steadfastly refused to write in cloistered garrisons far removed from the mainstream of life. This explains at least in part why his biographies form on the literary horizon of our century an imposing and high point, one that seethes with humanistic values and the vibrancy of warm and admirable human lives.

Part III
The World of the Novels

4
Themes and Variations—Novel by Novel

> The total is infinitely larger than the sum of the parts.
> Maurois, *Prométhée*

In the twentieth-century French novel André Maurois belongs to those novelists who consciously prolonged the fictional traditions they had inherited from the three preceding centuries. Deliberately, Maurois fended off the temptation to express himself in a completely new manner, to seek originality for the sake of originality, or to experiment with novelistic form. Alain had inculcated in him an indomitable respect for the proven virtues of Balzac, George Sand, and Stendhal, and, consequently, Maurois perpetuated in his novels many of the echoes of his predecessors. For the most part, his fiction is built along the conventional lines of the nineteenth-century novel; to these inherited ingredients he added his own personal qualities. The whole gives the impression of continuity enriched with a mild touch of modernity.

At the base of Maurois's philosophy of the novel is the fact that he regarded this genre as an already perfected species, one whose form had already been clearly defined. Maurois asserted too that the novelist of today should not modify this tradition until after he has fully absorbed the great masters of the past and appreciated their finest works. He informed the French Academy that "a novelist, like a painter, learns his craft by copying the masterpieces. Originality does not give herself to those who court her. She becomes an additional fringe benefit for those who work on the object."[1]

A. *Les Silences du Colonel Bramble* and *Les Discours du Docteur O'Grady*

Maurois's literary début was a late one. He was already thirty-three years old when he ventured into the arena of literature. For fifteen or twenty years the writer in him was maturing, and the blossoming young man was dreaming of writing books. His first title, *Les Silences du Colonel Bramble,* is composed with such care that it is hard to believe that this work marked the inauguration, rather than the apogée, of a career. André Chevrillon marveled at this feat: "When there appeared in 1918 this exquisite book *The Silences of Colonel*

Bramble, written at the British front where you served as an interpreter, everyone was astounded to find an accomplished artist in a beginner. People did not
realize how many years of preparation had been necessary to make possible this
perfect success."[2] The novel, published by the incipient publishing house of
Bernard Grasset, had a brilliant success: one hundred thousand copies were
quickly sold.

Maurois had barely been able to contain within himself the things he heard in
the barracks, the experiences he lived, the people he had met in the British
army, the sights, sounds, smells, and dramatic occurrences of the war. Too
preoccupied with warfare to begin serious composition, an accident, which
temporarily immobilized him, provided him with the conditions needed to
write. One day, after falling off a horse that had slipped in the mud, he found
himself nursing some serious wounds in the military hospital. He disclosed that
"this accident sent me to the Infirmary of the Division, in which I found some
doctors and some Padres whose conversation enchanted me. It was while listening to them that for the first time I got the idea of writing some dialogues
which would paint England and Scotland from the inside, without author's
comments, and that I composed a first chapter."[3]

A curious novel, devoid of a firm plot in the conventional sense, the *Bramble*
is a composition in which various male characters come and go, and they engage
in discussions with each other on a variety of timely topics. The book juxta-
poses three metaphysical points of view: Dr. O'Grady's materialistic and
scientific determinism; the padre's religious and spiritual faith; and the taciturn
and stubborn confidence in mankind's destiny held by the almost noncom-
municative Bramble.[4] Aurelle, the French liaison officer, prods these three into
debates of all sorts, mainly so that they can externalize their views of life.
Occasionally he plays the part of the "faux naïf" (or falsely innocent person),
pretending not to know or to understand much of what was being discussed
and forcing his friends to clarify controversial or unclear topics.

The book forms a mosaic of tiny dialogues that comprise a loosely defined
plot. An Anglo-Scottish brigade finds itself stationed in northeastern France
during World War I. The soldiers continually discuss a broad variety of topics.
Seemingly minor subjects are tossed about lightly—when in reality the author
is earnestly serious [for example, the love of land by the French, *Romans,*
(Paris: Gallimard, 1961) p. 913]. Homespun anecdotes mix with barracks quips
and some deeply philosophic discussion. Maurois shows quite easily that every
strongly held point of view has at least one detractor. For each debate he creates
two discussants for the purpose of expounding their contradictory points of
view.

Really a strange mixture of many physical structures, this novel is virtually
formless. Transitions from section to section seem nonexistent: poems are
followed by narratives in the third person, which in turn are followed by
letters, dialogues, pages from Aurelle's diary (See, for example, *Romans,*
p. 920). The book starts out with absolutely no preparatory chapter designed

to set the place, time, circumstances, or mood. We stumble onto the Scottish brigade in a Flemish barn watching a boxing match during one of the brief respites of the war. Before we know it, Major Parker, Aurelle, and Colonel Bramble are engaged in a heated debate on the differing mores of the French and the British.

National differences constitute one of the central themes of the book. The confrontation between Aurelle and his British friends represents the confrontation of life-styles and values between France and Great Britain. "We are funny people," says Major Parker. "In order to get a Frenchmen interested in boxing, you have to tell him that his national honor is involved in it; to interest an Englishman in a war, all you have to do is tell him that it resembles a boxing match" (*Romans*, p. 879). Maurois admires above all the stouthearted stoicism of the British in the face of pain and war: "They have spent their youth hardening their hide and their heart. They fear neither a blow of the fist nor a blow of destiny. They consider exaggeration as the worst of the voices and coldness as a sign of humor. When they are unhappy they put on a mask of humor" (ibid., p. 902). Conversations on hunting and fishing reveal the strong English propensity for sports and outdoor life (p. 888); others on polyandry, polygamy, and monogamy divulge their attitudes on marriage (pp. 916–17). Maurois lets his characters talk freely of the horrors of war and the glories of the military tradition (pp. 900–901, p. 932, p. 954), the role of superstitions in modern life (p. 941), and the absurd bureaucracy of both their own military establishment and of the French Ecole Polytechnique (pp. 934–35). Occasionally—and inevitably—the barracks talk degenerates into boastful tales concerning conquests of women, but Maurois quickly transforms the crudeness of these boasts into tasteful exploits (e.g., pp. 918–19). Never do these soldiers tire of listening to an old and well-worn disc of the "Destiny Waltz," played again and again in both the *Bramble* and the *O'Grady*. That the French Aurelle can derive pleasure from the same song as the English soldiers amuses the latter. Music becomes symbolic of their close human rapport, and this same melody will recur often in Maurois's later writing, manifesting the degree with which he loved to recall the happy, as well as the tragic moments of his association with the British Expeditionary Forces of World War I.

An unmistakable theme of the book is suggested by the title "Les Silences." Through his silences, the laconic Colonel Bramble expresses himself more meaningfully than others more articulate than he. Bramble usually spends his time simply listening to what his more loquacious friends have to say. Occasionally, he mutters a word or fragment of a sentence, but when he talks, it is a pithy and forceful utterance.

The final theme deals with war. It is the underlying event. Against the chattering discussions of the men in the barracks, the war continues to unfurl, taking a heavy toll in human lives. But somehow life continues to move forward, regardless of the debacle in which all of these figures participate. Human beings, with their love of land and life, will not all be destroyed by war. Many will manage to outlive the worst disasters. When an old French peasant tilling the fields is asked where the battle is, he replies: "The battle? . . . which battle?" Maurois's closing sentence summarizes his faith in the dogged continuity of man, as he adds: "And the people of Crécy went back to tying up in precise sheafs the wheat of this invincible earth" (ibid., p. 956).

The Discourses of Doctor O'Grady, written in 1922 to satisfy the still unsatiated interest of the public for war stories, is based on supplemental notes that Maurois had not used in the *Bramble*. The two books form an ensemble and should, for maximum pleasure, be read together. In the second book the characters are the same, and the events are sequels to the earlier occurrences. The contrasting titles "The Silences" versus "The Discourses" underscore the disparity between the two heroes: Bramble speaks very little, while O'Grady is the voluble type. On every conceivable topic, from religion (*Romans*, p. 976) to French cuisine (ibid., p. 989), from the goriness of war (p. 955) to the subject of human destiny (p. 996), and from British military hierarchy (p. 986) to modern music—especially that of Debussy (p. 992)—the garrulous military physican espounds his opinions copiously. Actually, the title, *The Discourses of Doctor O'Grady*, is somewhat of a misnomer; the book ought to have been called more precisely *The Dialogues of Doctor O'Grady and Aurelle*, for the two men are always at loggerheads with one another. Aurelle urges O'Grady to elaborate on the massive issues facing the world. Generally, the latter takes a hard-boiled view of humanity, while the former sees mankind in a more optimistic light. The British figure almost expounds a philosophy of nihilism. Here is how he describes the history of civilization: "Six thousand years of warfare, six thousand years of misery, six thousand years of prostitution; half of humanity busy asphyxiating the other half; famine in Europe, slavery in Asia . . ." (p. 1011).

A few of the characters from the *Bramble* have disappeared; some have been killed in battle. If the *O'Grady* takes place a bit later chronologically than the *Bramble*, a few incidents overlap. The principal casualty from the earlier volume is the Padre, who has died in the interim.

Structurally, this work is a precursor to some of the unorthodox and experimental novels of the period of the nineteen fifties and sixties. The text progresses with no apparent order of chronology or logic. Selected moments from the war succeed each other with little coherent sequence. Flashbacks into the past are interspersed with apparently new events. Then, with no preparatory development, we learn that armistice has suddenly been declared, and, in fact, the Colonel announces that "this peace arrives at a badly timed moment" (p. 1021). Just when the men were beginning to adapt themselves to a new way of daily life, to develop close human relationships with each other, they learn that the strange reality they had learned to accept, not without some sense of gratification, has been entirely shattered. But is this not a realistic presentation of life in the military forces? How often have men in the front learned that peace has been declared by the politicians, without their having the slightest notion of its imminent possibility?

The theme of the *O'Grady*, even more than that of the *Bramble*, treats of the necessity of establishing warm and deep human attachments, especially during the most demanding tribulations. Men need companions. And when the war ends, there is the mixed sentiment of separation. How sad it is to leave one's closest associates, men with whom one has shared so many pleasures and sadnesses! The reader experiences the melancholy atmosphere of the farewell party made by the British for their French interpreter, Aurelle: "Aurelle, very moved, looked over these friendly faces and thought with sadness that he was going to leave this little universe forever" (p. 1023). And time and men do not remain fixed. The Colonel Bramble of the first volume emerges at the conclusion of the second novel as General Bramble.

At the end, Maurois adds an epilogue, dated April 1920. Two years following the termination of hostilities, Parker writes to Aurelle to disclose that he has become a gentleman farmer. Aurelle, for his part, has become a French author. The final chapter describes a touching reunion of Aurelle, General Bramble, and Doctor O'Grady. The three exchange quips and some nostalgic references to the past over a glass of whiskey, and the whole affair ends in a spirit of bonhomie. This bonhomie between the English and the Frenchman conforms well with Maurois's philosophy of Franco-British conciliation.

Maurois's infatuation with his British friends did not halt with this book. Throughout his career his wartime experiences continued to linger. During 1939 he maintained a Wednesday series of articles under the rubric of "The New Discourses of Doctor O'Grady," in which the doctor returns to visit his old French friend Aurelle; both exchange notes about their respective lifetimes. This series appeared in volume form in 1950 and was published, symbolically, by Bernard Grasset.

The *Nouveaux Discours* demonstrate unequivocally that the young man who had begun as a charming novelist in 1918 and 1922 emerged decades later as a perspicacious essayist of human morality. If *Les Silences du Colonel Bramble* and *Les Discours du Docteur O'Grady* figure among Maurois's most light-hearted and enjoyable texts, *Les Nouveaux Discours* ranks among his most cerebral compositions. The first two works were included by Maurois among editions of his complete novels. The third work has lost all fictional resemblance and must be regarded as an essay.

B. *Ni ange ni bête (Neither Angel nor Beast)*

The Bramble O'Grady books are really bastard novels or mixtures of journalistic reportage and the novel. His first *pure* novel, *Ni ange ni bête*, is unadulterated by journalistic chronicles of the author's personal observations. He always regarded this novel with misgivings; it was his first fumbling effort at real fiction. In 1919 *Ni ange ni bête* failed miserably as a commercial commodity; only about seven or eight thousand copies were sold. Curiously, *Ni ange ni bête* was regarded as a work of sufficient merit to be reissued in 1962, more than four decades later, but this time among the popular Livres de Poche paperback series. Generally, this series is reserved for best-sellers. In 1962 it was reasoned that Maurois's reputation as an accomplished literary artist was firmly estabished, and the public might be curious to read his earliest pure novel. Actually the book enjoyed mixed success.

Though far from perfect, it marks the début of a writer who manifests a tight sense of control over his plot. In fact, Maurois's own lukewarm appraisal of his own work seems a bit harsh. In a preface to *Ni ange ni bête,* added to his *Oeuvres complètes* of 1950, he disclosed his hesitations: "It is a strange experience for a writer to reread one of his first books. He does not find himself in it any longer. He might wish to efface everything, begin again, and, yet, this imperfect work, he feels that it is very close to him."[5]

In another moment of candor the novelist suggested that *Ni Angi ni bête* ought to be considered as the product of the foolish and impractical idealism with which so many lycée graduates, unprepared for the hard realities of life, graduate from school. Here is how Maurois phrased the relationship between this novel and his own first disappointments with life: "Out of the lycée I went as a socialist; briskly transformed into an industrialist, I had found my ideas to be in conflict with my actions. A rigid theoretician, I had wanted to apply rational systems in my sentimental life; on all sides, I had encountered a living and sensitive matter, which did not bend to my logic" (*Oeuvres complètes,* 1:387–88) In the novel, Philippe Viniès reflects the silly idealism of the author; only Maurois transported him back in time, back to 1848. He believes in the feasibility of a genuine people's revolution that would, at long last, usher in an era of social equality, peace, and individual rights. Once the revolution has taken place—a movement in which the hero naively believed that he could make a significant contribution—the ruling and financial classes simply continue to rule as before, but under different labels. In the end the quixotic and disillusioned Philippe must flee to England as a *persona non grata.* With gentle satire, Maurois, who had since learned to be a realist, exposed his hero's extravagances. These are great all-conquering dreamers and lovers, who are more successful as conquerors in their dreams than in the reality of life itself. It was at this stage in life that Maurois wrote *Ariel ou la Vie de Shelley,* a book concerning another great dreamer: "I wanted at the same time to expose [the adolescent that I myself had been]," wrote Maurois, "to condemn him and to explain him. Indeed, Shelley had known the same failures, with a hundred times more grandeur and grace . . ." (ibid., p. 388).

When Maurois originally wished to write on this theme of disillusionment, he was stationed in a military base at Abbeville. Shelley would have been his great hero. But the requisite documents on the poet were unavailable to him in that small provincial town. So he translated Shelley's adventures into those of a purely fictional figure, Viniès, and clothed the British poet in the vestments of a nineteenth-century Frenchman. Thus Philippe Viniés incarnates both Shelley and the youthful Maurois. Maurois situates the locale of the novel in Abbeville. The parallels between the life of Philippe Viniès in *Ni ange ni bête* and that of Shelley in *Ariel ou la Vie de Shelley* form a pregnant topic for some novice doctoral student in literature.

Maurois utilizes *Ni ange ni bête* as a vehicle to satirize the small-town, narrow-minded, and money-oriented mentality of Abbeville. The satire is disturbingly imitative of Stendhal's depiction of an almost identical situation in Verrières, in the early pages of *Le Rouge et le noir (The Red and the Black)*.

Ni ange ni bête reminds us of still another author, Anatole France. Like the latter's novel *Les Dieux ont soif (The Gods are Athirst)*. Maurois's work conveys his own skeptical belief that violent revolutions could truly improve the human lot. Violence leads only to bloodhsed and seldom to reform. The novelist suggests that man can solve his most serious problems only by slow, patient, methodical, and above all peaceful reform. Maurois the future historian expresses himself in the following manner: "These industrialists, these workers, these factories, our frock coats and our jackets will disappear as certainly as the armor and the arquebuses, as well as the barons and the serfs. But you need time. One cannot throw away civilization like a book that has lost its appeal" (ibid., p. 403).

This writer knew that fiery words and clever slogans exist mainly as tools for opportunistic politicians and revolutionary agitators who seek only to arouse the gullible mobs to take lawless action. On the concluding pages of *Ni ange ni bête*, he insists that "all of our misfortunes . . . come from the fact that people use words which they have neglected to define" (ibid., p. 494). Thus, "Salvation and Fraternity" are empty goals for which Philippe has risked his life only to help bring on a new government which ironically regards him as an enemy of the state. If he continues naively to believe in these words, those who have seized power on the strength of his slogans were little more than callous cynics. Lust for power under the guise of idealism is the central thesis of the novel.

From the standpoint of form, *Ni ange ni bête* is completely conventional. The novel, told in the third person, describes a slice of the life of the hero, starting from the moment he arrives in Abbeville, where he has been appointed to serve the municipality as an engineer. Maurois then relates his marriage there, his associations with the local townspeople, his departure for Paris to take part in the Revolution of 1848, his failure to play a dramatic part in it, his disillusionment, and finally his exile. The last chapter assumes the form of an epilogue and consists of a bitter letter addressed by Philippe's philosopher friend, Bertrand d'Ouville to Geneviève Viniès, in exile with her husband in England; there Bertrand reveals that nothing has really changed in France as a result of the revolution. The letter is dated *Abbeville, October 1853*.

Maurois's Pascalian title *"Ni ange ni bête" (Neither Angel nor Beast)*, he has used over and over again in the texts of many of his subsequent works. Bernard Grasset, the publisher, always claimed that this title was the principal reason for the book's scant success. In a superb maxim, dropped at random somewhere in his thoughtful essay on "De Ruskin à Wilde," Maurois gives us his best definition of the title: "Man is neither an angel nor a beast, but it is a happy fact of life that when he acts like an angel, he acts a bit less like a beast."[6] This maxim accurately sums up a large part of the philosophy of life of Maurois the moralist.

Perhaps, in the long run, *Ni ange ni bête*—a book the philosopher Alain admired with surprising ardor—will elicit more esteem than the hypercritical Maurois thought it deserved. For the moment, however, it appears that the disciple was a more accurate critic than his master.

C. *Bernard Quesnay*

The subsequent novel, *Bernard Quesnay,* published in 1928, has continued to rise slightly but steadily in public favor and despite its moderate commercial success at first, it is one of Maurois' finest fictional compositions. If *Ni ange ni bête* carries undertones of Stendhal, *Bernard Quesnay* perpetuates the traditions of Balzac. Written with vigorously sketched characters and dramatically organized scenes, it possesses a robust solidity lacking in Maurois's other novels. In contrast with novels like *Promised Land* and *Family Circle, Bernard Quesnay* treats of the search for happiness of male characters; women in this novel play merely an accessory role. Maurois formulates detailed and Balzacian descriptions of the world of financial speculation and of industrial activities.

Bernard Quesnay is a "problem" novel. A Spanish critic, Miguel Pérez Ferrero, pinpointed the problem cryptically: the central issue is "Emile Herzog versus André Maurois."[7] Herzog symbolizes the young man who as an industrialist did not wish to break the ties between himself and the family business, whereas Maurois of course represents the writer stirring in his soul who struggles to express himself. In reality, Maurois dramatized his own personal crisis of conscience as a young man divided between two overpowering goals. But he splits himself into two brothers, Bernard and Antoine. The dilemma is summarized in a nutshell as Bernard recognizes the dangers of remaining in the provincial town of Pont de l'Eure: "No law in the world can force me to live in Pont de l'Eure. I am young, active; I would succeed anywhere. . . . But it seems to me that I am divided into two parts. One part of me says: 'The essential thing is that these looms keep turning.' Another part of me replies: 'Are you mad? You are making me lose all of my youth.' I am aware that the second personage expresses more truthfully my thinking and, in fact, I obey the first one" (p. 185). Later, the same dilemma is reemphasized by Françoise, Antoine's wife, who continues to agitate for an early departure from the town: "It was enough for me to have spent my youth buried in a countryside, linked to a man for whom I count less than his smokestacks and looms! I still have a few years of youth left. I wish to live" (p. 212). Finally, she does succeed in persuading her husband that for the sake of their children and the health of their family they have no choice but to depart for a more attractive environment. Antoine informs Bernard that he is resigned to living in Provence on less money than as an industrialist in Normandy. In the south he can make a stab at free-lance writing: "As for me, I love to be warm and provided that I have a car, a gun, I am happy. Françoise will have her children, a garden, some flowers; I shall keep a small foothold in Paris so that, during the winter, she can hear a little music and see her friends . . ." (p. 248). The entire drama of the book is contained in the foregoing citations. Bernard, for his part, even gives up his sentimental attachment to his beautiful friend, Simone, in favor of a life devoted entirely to the industrial firm and to his family tradition.

The central theme concerns the continuity of the family line. The Quesnays of Pont de l'Eure, like the Herzogs and Fraenckel-Blin clans of Elbeuf, possess a proud tradition of factory ownership. Wool weaving and marketing literally run through their blood. Their life unfolds against the background of the humming looms and the bolts of fabric. It is taken for granted that this all-pervasive life will be passed on from father to son. Bernard, following a most agonizing soul-searching, clings to the traditions of the family. Antoine becomes the first to break with the family chain. And when their grandfather, Monsieur Achille, dies, it is as if a monarch has just left behind him a kingdom that must pass on to his legitimate heir. At the funeral, Bernard is asked whether the factory can be expected to open at the usual time of 2:00 P.M. The book ends with his reply, "Naturally" (p. 261). And so continuity continues.

Michel Droit identifies the theme of this novel as "Fidélité," and emphasizes that it is consistent with Maurois's own lifelong obsession with fidelity as a cardinal force in life as well as in art. In real life Maurois remained faithful to his earliest friends. Never was there a break in his attachment to such friends as Alain. And though he could easily have permitted more dynamic publishing houses to publish his books, he never forgot that it was Bernard Grasset who gave him his earliest opportunity.[8]

Maurois treats yet another theme in *Bernard Quesnay*, that of relations between management and employees. This question haunted him throughout his career, as he so readily admitted in his *Mémoires*. We know that upon leaving the Lycée Corneille, he was imbued with socialistic fervor, thanks to Alain's precepts on the equality of all men. Determined to find a solution for the fundamental problem of human inequity, he entered the management of his family's firm only to discover that his relatives also worked long and hard through the hours of the night, seven days each week, in order to eke out a meager profit. He began to appreciate not only the grievances of the workers but also the fact that management too had its legitimate point of view. The climax of *Bernard Quesnay* is reached when the workers go out on strike, paralyzing the operations in the mill. Their dissatisfaction is not unjustified, but for management to yield to their demands would lead either to a further decline in the already meager profits or else to a rise in prices. This would place their firm in an uncompetitive position on the market, thus hastening an end to this company's existence as a successful industrial enterprise.

Bernard Quesnay, one of the most unjustly underestimated novels of our times, must be studied on several planes: as a historical *récit* of life in a small Norman industrial city in the early part of our century; as an ideological novel that dramatizes the confrontation of two doctrines: socialism and capitalism; as a sentimental and psychological novel in which the author studies the place of love in the lives of his busy industrialists; as a realistic account of the business world and the motivations of businessmen; as an analysis of the psychological stresses and tensions that divide generation from generation.[9]

The structure of the novel is orthodox: a third-person narrative, it is charged with many vivid dialogues and discussions. Incisively, Maurois plunges into his plot, and already in the very first scene the main characters are plainly visible. From the first pages we understand their interrelationships. And as the action progresses Maurois achieves a sharp degree of vividness by alternating lively spoken exchanges with descriptions of visual scenes.

Bernard Quesnay is a carefully written, carefully structured, in fact, nearly flawless work. It should be! Today's version represents the third published version of the novel, the first of which appeared in 1922 under the title *La Hausse et la baisse (Ups and Downs)*, the second in 1926, and the final and most successfully revised edition in 1929. Maurois remained modest vis-à-vis the work, although one detects his subtle degree of satisfaction with it: "*Bernard Quesnay* is not a 'great' novel, far from this; but it is an honest book, more true as a painting of the industrial world than the pamphlets written, under the guise of novels, by men who have not seen this life except from the outside and through their prejudices."[10]

D. *Climats (Atmospheres of Love)*

When the shrewd critic Edmond Jaloux predicted in his prophetic review of *Climats* that this novel "has every chance of enduring. It is a work which will count in the literary history of our time,"[11] he realized that *Climats* had the makings of a true classic of the twentieth century. If Maurois will be remembered at all for any novel at all, it will be for *Climats*. Here is a work that has good chances to resist both the corrosive forces of time and capricious fluctuations of future tastes. Of all of his fictional writings *Climats* has attracted the largest numbers of readers in France, Germany, Italy, Japan, Spain, Poland, and Latin America. When *Climats* first appeared in a Russian translation, the entire first edition of one hundred-thousand copies was exhausted on the very day the novel appeared for the first time in the bookstores of Moscow. In the Anglo-American world, however, under its title of *Climates of Love* or *Atmospheres of Love* it has never enjoyed the popularity that it deserves. Perhaps for English readers its delicate psychological shadings, its almost total interiority, and its lacy infrastructure are not appealing in an epoch that has accustomed itself to novels hewn out of gutlike, often violent language. Perhaps too the translations of the poetic prose cannot adequately be rendered in English. The Spanish edition, *Climas,* has already had at least fourteen editions, and in the Spanish-speaking world the book has continued to be regarded as a genuine master-work. In France, more than a million copies have been sold, and it ranks with the all-time best-sellers of French literature. Hardly any serious reader over the age of forty can be found in France who has not at some time read *Climats.* In 1961 the novel was transformed into a film, with Marina Vlady as Odile, Emmanuèle Riva as Isabelle, Alexandra Stewart as Misa, and J-P Marielle as Philippe Marcenat. The film enjoyed only moderate success, probably because the actors were not at all appropriate for their almost impossible roles. Also, this introspective and analytical work does not lend itself to being easily transferred to the external images of the screen. Some critics attributed this lack of success to the too numerous liberties taken by the producers of the film as they transformed a literary text into a different medium. Few who saw the film, including Maurois, were entirely satisfied, all of which proves once again that a great book may easily degenerate into a mediocre film.

No work Maurois produced has elicited more universal praise from the corps of critics. Because some of this praise helps explicate the book itself, it is useful here to quote a few of the critical evaluations.

André Chevrillon, in his French Academy address, implied that with *Climats* Maurois had at last come into his own as a novelist. With the *Bramble-O'Grady* he was still an able commentator of his own wartime adventures. *Ni ange ni bête* is a too-imitative pastiche of Stendhal to be taken seriously. *Bernard Quesnay,* with its strongly stereotyped characters, is a bit too reminiscent of Balzac. *Climats,* however, in spite of certain discreet Proustian echoes, is an original piece of fiction. Chevrillon notes:

> In *Climats,* the history of a passion, the point of view and the procedure are reversed compared with *Bernard Quesnay.* The characters are too complex to permit themselves to be sketched in a single stroke. They change, they evolve. You do not describe them; they study themselves, tell about themselves, confess themselves. Bit by bit, the depth of their souls, their most secret simmerings reveal themselves. We see the obscure birth of sentiments, their fluxes and their refluxes, the fleeting nuances with which these waves become iridescent.[12]

No longer is Maurois's narrative in the third person. His form, actually quite unique, is composed of a binary structure of which the first part consists of Philippe Marcenat's long confidential letter addressed to his second wife, Isabelle, describing his lingering attachment to his late first wife, Odile; and in Part II Isabelle discloses her own first-person version of her complex marriage with Philippe. What we have then is the effect of a kind of "diptych." In the first panel of the "diptych" we view Philippe as he chooses to describe himself, whereas in the second we see him through the eyes of his spouse. Similarly, Odile is first presented through Marcenat's eyes as an angelic but naughty nymph, whereas in Part II Isabelle reacts to the vestigial memory of Odile with a mixture of fascination and terror. While most of the critics have admired this unique construction, a few have considered its bilateral form to be an annoying and "artificial symmetry."[13] In an unpublished letter to Maurois, the discerning and candid critic Jean Paulhan clearly prefers Part I (Odile) to Part II (Isabelle):

> While reading *Climats*, I have passed through many different feelings. I know few works as poignant as Odile: it occurred to me, during the reading of this part, to think of *Adolphe*, of *Dominique*, to tell myself that this wise and clear voice conveyed a far-off message, that your account was neither less precise nor less happy than that of Constant or Fromentin, that the event which you choose was more serious perhaps, and almost more demanding than theirs: finally everything that bears upon the various languages, which responds to the different climates, appears to me to be particularly just and revealing (what you say, for example, on page 60, concerning the language of Marcenat). You succeed even in making one of your characters recite verses without this wager and this literary mixture, achieved in a strange manner, surprising or shocking us in the least.
> Finally I found in *Odile* a perfected art, and much more than art. *Isabelle* disappointed me all the more. I can't help but see in it a rejoinder, a kind of false window: I should prefer that she not exist. (Yet, I know that she is esteemed and loved by people who are more worthy than I).[14]

Those who share Paulhan's disappointment over Part II believe also that the symmetry between the two parts was a bit too tidy. Some, like Paulhan, preferred that the poignant first half constitute the entire novel. Yet it was an open secret that *Climats* contained more than a few autobiographical elements, that there were two marriages (two lives, so to speak) in Maurois's existence, each deserving of its own unit.

The novel depicts a man who, in a state of despondency, believed life to have reached its terminal point; suddenly, thanks to the stimulus of a new human being, life begins for him all over again. *Climats* represents a clear example of art imitating life. If the binary structure of the novel seems incredible and factitious, then Maurois's life too was equally incredible and factitious.

Furthermore, we cannot discern the power with which the climates of Odile's magical presence have imperceptibly (in Part I) adulterated the personality of Philippe until we have observed his modified behavior in Part II. The Tharaud brothers throw further light onto this complex question: "We have read with much pleasure your two elegies [Parts I and II of *Climats*], and we rejoice at their great success. My brother loves especially in Part I the finesse of the psychological analysis; my wife prefers the second part; . . . because you have rendered with admirable skill the impregnation of one human being by another; as for me, I was . . . enchanted by your peaceful and sure art."[15] "The impregnation of one human being by another." In these few words Tharaud has summarized the capital theme of *Climats,* a novel that treats of the ways in which people who live in intimate proximity with one another influence each other's "climates"—that is, their tastes in eating, decor, dress, music, reading, and their mannerisms of speech and daily behavior.

Perhaps the most refreshing quality of *Climats* is its total sincerity and its absence of stylistic affectation. Maurois finally ceased to imitate, consciously or unconsciously, Stendhal and Balzac. He had just undergone a shattering crisis in his own life (the death of Janine, his first wife). The anguish, the pathos of this young man, prematurely a widower, resounds in every sentence in *Climats.* So the novel becomes a faithful rendition of the author's own personal crisis. The events and details of reality have been transformed, but the poignancy of the crisis was authentic. Though he used fiction to distort certain events and details, Maurois could never convincingly deny the similarities between his own painful existence and that of Marcenat. Thus *Climats* possesses a depth of melancholy manifested in none of the other novels of André Maurois. Through the sincerity of this story the reader becomes irresistibly involved in the profound intricacies of a unique love affair. This is precisely the point that Paul Desjardins makes in his personal letter to Maurois:

> You were an author [before *Climats*] according to my taste, and it did not bother me that this taste was shared by hundreds of thousands of readers on this planet. However, I was beginning to concede something to the critics around me who were disturbed by your lack of distinctive and inborn imperfections. Here, in *Climats,* you have the presentation of a Maurois who has been renewed by depth, a more intimate, more tragic, and greater one, and without doubt one with a more precise resemblance with himself. . . . The book is therefore essentially the mirror of you.[16]

Desjardin hits the nail on its proverbial head. He senses exactly why *Climats* stands apart from the preceding novels.

Maurois, in an unpublished page bound in the personal edition of *Climats* of Madame André-Maurois, is remarkably lucid in his analysis of this novel. Even there, in a page destined only for the eyes of his wife, he refused to admit the strongly personal traits in the work. It was, in his opinion, a universal book treating of a universal, nonsubjective subject. He was only partially right. The moment he verbalized artistically the deep anguish of Philippe Marcenat, this feeling was converted from the autobiographical details of a single human being's existence to the universal heritage of all men. The sufferings of Philippe, the tribulations of Isabelle, the playfulness of Odile—these are traits that can be appreciated by readers at any given time and in any given land. Here is what Maurois wrote to his wife:

Climats is a novel, and a novel proves nothing. *Climats* is essentially the story of three people: a man and two women. But it is not a question of the classical triangle; the two women succeed each other in the life of the man and the second one has never met the first one. Philippe Marcenat marries at first Odile, a character out of a Shakespearean comedy, more an elf than a woman; then Isabelle, whom he also loves but in a very different way, and who is a reasonable French middle-class woman, more a spouse than a sweetheart.

Although a novel proves nothing, it is permissible to draw from it some observations concerning human nature. This one shows: a. that certain beings make us live in a "climate" which we need and in which we would love them in spite of their faults; b. that a man can be impregnated and transformed by a woman whom he loves. . . . c. that certain men attach themselves to that which makes them suffer and that there is in the love-passion an element of painful curiosity.[17]

This last point contains one of the most vital truths Maurois learned from the Proustian novel: love and suffering are linked by some mysterious and invisible chain of sentiments.

Without naming Proust, Edmond Jaloux instinctively pointed to the numerous Proustian tinges in *Climats.* Speaking of the tremendous role that time plays in shaping the form of Maurois's novel, Jaloux asserts that "the beauty of the book resides in the truth of the characters and the situations and above all in the study of the effects which time makes his heroes undergo. . . . This interesting and fierce force of each hour that passes. . . ."[18] To an exceptional degree, Maurois succeeds in making the reader conscious of the numerous transformations undergone by his characters, from month to month, from moment to moment. The Philippe who marries Odile is not yet the later version of the Philippe who becomes madly jealous of her once she embarks upon her stealthy relationship with François. Nor is this jealous Philippe the same man who later will become unfaithful to his second wife. Odile Malet is a strangely different girl from Odile Marcenat. These characters float in the incessantly drifting clouds of time. In his same essay on *Climats,* Jaloux speaks of Odile as "perpetually moving, perpetually ungraspable . . . slippery, discontinuous." The many combinations of characters form both harmonious and contrasting palettes: Philippe-Odile versus Philippe-Isabelle; Philippe-Misa versus Philippe-Solange; Isabelle versus Odile; Odile-François versus Odile-Philippe; Isabelle de Cherverny versus Isabelle Marcenat; the Philippe of Gandumas versus the Philippe of Florence, Italy. All of these combinations create a multiple series of overlapping, triangular love affairs and continually shifting personalities and climates. Of these perpetual shifts, Jaloux remarks that "the beauty and the strangeness of *Climats* arises from this play of oppositions, interferences, refractions, one of which is arbitrary or bookish, but born out of the very truth of the characters and the situations." These complexities accumulate on top of each other, layer upon layer, and defy easy analysis. The more one seeks to elucidate *Climats,* the more it becomes elusive. Here again we find another reason for the supremacy of *Climats* over Maurois's other novels: It will always defy critics by its manifold and shifting perspectives.

Climats is a masterpiece for still another reason: its universally recognized stylistic polish. While Jaloux speaks of a "purity of language," even of a "dryness" that will keep the novel from appearing dated stylistically, Louis Chaigne describes the lacelike finesse of Maurois's style in the following way: "The sketch of the characters is accompanied little by little rather than traced all at once. The scenes are reconstituted with a pen that is economical in its means, with all of the slowness and finish that one could possibly hope for. A supple, gradual rhythm; a tone always beneath that of emotion. . . ."[19]

The delicate style emphasized by Louis Chaigne is a faithful rendition of the delicate psychological analyses that this novel possesses. Amélie Fillon contends that *Climats* owes its uniqueness to the "fine analysis of subtle, nuanced, and precise traits." She points out also that Maurois comes dangerously close to overdoing a good thing. He pushes his rarefied and exquisite analyses to their absolute limit. Madame Fillon underscores Philippe's "delicate sensitivity, the exigent character of his love," and the fact that he almost sins through his "excess of analysis and clairvoyance."[20] The analyses are so dense that little room is left for external events. The result of all of this is that Maurois has produced a double novel (first, the tragic love affair of Philippe and Odile, complicated by two third parties, Misa and François; second, the almost futile love affair between Philippe and Isabelle rendered more intricate by the third party, Solange Villier) that is rich in psychological profundity and somewhat threadbare in external events.

This is a novel of love. The trouble arises when the wrong people love each other or the right people love each other at the wrong time in their lives. Also, one sweetheart loves the other one more than the latter loves the former. Philippe adores Odile more than she adores him. Odile loves François more than he loves her. Misa worships Philippe more than he worships her. Isabelle is more bewitched by the spell of Philippe than vice versa. Philippe pursues Solange, who soon tires of his attentions. All of these uneven, disparate affections create a concatenation of tragic frustrations. The characters wind up uttering words they soon regret. Love turns to anger and anger turns to love. Philippe states: "Then I kissed her. I felt before her such complex sentiments that I understood them badly myself. I detested her and I adored her. I thought she was innocent and culpable. The violent scene which I had prepared was turning into a friendly, confidential conversation" (*Romans,* p. 64).

Structurally, this two-act tragedy consists of two first-person narrations interspersed with poems, letters, entries in journals, lists of sentiments. Though these parts are joined by no transitional passages, they all fit together with symmetry. Part I is closely interwoven with Part II by the flashbacks and allusions in the second part to events in the first. Events in the first section recur in the second. Leitmotifs of all kinds return again and again. Odile takes delight in the Neuilly fair of Part I, while Isabelle loathes it in Part II. Odile detests visits to Philippe's family estate of Gandumas; Isabelle feels most comfortable there. Music, especially Wagner, recurs in both parts.

Better than anyone else, Maurois the omniscient self-analyst reveals the significance of his most effective title, *"Climats"*: "What I have understood for a year, and this is very important, is that, if one truly loves, one should not attach too much importance to the actions of people whom one loves. We need them; they alone make us live in a certain 'atmosphere' (your friend Hélène says 'a climate' and that is very correct) without which we cannot get along" (*Romans*, p. 151). This certain "atmosphere," this poetic ambiance in which his characters live their lives, forms the basis for Maurois's finest hour as a novelist, for he has written not only a novel but also a poetic novel! Never again was he destined to produce such a successful piece of fiction.

E. Le Cercle de Famille (Family Circle)

After reaching the summit with *Climats*, there seemed to be no place for Maurois to go but downward. Despite this peril, *Le Cercle de famille*, Maurois's ensuing novel, represents this author's largest-scaled undertaking in the realm of the novel. In contrast with its impressive dimensions, this work actually had very modest beginnings. Maurois often referred to *Le Cercle de famille* as the classic example of how a major work grew out of very minor origins. His frank chapter "Elaboration of a Work," in *Portrait of a Friend Whose Name Is Me*, is essential reading for anyone interested in the candid revelation of how a difficult work found fruition from its earliest inception until its final growth. It all started with a conversation he had had with a young woman concerning her embarrassing relations with her mother. Immediately, Maurois envisioned the possibility of a "a mother-daughter novel, which would expose without reticence the problem that would be new and true."[21]

The principal theme is that of a young girl who discovers with her own eyes—and to her horror—that her reasons for childhood anxiety were indeed well founded, for she actually witnesses her mother engaged in an act of infidelity with the village doctor. She also realizes to her even greater shock that her father may well be aware of this adulterous relationship, but that he is either too weak or too indifferent to halt it. Pont de l'Eure, her hometown, whispers about this scandal, and her family is the laughing stock of all of the puritanical townsfolk. The shame of this hypersensitive child will haunt the heroine all of her life, and her adulthood will be altered as a result of shame, resentment, and even hatred of her mother and scorn for her father.

Jacques Suffel remarks that of all of Maurois's novels, *Le Cercle de famille* is the most bitter and bleak.[22] Suffel's statement does not, however, hold true for large segments of the work that have little to do with the mother-daughter relationship described above. *Le Cercle de famille* also contains a broad histor-

ical panorama of business, banking, political, and educational developments in
the world of 1900–1930. Nor is it confined geographically to the small space of
Pont de l'Eure; it carries us from provincial Normandy to the university milieu
and the banking universes of Paris as well as to the Riviera. Moreover, the cast
is comprised of more than merely the group of characters of Pont de l'Eure; in
reality, we come into contact with a large (for Maurois) assemblage of characters from many walks of life. The attention of the reader oscillates between the
tale of Denise Herpain's bitter life and political topics like Aristide Briand's
unsuccessful bid for the French presidency, the pending financial crash of the
early thirties, the French role in foreign affairs, the state of psychiatry at the
time, aesthetic and literary questions exposed principally by Maurois's fictional
spokesman, the author Bernard Schmitt.

The families in Pont de l'Eure are identical to those of *Bernard Quesnay*. The
secondary educational program followed by Denise Herpain in her daily train
trips to Rouen is strikingly similar to Maurois's own educational adventures in
the same city. The university ambiance in Paris and later the scenes in the
glittering salons of the capital's high society also come out of his own personal
observations. Through the Baronne Choin, this novel is linked not only to
Bernard Quesnay but also to *Climats*, the baroness being Philippe Marcenat's
aunt. Furthermore, the widow of Marcenat, Isabelle, has remarried Bertrand
Schmitt (whom Maurois called a "projection of myself").[23] In *Le Cercle de
famille* Bertrand functions as the confidant of Denise.

Denise Herpain probably represents Maurois's most ambitious feminine
undertaking. She evolves in stages from childhood and adolescent revolt against
her parents and the whole adult world through a brilliant adolescence during
which she excels as a student; then she reaches a period of experimental amoral-
ity in college, followed by her married life—in which she alternates between
moments of avowed faithfulness to her husband to other moments of moral
lapses. Finally, when Denise realizes that if she continues to lead an ex-
tramarital life, her own child may someday discover her betrayal and will
harbor the same kind of resentment against her that she had once manifested
against her mother. Before it is too late she renounces all adulterous entanglements and devotes herself entirely to her duties both as a spouse and mother.
Learning from her own experience how easy it is for a human being to go
astray, she returns to her mother's home, after a lifelong estrangement, in quest
of reconciliation.

Le Cercle de famille necessitated several years of composition. As early as
1931 Louis Chaigne alluded to Maurois's involvement in a new novel, entitled
Jusqu'à la troisième génération (Until the Third Generation), a work that can
only be the earliest draft for *Le Cercle de famille*.[24] Unlike Maurois's other
fictional undertakings, which generally are confined to limited chronological
duration, *Le Cercle de famille* depicts three generations: Madame Herpain (the
mother), Denise (the daughter), and the latter's own child.

Like the title, this is a circular novel: Denise begins life within the Herpain family circle, then severs her ties with it for many years, and in the end returns to her childhood roots. Geographically circular too, the novel transports us from Pont de l'Eure to Paris and beyond, and then back to Pont de l'Eure. We find even an annular relationship between the first and last scenes. When Denise returns to her family, after having vowed never to set foot in that despicable setting, she witnesses her mother singing at the piano the same Duparc aria that many years earlier she had sung when Denise had accidentally observed her late father's rival, Docteur Guérin, kissing her mother's shoulder. But the bitterness had mellowed. As Denise recalls that scene, she is now a new woman: she has herself lived an active life and knows how frail human beings can be. Like a Proustian character, she reminisces over the preceding thirty years of life:

> Denise evoked an odor of earth and of rotted geraniums, a little girl in a too long nightgown, the thick and ruddy nape of the seated man and the waves breaking gently on the sand, with the noise of rustling paper. But in the tranquil beatings of her heart, in the graceful and calm movements of her hands, she recognized that the wound had been emptied of all of its poison, the sore was closed. (*Romans*, p. 441)

The circularity of the theme is further embellished when in the final scene all of the surviving members of Denise's family and all of their friends from Pont de l'Eure—the Quesnays, the Pelletots, etc.—reunite in one large circle at a reception in the Herpain home. The past, the present, and even the future roll on uninterruptedly in one unbroken circle.

A minor *Bildungsroman*, in it Maurois gathers and orchestrates the events of an entire existence, from birth to late adulthood. As the heroine moves from one point in life to another, the novelist places her in contact with an array of different people, each of whom plays his part on the stage of her life and then either withdraws entirely or else moves back into the penumbra of the background so as to allow some new personage to enjoy the spotlight. We witness first the families of Pont de l'Eure, then Denise's immediate family, then her earliest adolescent friends—the young Bertrand Schmitt, the English soldier Ruddy for whom she felt a strong, but unconsummated physical attraction; her first lover and almost-fiancé Jacques Pelletot, who prefers the security of his father's notary practice in Pont de l'Eure to the uncertainties of marriage with her in Paris; Ménicault, the intellectual *raté* who becomes her closest friend at the Sorbonne; Edmond Holmann, a banker's son whom she eventually marries; once again the more mature Bernard Schmitt, who now becomes her most trusted friend; and then Dick Managua, the international socialite-playboy-athlete who seduces her with his professional charms; the politician Monteix, with whom she engages in adulterous relations before realizing the folly of her actions. There are also the Holmann family, the group of habitués who gather at the Riviera home of Solange Villier, the group of *le tout Paris*, which frequents the dinner-parties of the Baronne Choin, and many other minor characters and servants.

Maurois also strays from the central theme of the book—the life and loves of Denise Herpain—to indulge in some lengthy and involved digressions concerning the political tensions between right and left, the fiscal policies of the capitalistic nations, the rise of the Communist world. These digressions, rare in his other more tightly structured novels, risk irritating the hurried reader who is anxious to follow the vicissitudes in the life of Denise. But the more patient reader will find in them a rewarding place to pause from time to time in order to linger over the happenings in the world of finance, government, and literature. In only one other novel, *Terre promise*, did Maurois even come close to accomplishing through discursive digressions what he has achieved in *Le Cercle de famille*.

These diversions affect the structure of this novel, for they explain the relatively large dimensions of *Le Cercle de famille*. He even opens the story more slowly here than elsewhere, with a lengthy passage on child psychology. He speculates on the role of childhood recollections in our later maturation as adolescents. A student of Proust, he knew the importance of tiny things—the *madeleine*, the flagstones leading to the house of the Guermantes family, the tune of Vinteuil—tiny sensations that were capable of triggering off our remembrance of things past. Here is how Maurois put it: ". . . we recognize in them [tiny sensations] the weakened waves of a perturbation which, thirty years earlier, agitated the groups of cells of which we are the descendants" (*Romans*, p. 265). Only after the long introductory section does the story get underway. Told mainly as a third-person narrative by an onmiscient and invisible storyteller who knows all of the facts in the existence of Denise Herpain, Maurois's novel shifts the narration to exchanges of letters between some of the principal characters (first-person exchanges between Denise and Jacques Pelletot, between Denise and her sister, etc.). At one point the narration is interrupted by a powerful hallucinatory passage: the heroine's nightmarish dreams during her breakdown; also there is a lengthy passage devoted to an anguished stream of consciousness experience as the heroine walks through the rainswept streets of Paris to a friend's home (Part III, chap. 13).

This supposedly traditionalist novelist tries a few intrepid experiments here: for example, the vivid scene of the dinner-party at the home of the Baronne Choin. These pages rank with some of Maurois's most advanced fictional endeavors. A motley assemblage of guests engage in a free-flowing multilayered series of conversations, all scrupulously interwoven and developing along different lines simultaneously. We move back and forth from one group of guests heatedly evaluating the implications of submarine warfare to another evaluating the political policies of Aristide Briand to another exchanging common gossip about mutual acquaintances to another evaluating the cuisine of the hostess's cook to a number of people discussing Denise's marriage with Edmond Holmann to a group of politicians tackling the question of tensions between capitalistic and communistic nations to a final group complaining about the inflationary trend of prices in France. Back and forth, the readers zigzag from group to group, none of whose conversations is followed through to its logical conclusion. We hear only bits of conversation here and other bits there. The effect of the collective prattle is powerful. At the same time, the juxtaposition of so many exchanges has an authentic ring. Surely this animated scene deserves a place among the finer experimental scenes of early twentieth-century fiction and reminds us of Michel Butor, at his best; for instance, in some pages of *Réseau Aérien* or *Description de San Marco.*

But there are several other major scenes in *Le Cercle de famille.* The one at the home of Baronne Choin is mainly aural. The discovery of her mother's unfaithfulness by the sensitive child, Denise, is chiefly visual and psychological. This scene is not without some similarity to another "discovery" scene involving a child in Edmond Jaloux's prize-winning novel, *Le Reste est silence.* There a little boy instinctively recoils in horror when he learns that his mother has been conducting a secret life unknown to his father. Another scene in *Le Cercle de famille* depicts the agitated child Denise attempting to disabuse her credulous father concerning his wife's immoralities. To her shock she discovers that this weak and passive man, whom she had always worshiped as a tower of strength, is unable to react to such a situation with the decisiveness she had expected.

Le Cercle de famille ends with one of the most poignant scenes in all of Maurois's novels, the reunification of an entire family after years of bitterness. So much is crammed into this thick and complex novel that even though it does not contain the same level of density, anguish, or artistic polish as *Climats*, it is the kind of work one can read several times, each time discovering a new perspective that had not appeared during a preceding reading.

F. L'Instinct du bonheur (The Instinct for Happiness)

L'Instinct du bonheur contrasts sharply with *Le Cercle de famille* in almost every respect. One of the author's shortest novels, it contains hardly more than a hundred pages. Whereas in *Le Cercle de famille* one encounters scores of characters, in *L'Instinct du bonheur* there are only four major figures and one minor one. In the earlier novel the action moves from place to place in France; in the subsequent work, the entire story is staged in a tiny corner of Périgord. *L'Instinct du bonheur,* like a classical tragedy, observes the unity of time, place, and theme. If *Le Cercle de famille* spills over into at least three decades, *L'Instinct du bonheur* (except for a few brief flashbacks) takes place within the space of a few brief days. Only two years separate the publication of both novels: the former appeared in 1932 and the latter in 1934.

Since *L'Instinct du bonheur* is so abbreviated, not a single page in it can be spared for digressions or introductory passages. From the initial sentence, the reader is engulfed in a conversation already underway between the hero and heroine, a middle-aged couple, Gaston and Valentine Romilly; the latter is taking her husband's temperature. Once Maurois has introduced us to his leading characters he transports us through an open window into the lovely Dordogne landscape, with its soft bluish colors, the rustling trees and birds, the perfumes, and the old buildings that constitute this unique setting. Here, more than in any other Maurois novel, the setting plays a pivotal role. The Romilly couple itself reminds us of Maurois's second marriage: the novelist, like Romilly, hailed from Normandy (Pont de l'Eure/Elbeuf) and Simone Maurois, like Valentine, originated in Périgord. Maurois makes his Périgourdine heroine speak like a native, giving her both the intonation and the peculiar vocabulary of the inhabitants of the region: she uses the adjective *brave* where other Frenchmen say *bon*. All in all, if *Bernard Quesnay* is mainly the novel of Normandy and *Climats* of Paris, *L'Instinct du bonheur* is a novel about Périgord.

The two principal properties depicted here are the small estate, Preyssac, belonging to the Romillys, and the splendid fortress-type of chateau perched on a mighty hill, the Chateau de La Guichardie, modeled after the similar chateau of Hautefort situated very close to Maurois's own Essendiéras. Readers of *L'Instinct de bonheur* who approach the Chateau de Hautefort, seeing it from its many angles along the circuitous drive leading toward it, readily recognize the very marked similarities between the fictional rendition and the real model.

Structurally, this novel is a conventional, even banal, third-person narrative. Frequently Maurois interrupts his tale to let us hear the vivid exchanges of speech between the principal characters. Within the heart of this mini-novel, Maurois composes a smaller novelette (chaps. 15–20) that consists of the confession of Valentine Romilly made to Madame de La Guichardie concerning her past culpabilities. This flashback carries us back to the days when Valentine as a single woman had allowed herself to become the mistress of an older man who is the father of her only child, Colette, born soon after her marriage to Gaston. This confession, a first-person subnovel, ties in neatly with the outer framework of the larger work.

The theme of the novel resembles that of Maurois's other novels. How can a happy marriage be prevented from going asunder when threatened by formidable external obstacles? The true paternal circumstances surrounding Colette can no longer be kept a secret. The facts are beginning to leak out. Colette wishes to get married, and the vital statistics of her background must be recorded. Valentine has no idea whatsoever that her husband had known the truth all along, but that he had chosen never to divulge this knowledge to his wife. Separately, Valentine and Gaston attempt, each in his or her private way, to keep this unpleasant truth from reaching the ears of their daughter, Colette. They do not realize that she too has discovered the secret of her origins and has already openly discussed this matter with her fiancé. Only the wily Madame de

La Guichardie, who serves as the confidant for all three, knows that they all know. What matters above all is how to save the reasonably satisfactory Romilly marriage from cracking under the stress of a tragic crisis in the making.

A second, but related, theme is that of silence. If the truth concerning Colette were discussed too overtly, the characters would be so embarrassed that their pride, once the truth had been exposed, would probably make it impossible for them to preserve the family unit. Valentine remained silent regarding her past when she married Gaston, stating that "it seemed to me that the confession would be useless and cruel" (*Romans*, p. 503). Romilly too avoids a frank confrontation with his wife. For him, "these discussions on the past" would be "vain, painful, and would uselessly ruin our life" (p. 521). Silence thus preserves the marriage, whereas too much talk might have converted it into a tragedy. "There has been in my life," Gaston informs Madame de la Guichardie, "a frightful tragedy, but because it has always remained mute, it has now become something foreign" (p. 523). The instinct to remain silent emanates from the instinct to save at all costs happiness by not "rocking the boat." Gaston returns to his wife and says nothing to her: "This time again, a stronger instinct than that of pain, stronger than the need for knowledge, had closed his mouth . . ." (*Romans*, p. 525). The title of the novel summarizes Maurois's basic credo of life: We must work hard to achieve happiness in life, and once we reach its blissful state we must work even harder to hold onto it. Maurois refers to this struggle as "an instinct for conservation" (p. 518).

L'Instinct du bonheur, certainly not one of Maurois's most significant novels, may well be his most typical one. It mirrors the landscapes of his beloved Périgord, treats of his favorite subject—happiness in conjugal life— and echoes some deep-seated personal sadness on his own part. Finally, it illustrates very effectively one of his basic tenets: too much candor, too many words, may harm us. We must from time to time conceal ourselves behind a mask of silence. Truth and excessive candor may end up by destroying our lives.

G. *Terre promise (Promised Land)*

Maurois's second longest novel, written in America during the War of 1940– 45, represents his desire to return to the heartland of France, which he missed very much during his four years of exile. The first third of the novel takes place in "Sarrazac," a realistic but fictional transposition of many of the domains in the Limousin and Périgord regions that he knew intimately.

The work concerns the psychological development of a heroine—in this case, Claire Foregeaud—from early childhood until about 1944, when she reached her mid-forties. Thus *Terre promise* too must be regarded as a feminine *Bildungsroman*, which, unlike *L'Instinct du bonheur* or *Climats*, covers a much longer segment of time and portrays much more than a single emotional crisis at its peak. Here, in fact, there are several scattered crises in the lifetime of Claire. Chronologically the story opens when Claire is five or six years old (she was born in 1896). In chapter 9 Maurois leaps quickly to her seventeenth birthday, after lingering at length around her tenth year of life. The final chapters end during the waning months of World War II.

Geographically the book follows the peregrinations of Claire: her childhood and formative years took place in the provinces; then her first social party in Paris; her two successive marriages in Paris; the brief vacation she spent on the Channel coast and her visits with her family in Sarrazac; finally, during World War II Claire finds herself a widow in New York City.

Of all of Maurois's novels, *Terre promise* manifests his fullest psychological study of the evolution of a character. With slowly cumulative details, he describes the subtleties in Claire's unhealthy attitude toward sexual relations, an attitude arising from the stringent discipline and stern domination of her ex-soldier father, the puritanical prudishness of her mother, and the hysterical fear of men on the part of Miss Brinker, Claire's childhood nurse. Rather than instill in her positive attitudes toward men, these persons have filled her soul with a terrifying mistrust of them. For Clarie sex becomes an almost criminal act, a virtual taboo. Fears invade her imagination, until the very physical presence of men begins to horrify her. Like Miss Brinker, she starts to believe that physical love even with one's legally married husband signifies the sacrifice by the wife of her womanly integrity: the latter places herself at the mercy of an egotistical, pleasure-loving male obsessed with little more than self-gratification. In contrast with Flaubert's Emma Bovary, who dreams of exciting, romantic courtships with men, Maurois paints a tableau of a hyper-imaginative young lady who fantasizes about the horrors of romantic involvement with men. Maurois devotes a great deal of time to his delineations of Claire's imagination; for example: "She introduced into her reveries some characters drawn from the tapestries of the living room. She had given them names . . ." (*Romans*, pp. 543–44). As in the case of Emma Bovary (but for a contrary reason), "Claire fills her life with an image of love which she has formed through her readings, through her dreams" (p. 693). Her second husband has finally realized that her entire attitude toward physical love has been improperly conditioned by her formation and imagination. In a letter to her he writes: "You have been led astray by a puritanical education, by a romantic kind of instruction which seems like a contradiction and isn't one, for both forces have directed your attention to you yourself, the one to teach you to hate yourself, the other to teach you how to become affected" (pp. 709–10). On the other hand, she has a terror concerning physical love; on the other, literature has kindled in her a curiosity about spiritual and romantic pleasure. But she fears the physical aspects of these experiences, which excite her when she reads about them. Claire is even warned by her nurse to look at the ceremony of marriage as society's manner of camouflaging something shameful: "Don't you understand that this ceremony, this music, this incense, these white flowers are there only to mask the horrible act which is about to be accomplished? Think of that frightful scene which will unfurl this evening, for your cousin who has been surrendered [by her family] defenseless to that man! Don't you know what a honeymoon night is? Can you imagine the humiliation of getting undressed in front of a man? Of being at his mercy completely nude? . . . Oh! the horror of all of that!!" (p. 572). Filled with such dire warnings, it is no wonder that Claire approaches her own sexual relations with her first husband, Albert Larraque, with real trepidation. The latter does not help assuage the situation either. So completely engrossed is he in his own gratification that he treats Claire with total insensitivity; he assumes that merely because he has been satisfied she automatically has also been satisfied. Actually, Claire appreciates in Larraque many of his admirable qualities as a human being. Her marriage with this gifted automobile executive is universally regarded by high Parisian society as an unmitigated success. Claire alone knows that the success is only on social, material, and platonic levels.

The heroine has been taught to separate physical from spiritual love. Maurois, the specialist of conjugal bliss, knew that to be perfectly happy a husband and his wife must fuse these two loves into one indivisible entity. Claire's mother tries with naïveté to save her daughter's financially attractive marriage to the industrialist by counseling her to content herself with spiritual and social felicity alone; "Listen Claire," Mme Foregeaud admonishes, "I am going to tell you a thing which few other mothers would tell you, but something that is true. If you do not love your husband 'physically,' as you put it, and if you cherish him sentimentally, affectionately, simply pretend that you desire him. . . . It is so easy! . . . Men are so naïve in this respect!" (p. 648). But Claire rejects this hypocritical kind of life. She keeps searching for total happiness, one that weds the physical to the spiritual, as was the lesson of the fairy tales she read as a child. At first she is unaware of the tremendous psychological hurdle she bears within herself; this hurdle prevents her from indulging in any intercourse that is free of fear. In fact she almost fails in her efforts to be happy with her second husband, the sensitive poet Christian Ménétrier. Like Emma Bovary, she too has been ineradicably marked by her childhood formation and by her readings, whose themes keep recurring later in her life. The perspicacious Christian diagnoses her problems and tells her that "You remain a child . . . and you seek to live the fairy tales. You must live life, Claire, and understand that it is beautiful, in all of its forms" (p. 673).

These resemblances, accidental or otherwise, between *Terre promise* and *Madame Bovary* are impossible to ignore. For example, just as the provincial Emma discovers high society at a fashionable ball, there is in Maurois's novel an equally important ball: Claire, as a maid of honor at the wedding of her Parisian cousin, Sybil, is exposed to the exhilarating social world of Paris at a fashionable wedding party. Upon her return to the provinces, life becomes unendurable: "After this month in Paris and this intoxicating happiness of pleasing people, Sarrazac seemed rather colorless. The image which Claire had at one time formed of life now seemed to her to be naïve and false" (p. 573).

Once more Maurois's principal theme is the search for happiness by a heroine unfavorably conditioned by an unfortunate childhood. The biblical title suggests that the principal character stands at the brink of achieving the fruition of her dreams in the promised land. She perceives the promised land in the near distance, but something within herself prevents her from penetrating into its blissful confines. Composing a little poem, she acknowledges the unlikelihood of entry into this terrain of happiness: "Et vers le soir, à l'heure où le soleil décline,/ Je frissonne en voyant de l'aride colline/ Tous ces verts paradis où je n'entrerai pas." ("And toward the evening, at the hour when the sun is setting, I shudder when I see from the arid hill/the green paradises which I shall not enter") (p. 641). The more she tries to achieve her goals, the more she fails. The promised land is attainable only through spontaneous, natural ardor, unobstructed passion, intensity of life, all of which would make physical fulfillment of love easily possible. But Claire is too intellectual, too analytical; somehow she cannot bring herself to a point where nature is unfettered by anxiety. The heroine even tries to find happiness by remarrying: ". . . it is a strange thing that I have never been nearer to the Promised Land. The tears, the grief, had given me some sort of ardent and unhealthy madness. Nevertheless, I have not crossed 'the iron gate,' but I *know* that marriage will give the key for it" (p. 686). Even in her second marriage, with a totally different kind of husband, one for whom she experiences genuine love, she continues to stand at the precipice overlooking the *promised land:* "Nonetheless, she continued, from the summit of these sterile hills, to gaze with desire at the delightful valleys and the perfumed woods of the *Promised Land*" (p. 695). Modern woman that she is, she even tries consultation with a distinguished analyst. Later she seeks advice from the ubiquitous novelist Bertrand Schmitt. At the end, just when Claire seems on the point of resolving her deeply rooted problems with her poet-spouse, he dies from an infection caused by a rose-prick. And the novel ends with the futility of this marriage too. (We may well compare this premature death with that of the hero of *Climats.*)

But *Terre promise* is much more than the story of a heroine's struggle to achieve happiness. It contains some of Maurois's most realistic descriptions of the social milieux he knew so well: the domains of Périgord, the sophisticated social world of Albert Larraque, the fascinating universe of the hermetic man of letters Ménétrier, and the French colony in New York City.

Terre promise offers nothing novel in the way of structure. It begins instantly, in the midst of a dialogue that had already started, and consists mainly of a third-person narrative interrupted repeatedly by first-person revelations of Claire's inner self from the pages of her diary and correspondence. Maurois adds an epilogue dated 1944 in New York. We learn in it that Christian has died, that Claire has escaped the German occupation to go to New York, where she devotes herself piously to the promulgation of her husband's poetry and to the preservation of his reputation among literary circles in America. While she did not entirely succeed in being a perfect wife, it is ironic that she is "an incomparable widow." *Terre promise* represents Maurois's most important fling in the domain of the psychological novel.

H. *Les Roses de septembre (September Roses)*

André Maurois' final novel differs from all the others because of the age group depicted in it. We have here not young men and women in their prime of life all groping to resolve the problem of romantic happiness, but rather an approximately seventy-year-old Academician, Guillaume Fontane, who—after years of a seemingly happily married life—finds himself tempted by a love affair with a much younger Latin-American actress. The title poetically conveys the theme of the book: the hero is in the autumnal stage of his career. The roses, symbolizing love and feminine beauty, are the last ones he will gather before the winter of his life. Momentarily refusing to recognize the realities of his marital and social position as well as the debilities of his age, he makes one last leap into the wonderful abyss of romance. The young lady sees in Fontane a glamorous attachment with a world-famous and successful writer. The encounter between Dolorès (Lolita) and Fontane is brief, spirited, and comes to a sudden halt when the former, thanks to the clever tactics of Mme Fontane and to her own good sense, realizes the folly of pursuing any further an impossible situation. She leaves her Academician-lover and will presumably lead a life with men of her own age.

Les Roses de septembre, like *Le Cercle de famille,* follows a circular construction. In the opening paragraph the budding author, Hervé Marcenat (the younger brother of Philippe Marcenat of *Climats!*), strolls through the Bois de Boulogne with Fontane. Marcenat seeks some data on Fontane's aesthetic philosophy to incorporate in his proposed book on him. After a dozen chapters devoted to the life of Fontane in the world of *le tout Paris,* Maurois transports us into the core of the novel: a description of Fontane's lecture tour throughout South America. This geographical dislocation is the most vital example of exoticism in all of Maurois's novels, most of which take place on French soil. The trip is a necessary ingredient in the plot, for Maurois has to justify the otherwise unlikely metamorphosis undergone by Fontane once he reaches the western hemisphere. In the end, with his lecturing tour finished, the elderly hero returns to Paris to regain Pauline, his wife, who had not accompanied him on this trip. The circular structure is accomplished in the last scene, which carries us back into the verdant Bois de Boulogne: Now it is Guillaume and Pauline Fontane who stroll through the park, reminiscing over the strange and menacing cloud that had hovered over their recent past; both are grateful that reason has prevailed. Time cannot be held back. September is fleeting, and soon there will come October. Even the loveliest roses wither and fall from their branches. The indomitable passage of time is emphasized by the final statement of movement: "Un cygne glissa" ("A swan glided" [*Romans,* p. 876]). Actually the title is fully explained in a tiny poem Fontane writes to Dolores: "Hélas! les roses de septembre / Aux premiers vents vont défleurir. / Lolita, j'ai peur de décembre / Et je voudrais ne plus vieillir." ("Alas! The roses of September / In the first winds will fall apart./ Lolita, I fear December/ and I should prefer not to grow old") (p. 835).

Maurois's attempt at exoticism comes off very well indeed. He describes in detail the life and customs of Latin America and injects many Spanish terms into his dialogues to create a vivid sense of realism. What he emphasizes above all is the encounter of two cultures, French (Fontane) and Latin American (Lolita). "These statues under the trees [in Peru]," declares Fontane, "remind me of our gardens of Luxembourg, which I certainly hope to show you some day. . . . Over there we are classicists, we French, and you . . . oh . . . you are romantics." Dolores, not satisfied with this generalization, retorts: "No, . . . we would rather be people of the middle ages. We do not have measure; we do not love it; we wish to taste everything in life, even briefly, with passion, with fear because we would risk eternal damnation, but also with hope, because all you need is an instant to repent in order to obtain divine mercy" (p. 790). Two attitudes, two culture systems, two sets of values confront each other. If Fontane falls in love with Dolores, it is because she incarnates all that is lacking in his routine, steady, unexciting existence in Paris; and she falls in love with him because his orderly life and his many international honors represent for her an element of stability lacking in her turbulent life.

The novel, like a classical play, is divided into three clearly defined sections. Part I consists of the Paris segment, during which Maurois anticipates the hero's overseas trip. The section is essential, because it discloses certain clues concerning the nature of the marriage of the Fontane couple, clues that justify some of his conduct once he is distant from his wife. Part II features the infatuation between Fontane and Lolita in South America. Part III forms the dénouement, the return of Fontane to Europe. It is then that he discovers that he is really an integral part of an old, refined society in France. In that society the lively, tempestuous Dolores Garcia would be out of place.

Once again the novel is in the third person. Once again the lively dialogues and conversations break the monotony of the narrative. On one occasion with no transition, Maurois leaps from the thread of the story to an exchange of letters between the principal protagonists.

The theme centers around a classical triangle: the dashing Lolita is pitted against the gracefully serene and sophisticated Pauline Fontane in a battle to win the affections of Guillaume. More is at stake than merely a competitive struggle between two women: each symbolizes her own culture, her own way of life, her own values. Lolita represents "an adventurous life, free, passionate . . . some instants of marvellous happiness; she also offers frightful despair," while Pauline represents "a manner of living, a respectable and conventional manner" (p. 871). If there is a message in this mature novel by a mature novelist, it is that there is an age for everything, above all—for people in their seventies—an age for tranquillity, wisdom, moderation. The novel ends as soon as the hero accepts this truth.

I. Maurois, or the Novelist as a Pedagogue and Purveyor of Clarity

Like his biographies and histories, Maurois's novels are models of limpidity of expression. Even in his fiction Maurois assumes the stance not only of a story-teller but also of a pedagogue. Anxious to make his readers comprehend what is taking place in the plot, and to do it with clarity, he halts from time to time, like a teacher giving a course, to summarize the story up to a certain point before going farther and to fill us in on certain background data. How different is he from so many contemporary novelists who seem deliberately to create complexities for the sake of forcing their readers to work at demystification. In Maurois's case, it is not enough to write with simplicity and intelligibility; he actually structures his novels around his central goal of clarity and simplicity.

Occasionally, Maurois senses that the threads of his intrigues begin to get a bit too tangled or too loosely separated. This is especially true in the longer novels, where we have many major characters. Before proceeding with the subsequent stage of the novel, this author pauses briefly for a paragraph or two to make his characters think aloud or to meditate over the events that have just transpired and to prepare for their possible courses of action in the days ahead. (See as samples of this type of summary *Le Cercle de famille* in *Romans*, p. 339, and *Terre promise*, in ibid., pp. 617–18)

Maurois wished to provide his readers with total knowledge. There was nothing he desired less than to confuse those who read his novels. He related interesting stories about the search of very fallible human beings for happiness. But he desired much more than to relate a story. Indirectly, he wished to teach us a friendly and (he hoped) useful lesson: Happiness is attainable only if we are willing to make certain sacrifices, only if we understand that some measure of suffering is inevitably involved in our quest. Nothing worthwhile can be achieved without exertion. It is this central lesson that unites all of his novels into a single but minor *Comédie humaine*.

Maurois's fictional world might not have ended if the eighty-two-year-old novelist had had time to live an eighty-third year. At the time of his death he dreamed of expanding this world by bringing it up to date. In a personal conversation he once confessed his intention of picking up Bertrand Schmitt where we had last left him right after World War II, in New York. Then he could paint this writer at the pinnacle of his career and also his reception into the Académie Française. He would have liked also to return to Bernard Quesnay as an old man, still devoted to the wool mill in Pont de l'Eure, perhaps as a kind of subdued plant-owner. Quesnay might have witnessed the era of synthetic fibers, and tried to save the disintegrating wool empire of the family by adapting it to modern technology. Maurois confided further: "The Novel which I should have liked to do—it is the one which I could take all of the people of the world I had created, then show what they have done in 1938, then during the war, and to demonstrate that after the war their destiny had changed. But unfortunately, I am perhaps too old. But one must begin, nevertheless, and stop on the way—if necessary."[25] Regrettably, even robust writers have limited endurance, and their dreams are not always fulfilled.

J. The Novel as a World

All of his life Maurois was obsessed with the dream of utilizing the novel as a means of creating a new world. Alain had taught him to admire the demiurge who had created *La Comédie humaine* precisely because in it there was an entire world of vivid people. Maurois longed to accomplish a similar miracle. On reading Maurois's fifth novel, *Climats,* Alain was favorably impressed by the style, which he compared to "the grace of Bramble"; but he also issued a challenge: "And now you must give birth to a world."[26] Maurois accepted this challenge. That he failed to meet it, he is the first to admit. Yet all of his life he never gave up the struggle. Maurois's world is too small, too uniform, when compared with that of Balzac. In the history of French literature there is only one Balzac. Certainly no one can fault a novelist of talent and ambition for seeking to emulate the greatest model of the French novelistic tradition. Nor should one blame Maurois if he did not entirely succeed in fulfilling his Promethean goal. Besides, as I shall demonstrate below, Maurois's nine novels, in conjunction with his hundreds of short stories, do comprise a mini-world, limited in scope, but one that contains an interlocking tightly woven web of the same characters, similar events, almost identical settings and places, and a uniform atmosphere that holds the whole series of novels together.

Maurois's fictional universe is no accidental assemblage of motley people. Nor are their interrelationships forced by the heavy hand of a too-deliberate artist. On the contrary, these characters fall neatly into place vis-à-vis each other. The experiences in their lives, recounted from novel to novel, follow a consistent and natural pattern. We find no glaring contradictions between the behavior of a character in one novel and that same character in another. Despite the overall unity of these works, they need not be read in chronological order or read *in toto;* they can be appreciated individually. Each individual novel is both part of an integrated whole and also an autonomous unit. If the names of the characters and places recur, the plots are self-contained. In each novel Maurois depicts these persons at different stages in their lives and under a new set of circumstances. Only *Ni ange ni bête* and the Bramble-O'Grady cycle do not fit in the compact little world of Maurois's novels and short stories. Michel

Droit emphasizes the unity of Maurois's collected fiction, but he does so a bit too forcefully:

> No fatalism. Nor irreparable fact. On the contrary, an absolute rigor which is almost mathematical in its determination. Each event of the world, each event of the heart possesses its cause, produces the effect that a logician might expect. With his *world subjected to the laws of the mind,* he stands in opposition to most of the contemporary novelists for whom the mind is subjected, on the contrary, to the chaos and the wills of the world that surrounds it.[27]

While we may dispute Michel Droit's pretensions that Maurois's world of fiction is controlled by the rigorous laws of mathematics and logic, it is true that he seems totally unlike a Gide, for example, who, in *Les Faux-Monnayeurs,* assumed the pose of a novelist unwilling or unable to predict the subsequent moves of his characters. Maurois's light hand remains in control of the destinies of his characters, and never does he grant them enough freedom so that they might go astray. Droit seems also to overstate the theory of "effects after causes," for these novels contain surprising, unpredictable incidents. But these incidents are orderly, and never throw the novels into chaos. This neatness harmonizes with Maurois's conviction that a work of art must be constructed with loving care; the artist should leave as little as possible to chance: "I discovered the joys of the author: to compose, to set in order, above all to find a refuge in a world created by himself."[28] In a probing investigation of the art of Balzac, he elaborates on the need of the novelist to organize or arrange his facts in some organic pattern: "But it is not a question of transporting an entirely bare reality into a novel; it is a question of organizing, accentuating certain lights and types. . . ."[29] Maurois attempted to create a kind of coherence in this world by distributing his characters among various families: the Quesnays, Guérins, Pelletots, and Louviers from Pont de l'Eure; the Marcenats, Romillys, and Forgeauds of northern Périgord and southern Limousin; Larraque, the Fontanes, the Schmitts, the Holmanns, and Choins of Paris; Solange Villier, Dick Managua, and a great many other playboys and playgirls of the Côte d'Azur and of the other international resorts; the Brambles, O'Grady's, Parkers, and Dundas from the British scene. These people from Maurois's own fictional world could be at home in the universe of no other novelist. They think, talk, love, eat, and breathe in the style of Maurois. They reflect the habits, sentiments, and attitudes of Maurois himself and of the many associates in his life. Candidly he admits a real sense of satisfaction: in *Le Cercle de famile* he began to experience the pleasure of having created his own unique little cosmos: "I began to measure the strength a novelist acquires when he has *his* world. By now mine already possessed *its* physician (Doctor Gaulin); *its* priest (Abbot Cenival), a transposition of our friend, le chanoine Mugnier. Without the Second World War, I would have multiplied these links and woven a tighter fabric. It is relatively stable societies which make possible the long novelistic continuations. I am not sure whether Balzac, following the Revolution of 1848, would have been able to continue his work."[30]

The desire to produce his own world continued during the war years in America. Although busying himself as a college professor, publishing extensively, and traveling frequently, he had been able to find the time to continue the fabrication of his little world: "Suddenly, I had the desire to create a world, and a French world. . . . "[31] From this sudden impulse emerged *Terre promise.*

No demiurge in the Balzacian sense, Maurois limited his fictional arena to only nine novels and a few volumes of short fiction. In contrast, complete editions of Balzac's *Comédie humaine* range from the Hazan edition of twenty-five volumes up to the Conard edition of forty volumes. If no other factor distinguished Maurois from his idol, the difference of quantity alone is striking. But there are other factors, too. Maurois's characters almost all belong to the upper middle class or to high French society. Balzac painted vigorous tableaux of all social classes and milieux, ranging from peasants to businessmen and notaries and noblemen. Maurois marveled at Balzac's uncanny ability to remember vividly all of the different types of people he had ever met, even superficially, and to paint with equal authenticity the lowliest pauper and the loftiest artistocrat. While the author of *Climats* had personal tragedies that were as poignant as those of Balzac, he was never compelled to struggle against financial hardships that filled Balzac's life. If he gathered his materials from the raw materials of life during his stints in the army and at work in his family's wool mill, Maurois seemed most comfortable in the portrayal of people from his own personal social milieu of the upper middle class. This is a restricted repertory of characters. Of Balzac, Maurois wrote with amazement that "an absolute master of a people who lived within him, he had only to select among his creatures the characters for a new tale."[32] Maurois too could make similar selections, but, in his case, the options available to him were severely limited.

Maurois expanded his thinking on this subject in his writings on another Promethean novelist, Tolstoy, for whom he expressed endless admiration. The Tolstoyan monument in fictional literature could have been erected only by a novelist endowed with the vision to conceive an immense community of characters, all of whom were "raised by humanity, true men, true women; love and hate; ambition and frivolity; the elite and the popular masses; birth and death; work and thought."[33] Besides this vast assemblage of people, events and emotions, the demiurge-novelist, in Maurois's judgment, should be able to engender in the life of his novels "the religious, political, social ideas of his era, which he has mingled with existence and incorporated with this moving and ebullient substance, as they are in the real world."[34] In *Le Cercle de famille, Terre promise, Ni ange ni bête* and in *Bramble-O'Grady* Maurois does indeed inject ideological, sociological, financial, and political themes into the human plots. On the other hand, *Climats, L'Instinct du bonheur,* and *Les Roses de septembre* focus the author's attention exclusively on subtle psychological analyses of character. These works belong more to the tradition of *La Princesse de Clèves* and *Manon Lescaut,* in which the texture of the work hardly moves beyond the frontiers of character analysis and relationships of sentiment. As a matter of fact, more than any of his novels, *Le Cercle de famille* and *Terre promise,* come closest to being *total* novels, that is, works that depict not only the fortunes of a relatively large group of characters whose destinies are interwoven but also a wide range of the historical events of the era in which these destinies evolved.

Throughout André Maurois's writing we discern his refreshing objectivity with regard to his own books and his candor in admitting his own shortcomings. At times he was a bit too harsh with himself. His appraisal of his poet-hero Christian Ménétrier (*Terre promise* and many of the short stories) is lowly: "I am not very satisfied with my poet: Christian. I can see how he is made. Some memories of Rilke, and also of Valéry, entered into his composition, but I am afraid that he may not be a person of flesh and blood ("un être de chair"), which is what Rilke and Valéry were."[35] Maurois's self-disparagement notwithstanding, Christian is, in effect, one of the most engaging male creations Maurois managed to formulate.

"Un être de chair!" It is true that the successful demiurge knows how to paint his portraits with vigorous strokes of the pen; he makes them stand out in relief; to their gestures he adds vivid movement. Maurois's characters do seem somewhat flat, grayish in tone, slightly sluggish in gesture. Many are thinkers, meditators, people blessed with the leisure needed to analyze themselves and each other; some spend overly prolonged amounts of time in conversation, even bantering; others have the financial ability to cultivate the arts and the art of lovemaking with a bit too much attentiveness. These characters resemble more the exquisitely refined protrayals of a Henry James than those of demiurges like Balzac, Zola, or Tolstoy. Maurois's fictional society was not very different from the world of Henry James, as he himself described it: "Henry James reached a point where he thought that only a society of leisure, one which has inherited a long civilization, constitutes a milieu that is favorable for sentiments."[36]

Because Maurois felt that he could most completely deal only with French society, he seldom attempted to describe non-French milieux. He feared that he could not do justice to the mannerisms of Germans or Americans or Russians. He did not fully comprehend them. Thus he was not surprised that the Russian, Tourguéniev, who spent so much time in France, hardly wrote about Frenchmen and preferred to paint Russians: ". . . although he lived in France," wrote Maurois, "Tourguéniev sought the substance for his work only in memories of Russia."[37] In *Bramble-O'Grady* Maurois did utilize non-French nationals extensively. In this case, however, he had already lived for four years side-by-side with his English soldier friends in the intimacy of their barracks, and the experience was still very fresh in his mind as he wrote these books.

Maurois's French society is coherent and nearly monochromatic. First, it is composed of the same several people who come and go. Always do we en-counter in his fiction the wise and indulgent writer, Bertrand Schmitt, whose acquaintance we make in many of the short stories as well, and who in the *Bramble-O'Grady* wears the mask of Aurelle. The latter, calling himself Schmitt, makes an important reentry into the plot of *Le Cercle de famille*, where we learn that he has spent World War I serving the British as an interpre-ter. By the time we reach *Terre promise* and the forties, he is mature, successful, and talks, acts, and writes much like Maurois in real life. Then there is the temptress and siren, Solange Villier, who uses the same techniques of seduction and enunciates the same lax morality in *Climats* as in *La Cercle de famille*, not to mention the short stories. By the time we reach *Terre promise*, Solange would have been too advanced in years to remain as active in her amorous pursuits as before, so Maurois has reincarnated a younger version of the same aggressive female-type, in the disguise of Rolande. Fabert, the eternal Don Juan type, in the short stories is only another name for his counterpart, Dick Mana-gua, in *Le Cercle de famille*. Isabelle de Cheverny, who becomes Isabelle Marcenat in *Climats*, links this work with all of the others when, thanks to a third marriage—with Bertrand Schmitt—she makes repeated appearances in almost every subsequent work of fiction.

The same names, the same types form small, intimate circles. Maurois makes use of many fictional devices to group his characters into little interlocking clusters. The distaff characters from more than one novel make use of the same couturière (in *L'Instinct du bonheur*): "Suddenly all of the women of Paris met each other in the salons which had become too small. Hélène de Thianges is reassured because she notices Denise Holmann, and Denise Holmann because she finds there Isabelle Schmitt" (*Romans*, p. 463). Maurois also seemed ad-dicted to the use of gossip as a tool to tie together the characters from more than one novel. In *Terre promise*, Madame de Saviniac, an almost professional gossip, arrives at Claire Forgeaud's chateau and relates the highlights of the plot of *Climats* (*Romans*, p. 562). At least three times the novelist uses his remark-able dinner hostess, the Baronne de Choin, as the key figure responsible for rounding up his world of characters, all of whom gather at her festive banquets on regular occasions. There can almost always be found representatives from the Holmann and Marcenat families, the Bertrand Schmitt couple, Solange Villier, Claire Forgeaud, and even such real life characters as Paul Valéry, Léon-Paul Fargue, François Mauriac, Fernand Léger, and Darius Milhaud (*Romans*, pp. 654–55). Maurois's world of bankers, diplomats, and financiers is merged with the Holmanns and Hélène de Thianges and Solange Villier and others, thanks to another fascinating dinner party given by the tireless Baroness Choin in *Le Cercle de famille* (*Romans*, pp. 338–85). In his post-World War II novel, *Les Roses de septembre*, the author creates a luncheon affair given by Madame Fontane to gather at the same table and at an identical social function various characters whose acquaintance we have already made in earlier novels (Chris-tian Ménétrier, Bertrand Schmitt, etc.) (*Romans*, pp. 866–67).

Basically, if these novels are remembered, it will be for their concrete character and situations and not for their ideological content. People and décors rather than philosophical systems predominate. Maurois contended throughout his life that the fine novelist was he who could vividly portray the existence of characters and not ideas. The essay, rather than the novel, was, in his judgment, the most appropriate literary vehicle for an author's thought. The novel's prime raison d'être is to serve as a universe of active people: "The function of the novelist is not to expose philosophy, but to give it [the novel] the solidity of beings and things."[38] Elsewhere he goes as far as to equate a novel with a three-dimensional substance: "In fact, I require of a novel three dimensions: There is the line of the tale, the social level and the depth which adds the finishing touch to the volumes. . . . But it is essential still that this volume be presented in such a way that we are sensitive to it and can explore its dimensions. That is possible only through a central character with whom the reader can identify himself. . . . A well made novel is never a flat tableau."[39] Rather should we compare a novel with a piece of sculpture. A great novel must possess a pithy texture, a "meatiness," and the reader must have a substantial core into which he can penetrate profoundly.

Not always did Maurois succeed in attaining the three-dimensional solidity he esteemed so highly. *Ni ange ni bête* is somewhat anemic in that Philippe Viniès, the hero, is traced with inadequate clarity. In *Bernard Quesnay*, there are two almost equally vital heroes who nearly eclipse each other: Bernard and Antoine; our attention leaps from one to the other, so that it is hard at times to identify sufficiently with either of the two. André Maurois does usually excel in his "récit": he is a master storyteller. And he does manage to paint a convincing "social level," which, although limited in scope, is, nonetheless, clearly defined; but occasionally his novelistic chemistry lacks the "depth," especially the depth that derives from the study of disturbing philosophical situations or the human condition. Yet most of his main characters are infused with Maurois's personal warmth, a quality that derives both from his sympathetic attitude toward them and from his technique of accumulating minute details to describe their personality and appearance. At all costs he seeks to avoid abstractness: "I love little concrete details which make a character live and which thrust the reader back into reality."[40]

Indeed, Maurois was really concerned with realism. He wished to render a realistic interpretation of the universe he knew. In this respect, his novels, in their limited way, represent little more than a twentieth-century prolongation of the realistic trends started by Balzac, Stendhal, and Flaubert. If his works are at all vivid, it is because he refused to exit from the worlds he knew and observed at first hand. He refused to describe a world he could only vaguely imagine. What he wrote of Proust applies to his own work: "A very thin cut into French society. But that matters little. He is going to exploit his lode not in breadth, but in depth, and besides the subject in art is nothing. It was with three apples and a plate that Cézanne has composed masterpieces."[41] And with the formula that consists of the exquisiteness of an Odile, the seriousness of an

Isabelle, the self-torment of a Philippe, and the half-airy, half-weighty charm of a Misa, Maurois has succeeded in rendering a masterpiece like *Climats*. Clouard, the literary historian, wisely refers to him as a "middle-class novelist of marriage and family life."[42] There is no reason why a human comedy cannot be built around the subject matter of marriage and family life in bourgeois society.

In the final analysis, the cumulative novels of André Maurois must be regarded as yet another link in the long French novelistic tradition of *le roman d'analyse* (the novel of analysis), a tradition deriving from the seventeenth century in France. Maurois excels in his portrayals of the emotions of human beings, their psychological motivations, sentimental interrelationships, inner reactions to one another, shifting moods, human consistencies and inconsistencies. The psychological analyses in these novels are far more significant than the episodic substance of his plots. Because these works of fiction are so intensely analytical, and because current tastes appear to be tilted toward novels heavily laden with dramatic events and occurrences, the human comedy of André Maurois has lost much of its former appeal in the eyes of most contemporary readers in the Western countries. Is this a temporary phenomenon? Only time will solve this riddle.

Part IV
The World of Short Stories

5

André Maurois as a Writer of Short Stories

Tighten, condense, and end with a punch.
Alain, quoted in *Portrait d'un ami*

During his long and prolific career, André Maurois demonstrated an unswerving devotion to the art of the short story. Already at the turn of the century he made his literary début with an ill-fated collection of short stories, which, to the day of his death, remained a well-guarded secret to all but his closest friends. In 1904 the nineteen-year-old lad Emile Herzog ceased to dream of a literary career and took the necessary action of writing. Seeking a publisher for the short stories he had been jotting down in his notebooks, he submitted his manuscript to the only firm he knew in Rouen, the firm that had been publishing the *Bulletin of the Alumni of the Lycée of Rouen*. Like François Mauriac, Marcel Proust, and André Gide, he too was forced to draw from his personal savings, recently accumulated from his salary at the wool mill, to cover part of the cost for the publication of the work. When the adolescent author received his proofs, he was so disappointed at the way his first opus read that he refused to permit the publisher to go ahead with the printing. With embarrassment young Herzog carefully hid the proofs, and few have seen them since.

For years afterward he continued to suppress within himself the urge to write. Ingenuously he revealed that "My story is simple. . . . It is that of a provincial industrialist who wished to write since he was a child, and whose dream was accomplished."[1] We know that when he finally did embark upon a literary career it was not as a writer of short stories, but rather as an author of a chronicle/novel. His real beginning as a writer of short fiction he postponed until 1927, when he finally mustered enough courage to publish a Swiftian satire entitled *Voyage au pays des articoles*.

During the ensuing years he produced with varying degrees of success an endless chain of all sorts of short fiction. Among these figure a number of sophisticated tales for children (and their parents): especially *Le Pays des trente-six mille volontés* (1928) *(The County of the 36,000 Wills)* and *Patapoufs et filifers* (1930) (This latter work was beautifully illustrated by the then-painter Jean Bruller, today known by his pen name of Vercors.) During the thirties, Maurois's reputation as a short-story writer was partly based on two successful

169

tales of science-fiction, *Le Peseur d'âmes (The Weigher of Souls)* and *La Machine à lire les pensées (The Machine for Reading Thoughts)*. In effect, he must be ranked with the most significant and most popular French authors of science-fiction of our century. Most of his stories he composed not so much for inclusion in specific volumes but rather at scattered moments throughout his career and as part of his fulfillment of contractual obligations with several newspapers and magazines, among which were *Paris-Soir, Marie-Claire, Candide*. Later he gathered these isolated stories as the basis for his first anthology in America during 1943. This title—*Always the Unexpected Occurs*—aptly sums up the tone of most of his stories. In the preliminary note for this collection Maurois contrasts the lighthearted tone of these stories with the gravity of the era when they were published: "All were composed during days of easy and happy life. This is what explains the tone that surprises me today more than anyone else." After the liberation of France, with many of his prewar works of science-fiction and fantasy out of print, Gallimard wisely decided to gather Maurois's major selections in the genre and to publish them under the heading of *Les Mondes impossibles (The Impossible Worlds)*, an impressive volume that combines "Le Peseur d'âmes," "La Machine à lire les pensées," "Voyage au pays des articoles," "Le Pays des trente-six mille volontés," and "Patapoufs et filifers" (which, in this edition, is regrettably unaccompanied by Jean Bruller's superb illustrations). During the two decades following World War II, Maurois continued indefatigably to inundate his faithful public with a flood of short stories, most of which first appeared in the leading periodicals of the day.[2]

Finally, in 1960, the publisher Flammarion persuaded this author to collect most of his finest short stories—including a group of miniature fictional sketches and all of *Toujours l'inattendu arrive*—for a densely packed and large-scaled volume, *Pour piano seul (For Unaccompanied Piano)*, a volume that to this very day remains his most complete collection of short fiction.

Readers who find themselves overwhelmed before the swarming array of short stories and titles produced by this perhaps overly energetic author are advised to limit themselves judiciously to only two volumes, which together contain the cream of Maurois's short fiction: *Les Mondes impossibles* and *Pour piano seul*.[3]

A. *The Appeal of Short Fiction*

The genre of the short story held for Maurois a strange, irresistible fascination. As a favorite pastime in his personal life he often read the short stories of other writers. In his *Mémoires* he discloses his predilection for the tales of Voltaire, Chekov, Mérimée, and Katherine Mansfield, all of whom he consciously or unconsciously sought to emulate. Short fiction represented also an exciting challenge. Maurois the artist functioned most effectively when confronting seemingly insurmountable obstacles. He thrived on difficulties. And this particular literary genre demands the finest qualities of the creative artist. Brevity calls for sustained meticulousness in style and structure, from beginning to end. In a vast novel, the novelist may allow himself the luxury of relaxing stylistically in the sheer mass of his prose. But in the short story there is no room for banality or relaxation. Yet Maurois was often tempted to consider the composition of short stories as representing a somewhat less taxing task than that of the novel. Sometimes he found it impossible to maintain the same high level of polish throughout the composition of a lengthy novel, whereas he could easily endure the most demanding efforts within the more restricted dimensions of the short story.

Maurois considered the short story both as a vehicle that enabled him to escape from the tensions of his professional life as a biographical and historical researcher and also as a medium that made it possible for him to express his personal interests. Exhausted by the serious business of writing a six-hundred-page life of a George Sand or a Victor Hugo, he found temporary relief through self expression in the free and relatively more imaginative realm of the tale. There he did not have to worry about footnotes, documentation, or authenticity.

Since his days at the Lycée Corneille, he had manifested a more than passing interest in the sciences, and his bedside reading often consisted of books of science and science fiction. Like the protagonist in *La Machine à lire les pensées*, who resembled him in so many different ways, Maurois could say also: "I have always had a vivid taste, in spite of my ignorance, for scientific subjects. . . ."[4] In his daily life too he manifested a keen curiosity about all that occurred in the scientific world, a curiosity that must have been a major factor in the success of his biography of Fleming, the discoverer of penicillin, and also in that of his science-oriented stories.[5] Frédéric Lefèvre once remarked to Maurois that "you have a constant and lively taste for those stories which are halfway between the scientific novel in the manner of Wells and the fantastic *récit* in the manner of Poe. . . ," to which Maurois replied in these terms: "Nothing is more relaxing, after lengthy research, than to give oneself for a few weeks to a task of pure fantasy in which the mind employs no other matter except its imagination."[6]

The short story as a genre approaches Maurois's own personal definition of literary art in general. The story is a valid art form simply because it is pure art and not because it is a tool that allows the author to demonstrate a favorite notion or theory. In his dialogue with Lefèvre, he emphasized that, in his short stories, "I have not wanted to prove anything. The idea of proof and that of a work of art are incompatible, contradictory."

B. Varieties and Classifications

The collected body of Maurois's short fiction is astonishingly heterogeneous in the length of the texts, their structure, form, mood, and subject. *Pour piano seul* alone consists of forty-four selections ranging in length from miniature sketches of one or two pages (e.g., "La Pèlerine," "Les Lettres," "La Cathédrale") to more complex and structured works like "Le Dîner sous les marroniers" (18 pages) and "Par la faute de M. Balzac" (26 pages); most of the items are ten or twelve pages in length. The tales of science-fiction in *Les Mondes impossibles* are all quite lengthy: "La Machine à lire les pensées," is some one hundred pages long, while the fable for youngsters "Patapoufs et filifers" is comprised of some fifty pages of text.

In his chapter on Maurois's short stories, Jacques Suffel compiles a long list of types that illustrate the author's diversity: "Children's tales, fantastic stories, philosophical stories, accounts of anticipation, psychological studies, studies of human mores, novelettes in the English manner, historical novelettes, dramatic legends, romanticized news items, he has with consistent success grappled with almost every variety."[7] Suffel does well to accentuate the multifaceted nature of Maurois's short fiction, for Maurois has indeed experimented with virtually every kind of short story.

Nevertheless, it would not be unfair or simplistic to divide this vast production into two general categories: on the one hand, the tales of fantasy and unreality; on the other, the tales of reality and psychological analysis. Into the first category fall the following items: his stories of science-fiction, those intended primarily for juvenile readers, his satirical compositions in the manner of Anatole France and Swift, his macabre and eerie adventures like "Thanatos-Palace Hotel," ghost stories like "Le Coucou" and "La Pèlerine," and the wildly surrealistic compositions like "Le Départ."[8] No less varied is the realistic category. Here we may justifiably place Maurois's dozens of "drawing-room" stories, all of which deal with men and women drawn from his personal social set. These are people who discuss various human themes—generally dealing with love and romance—while sipping cocktails or tea in a salon or while enjoying a splendid dinner in the dining-room of a great *hôtel particulier* or on the terrace of some posh Bois de Boulogne restaurant. In most of these stories we have subtle psychological analyses of the sentimental relationships between men and women, their jealousies, infidelities, amorous entanglements both in and outside of marriage. This group of tales can properly be labeled "realistic" because in them Maurois portrays with precision the world of writers, artists, Academicians, politicians, diplomats, and wealthy families who comprised his own social milieux.

The characters from this miniature "comédie humaine" bear the same names as the heroes and heroines in the slightly larger "comédie humaine" of his novels. Again and again we stumble into Christian and Claire Ménétrier, from *Terre promise;* Bertrand Schmitt from *Le Cercle de famille* and *Terre promise;* Bertrand's wife, Isabelle, whom we knew formerly as Mme Marcenat in *Climats;* Antoine and Françoise Quesnay, from *Bernard Quesnay;* Denise Holmann, the heroine of *Le Cercle de famille;* Hervé Marcenat, the young writer in *Les Roses de septembre;* the charming middle-aged couple, Gaston and

Valentine Romilly, from *L'Instinct du bonheur;* even Bramble, who has since been promoted from colonel to general. And no sentimental story was complete without the seductive tigress, Solange Villier, who played such a disruptive part in *Climats* and *Le Cercle de famille.*

The geography of these stories reflects quite faithfully both the wanderings of André Maurois and also the places depicted in his novels. In addition to his favored haunts of Périgord, Pont de L'Eure in Normandy, Neuilly-sur-Seine and Paris, we travel with him to the London Airport ("L'Escale"), the sumptuous home of Lady Hampton in London ("Pour piano seul"), the opulent social world of the Philadelphia mainline ("Love in Exile"), the former French West-African colonies ("Raz de marée"), the French population living in exile during the war on the upper east side of New York City ("La Jeune Fille dans la neige"), and the desert region of southern New Mexico ("Thanatos-Palace Hotel").

In these "omniformed" stories we find every conceivable narrative device. Some are accounts in the first person, others epistolary exchanges between two (or occasionally more) correspondents, still others entire dialogues or sprightly conversations. A few tales are built around ominous leitmotifs and portentous shadows that add to the somberness of the tone. A few are comprised mainly of jovial wordplay. Some of the more significant works (e.g., "Le Dîner sous les marroniers" and "Par la faute de M. Balzac") open with elaborate frame stories: a group of guests is gathered around the dinner table exchanging stories that illustrate some moral lesson. "Le Dîner sous les marroniers" opens as the diners take their hors d'oeuvres and ends with the service of the desserts. As the various courses are eaten, the guests compare and contrast anecdotic tales. "Le Commencement d'une femme" depicts at the outset a young girl who reads the diary of a heroine who lived many years ago; the principal plot is developed in the diary. In "Biographie," the hero, Hervé Marcenat, peruses the memoirs of one of the alleged mistresses of Lord Byron, and the theme is stated not so much through Marcenat's adventures as through the text that he reads.

Maurois has himself in an unpublished letter classified his short fiction into three subgenres based on their physical form: "contes," "nouvelles," and "récits." He volunteered to define each of these terms in the following manner:

> I call "conte" that which you have called in America "a short, short story," a simple account of facts without any effort to analyze the characters.
>
> A "nouvelle" is for me just like the *priming* ["*amorce*"] of a novel; it is shorter than the novel itself, but stems a bit from the same technique. [Presumably in the "nouvelle," he does analyze his characters psychologically, developing them into complex beings as he renders more than cursory descriptions of their physical and personal characteristics.]
>
> As for the "récit," it is a very general term which can also be applied to the "conte" as well as to the novel, provided that it is a question of a story told by one of the characters.[9]

Following his definitions, some of his longer stories belong under the heading of "récits." "Le Peseur d'âmes" opens with a first-person statement by the narrator, a Frenchman who visits London on a business trip: "I have hesitated for a long time before writing this tale" (*Les Mondes impossibles*, p. 11). Similarly, "La Machine à lire les pensées" is recounted by the author himself, disguised as a French professor invited to teach French on an American college campus: "Although I am a professor of French literature and my thesis on the sources of Balzac has been received with favor, not only by my colleagues, but by some frvolous critics, I have never myself written a work of imagination" (p. 75). With the group of "récits" belongs *Voyage au pays des articoles*, which begins like this: "I do not wish to talk here except about the mores of the Articoles and of my adventures with them; I shall withhold the tale of what preceded our arrival" (p. 178). On the other hand, his most important fairy-tales for children are essentially "nouvelles." "Patapoufs et filifers" and "Le Pays des trente-six mille volontés" are relatively lengthy and permit the author to create a string of far-fetched and complex adventures and extensively to develop the characters of his heroes, Edmond and Thierry Double in the first work, and Michelle, Gérald, and Olivier in the second.

In *Pour piano seul* we find several impressive "nouvelles." "Ariane ma soeur" consists of an epistolary exchange between two women and one man, with the male seen through the eyes of his two different female observers. The touching tale "Pour piano seul" easily qualifies as a "nouvelle," if not a novelette in the Anglo-American sense. Chronologically spanning several years, its dozen pages uncover first the complex love affair between the mainline dowager and patron of the arts, Kitty Robinson, and her internationally famous pianist-sweetheart, Boris Rosenkraz; then in the second part we read about the pathetic marital relations between Kitty and her noble and overly trusting husband. "Une carrière," a miniature *Bildungsroman* of some twenty pages, traces the chronological stages of development, from birth through childhood, maturity, and final failure of a fascinating anti-hero type, the parasitic and *raté* Chalonnes. On the other hand, the lengthy story "La Vie des Hommes" is, by Maurois's definition, little more than a large-scaled "conte"; here the author makes no attempt at character analysis and is content to itemize an impressive array of fantastic events as witnessed through long-range telescopes by the inhabitants of Uranus and told in the manner of Anatole France.

C. The Craft of the Short Story

No matter which of Maurois's stories we read, we sense instinctively that these are works composed by a deliberate and conscious craftsman of short fiction. Almost always the particular craftsman's hand seems steady and able to meet the most exacting exigencies of the genre. Everywhere we discern the artist's most characteristic qualities as a writer.

First, we note Maurois's apparent fetish for the economy of expression, for compactness and rapidity. Always he seems to strive to say as much as possible in as few words as possible. Avoiding lengthy introductions and detailed transitional passages, he plunges incisively into the heart of the tale and leaps from section to section and paragraph to paragraph with almost no connectives. And when, in his opinion, he has said all that needs to be said, he halts with breathtaking suddenness. If Henri de Régnier once complained that Maurois's "language is sometimes a bit cursive,"[10] in reality, this quickly paced, staccatolike tempo is ideally suited to the art of short stories.

In some of the shortest "contes" and "nouvelles," Maurois has, to a surprising degree, succeeded in conveying the illusion of a considerable flow of time and a complex web of human entanglement. He ardently admired the Russian storyteller Tourguéniev for his ability stringently to restrict the dimensions of his text: "Tourguéniev almost always plunges briskly into the subject."[11] Often Maurois's stories commence in the midst of a dialogue that has been underway for some time, as in the case of the sad tale of frustrated love, "Les Violettes de mercredi," which opens like this: " 'Oh! Jenny, stay!' Jenny Sorbier had been dazzling throughout the entire dinner" (*Pour piano seul*, p. 238). She does leave the room, and after her departure the other guests indulge in a tale about Jenny that develops into a flashback into her past. "Le Dîner sous les marroniers" also begins during the course of a conversation that had already been taking place. As the curtain rises a waiter offers second portions to one of the guests: " 'Still a bit more of the *petite marmite*, Monsieur Ménétrier?' asked the waiter. 'No thanks,' Christian said" (*Pour piano seul*, p. 119). The initial sentence of "Bonsoir Chérie" is a question: " 'Where are you going, Antoine?' Françoise said to her husband. 'I am going to the post office . . .' " (*Toujours l'inattendu arrive*, p. 109).

At other times Maurois forces his reader to penetrate deeply into the secret souls of his protagonists, with little time lost for preparatory development. The novelette, "Tu ne commettras pas d'adultère," portrays in its opening sentence a Wagnerian soprano sprawled on the stage of the Paris Opera House, while the soaring music hallucinates everyone in the audience. Before Maurois reveals these elemental facts to us, he first leads us into the mind of the soprano, who is meditating like this: " 'I have sung well . . . I have sung well. . . .' She remembered with a heartrending pleasure that great river of sounds that had just crossed through her chest, her throat, her mouth."[12] Then suddenly, with no transition, we move alternately from the thoughts of this Brunhilde (in the process of singing) to the music itself, and then to the reactions of the audience, only to be carried into descriptions of the dancing flames of the immolation scene and back again to her personal meditations and the leitmotifs in the score.

Maurois's conciseness is based partly on his technical mastery of the dialogue form. Lively, fast-moving, spoken exchanges between the protagonists, uninterrupted by any sort of descriptive narration, form the essential substance for many of his stories. (See the seven pages of incessant dialogue in "Bonsoir

Chérie" in *Toujours l'inattendu arrive,* pp. 114–21, as a typical sample of unbroken speech.) His dialogues vary in tone from frivolous bantering and witty
gossip to searching discussions on aesthetic problems in painting and literature.[13]

These short stories are remarkable also for their extremely taut sentences and
tidy little paragraphs. Between sections and sentences we find only the most
indispensable connective terms. Swiftly one event leads to another. Maurois
knew of no other way in which to relate, in a limited number of pages, a group
of complex occurrences. In the morbid tale "Le Peseur d'âmes," the narrator
one day encounters the merchant Mr. William Slutter in apparent good health
in a London boutique; the next day he stumbles into him in the hospital, where
he is being treated for pleurisy; that very night, however, he notes that Slutter's
face is enflamed with fever. In less than a second Maurois leaps over the
precipice: "I saw him again the following evening, at midnight, in the dissec-
tion room" (*Les Mondes impossibles,* p. 44).

The contracted sentences of André Maurois make for exciting reading.
Never do we feel that we have bogged down in the mire of heavy prose. As
pulsating as his introductory sentences are, they are only a faint hint of the
sledgehammerlike sentences with which he ends his tales. Seldom does he
compose a short story without remembering Alain's words, scribbled in the
margin of one of his schoolboy notebooks: "Serrez, condensez at terminez en
coup de poing" (Tighten, condense, and end with a punch). This challenge had
become the guideline for André Maurois's art of short fiction. So many of his
stories jolt us at the conclusion. "Le Seigneur des ténèbres" opens with a bland
presentation of a culpable love affair between the married Françoise Quesnay
and the irresistible lover, the playwright Fabert. The former has been warned
against becoming involved in a dangerous amorous entanglement with Fabert,
who has the reputation of bringing misfortune into the lives of all those women
who have been seduced by his smooth and polished overtures. In the case of
Françoise, we have every reason to suspect that at last destiny will be defied,
and that she will succeed in escaping almost inevitable disaster. But she yields to
Fabert. The story concludes with two brisk, unexpected sentences: "She died
during that year. The poor woman had cancer" (*Pour piano seul,* p. 41). The
astonished reader is left to draw his own conclusions: Did Françoise know that
she had incurable cancer and chose, therefore, to take advantage of her few
remaining days to indulge in a dangerous but delectable relationship? Or was it
true that tragic destiny inevitably pursued all those who fell under the spell of
this professional Don Juan? Thus the cancer could be interpreted as an expia-
tory after-effect of the affair. In another tale, the three-paged "La Ceinture
verte," the heroine, Nathalie, appears to have too quickly overcome the grief
she suffered at her husband's premature death. She seems to suffer from no
obvious signs of undue despair. Cheerful, eating heartily, she even wears an
outlandishly bright green belt over her traditional black mourner's dress. But
then comes the unanticipated jolt: "A few days later, they learned that Nathalie

had swallowed three tubes of barbital and that she had died" (*Pour piano seul,* p. 371).

D. The Short Stories as Faithful Reflections of Maurois Himself

The short stories of André Maurois, perhaps more so than his biographies, novels, and histories, reflect with the greatest fidelity the personal traits of this artist as a human being. In his stories his prose is enveloped in a patina of deliberately simple elegance. The graceful overlay is at the same time correct and casual. Yet, barely concealed beneath this surface, we confront a tight concatenation of jagged sentences and paragraphs whose inner tension seems on the verge of bursting forth from beneath the polished veneer. This tension is felt in the many brief, syncopated sentences and dialogues, the abrupt ellipses, the dramatic punchlines at the end of paragraphs and stories. Maurois the man, in real life, also gave the impression of fusing a façade of relaxed grace with internal tenseness. Speaking with his interlocutors, he manifested an apparent ease and grace, but his restless fingers and slight movements of the feet, not to mention his darting and penetrating eyes, betrayed by their barely discernible movements the tremendous energy stored up within him. His relaxed casualness was little more than a veil behind which lurked a fount of vigor ready to spring forth at any moment. In one of the most accurate verbal portraits ever rendered of him, an American journalist admirably summed up this unique combination of external grace and inner tenseness, a combination noted both in the behavior of the man and in the style of his short fiction:

> M. Maurois is the keen and sensitive type of Frenchman, a man whose appearance and every gesture exhibit a nervous, driving vitality leashed by a sympathetic understanding and yet scholarly mind. In repose he is likely to slump back in his chair, his body relaxed and only his fingers tightly interlaced, betraying the tightly coiled energy he will display a moment later when he bends forward and sits on the very edge of the chair to speak. Then his gestures are quick and his phrases direct, unequivocal, and penetrating as his own writing.[14]

For Maurois the short story is a condensed, compressed art form tightly packed with energy and complexity, but told in an outwardly polished and often deceptively simple way.

The art of writing was for André Maurois both a means of self-expansion and also a way of constraining certain personal tendencies. He admitted that "it is true that I have held back rather than pushed my style forward."[15] In all likelihood, as he composed his short stories, he struggled to control, to contract the force of an overly ebullient mind. His manuscripts are tangible evidence of his incessant attempt to restrain his style. Always he seemed to be driving toward greater compactness. In one manuscript he crossed out the first five sentences, preferring instead to dive immediately into the marrow of his plot. The manuscripts are a patchwork quilt of variants crossed out to make way for new variants. In every case, his changes represent a deliberate effort to eliminate the redundant, to suppress the overly flamboyant, to clarify what may be too complex. What he had to say of his style in his final diary, *Choses nues*, was a fitting epigraph for the dominant style of his short stories: "Its nudity will be its only adornment."[16]

Even his handwriting betrays his struggle to constrain himself. The overall appearance of the manuscript is one of flowing grace. But on examining the miniature letters more closely, we note in the minute curves and curls of the words that each letter has been carefully and nervously formed. It is almost as if he were consciously holding his pen back from flowing too rapidly. When Alain warned him against his "frightful facility," he may have had in mind not only his pupil's boundless array of ideas but also his ease of verbal expression.[17] Maurois never forgot Alain's admonition.

E. Realities and Unrealities

Maurois's tales of science-fiction and fantasy are models of restraint and discipline. This is ironic when we consider that these types of stories, by their very nature, lend themselves freely to unbridled imagination. Rather then invent wholly original characters, he borrows those people whom he knew in his own daily existence. "Patapoufs et filifers," an amusing tale satirizing international tensions in Europe, was written to entertain his own children first. The names of the two youthful heroes, Edmond and Thierry, are thin veils disguising the true identity of his own sons, Gérald and Olivier. In "Le Pays des trente-six mille volontés" he has entirely lifted the veil and not only is the story dedicated "à ma fille Michelle," but all three children, Michelle, Olivier, and Gérald, are, in fact, the three principals. The sophisticated novelette, "La Machine à lire les pensées," is—in spite of the immense dosage of science-fiction in it—almost disturbingly realistic, if not semi-autobiographical. The setting, that of an American college town and campus along Ivy League lines, replete with faculty-wives' teas, faculty committee meetings, football rallies, petty campus politics, sessions of the Board of Trustees, and even a corner drugstore "hangout," reminds us continually that, though the events take place in "Westmouth College," Maurois and his wife once spent a happy period of residence on the campus of Princeton University. If "la machine" had been eliminated from the science-fiction, what we would have left is a realistic piece of fiction, even an authentic portrayal of life in a small eastern college town in America. Even in the macabre "Le Peseur d'âmes," much of which develops in the morgue of St. Barnaby's hospital in London (almost certainly modeled after the real St. Mary's hospital there), he conjured up the fantastic situation of a physician who had invented a device to weigh the souls of recently deceased patients. His physician's name is Doctor James; many readers of Maurois are aware that the noted British psychiatrist, Dr. G. W. B. James, one of his closest English friends, had already served as the most important model for the now famous Dr. O'Grady in *Les Discours du Docteur O'Grady* and that he makes a fleeting reappearance in Maurois's celebrated *Vie de Sir Alexander Fleming*. In spite of the almost incredulous theme of "Le Peseur d'âmes," the work contains some carefully wrought, authentic descriptions of the City of London: the right bank of the Thames, Blackfriar's Bridge, the Strand, an open-air market. Maurois is careful not to let the theme of the "weighing machine" become so all-pervasive that it effaces the realism of the hospital setting, with its inescapable odors of chloroform and ether and its white-garbed nurses performing their errands along the dimly lit corridors.

One of his most powerful works, "Thanatos-Palace Hôtel," is a ludicrous tale situated in a strangely convincing setting, that of an elegant resort hotel. With its concierge, social activities programs, verandas lined with rocking chairs, terraces, hiking trails, and tennis courts it is reminiscent of hundreds of Old World hostelries Maurois must have visited personally in Switzerland and on the Riviera. But the hotel is located in some remote corner of a New Mexican landscape dotted with barren buttes and mesas. The outlandish fantasy of the plot is tempered by descriptions of very real settings; the hotel is, however, no pleasure palace in the conventional sense, but really a resort to which people, tired of life, go to commit suicide effortlessly, scientifically, and in dignified fashion.

Since most of these fantastic stories take place in true-to-life places—the metros of Paris, small Parisian apartment-building elevators, ateliers of the couturiers—they contain the familiar accoutrements from the existence of an author who lived in Neuilly and Paris.[18] We must, therefore, look to the plot (and not the setting) for the requisite elements of fantasy or science-fiction. Occasionally, however, Maurois performs the reverse operation: he transports us into a totally fictitious realm, in which a realistic plot evolves against the backdrop of a fanciful world. Such is certainly the case in "Le Voyage au pays des articoles" and "Patapoufs et filifers," both of which take place far removed from the familiar haunts of Maurois's Paris. Not once can we find a case when this author's sense of controlled proportion permits him the freedom to create *both* a far-fetched plot and a far-fetched decor.

The delicate equilibrium between reality and fantasy forms a legitimate subject for a more detailed study of Maurois's works of short fiction. This author prefers to start his fantastic works in a realistic manner, avoiding any abrupt shock for the reader. Gradually, unobtrusively, he injects first one slightly unreal detail, then another and another; soon the unsuspecting reader confronts not at all a psychological drama of middle-class Paris society, but rather a series of fantastic adventures. By this time it is too late to withdraw from a story that might otherwise have been too difficult for a sophisticated reader to swallow, had Maurois not resorted to a realistic opening passage in the first place. Our interest is so aroused that we wish to proceed to the very end in order to discover the dénouement. Maurois himself admits to this technique of surreptitiously converting a realistic episode into an unreal one: "The best method is to begin by a simple tale, in which no unreal element is present and then to introduce the extraordinary elements only in growing doses which are gradually incorporated into the paste. The mind succeeds then in accepting and even in enjoying doses of aesthetic untruths, which if they are injected in massive form, might kill the credibility from the first line."[19]

"Le Peseur d'âmes" illustrates clearly Maurois's blending of reality with unreality. The story opens with an almost painfully detailed account of a visit by the French protagonist-narrator to London's St. Barnaby's Hospital, where he goes to find once again his old friend, the physician Dr. James. Both men embark upon a philosophical and pseudo-religious discussion one rarely expects to find in science-fiction. Casually the doctor alludes to his "scientific" investigations into the weight of the human soul. Before we realize it, we follow with indomitable curiosity each step of the outlandish experimentation, and science has been discreetly transformed into science-fiction. At the beginning of "Le Pays des trente-six mille volontés" the heroine, Michelle, finds herself in bed, gradually dozing off. Insidiously Maurois converts her conscious thoughts into a weird dream: "She remained for a long time with her eyes open, perhaps for ten minutes, then it seemed to her that a ray of light which, from under the door, was coming from her parents' bedroom, was getting larger and was becoming sunlight. At the same time, the white sheet of the bed was becoming covered with sand and Michelle found herself alone, standing in the midst of an immense expanse of sterile earth. 'Gosh,' she said to herself, 'it is a desert!' " (*Les Mondes impossibles*, p. 218).

One of this writer's most compelling short stories, entitled "Le Départ," consists of a dream sequence of a dying man. As the curtain rises the hero lies in a serious coma, barely able to comprehend the muffled words of his physician and family, gathered at his bedside. Then he feels the need to get out of bed and leave the room: "But at the moment when I was going to reach the door, my hand bumped into my body and I felt with surprise that I was already dressed" (*Pour piano seul*, p. 174). A second later he finds himself in an airport terminal, forced to undergo the most anguished Kafkaesque experiences imaginable. Reliving symbolically life in the twentieth century, he waits in all sorts of lines, deals with various callous bureaucrats, especially airline and customs officials, nervously fills out multitudinous forms, fights through one crowd after another, considers the advantages and disadvantages of affiliating with the gamut of Protestant cults, from Presbyterianism to Unitarianism, and always feels uneasy about the growing possibility of missing his plane. Maurois constructs a series of frightful experiences that are now sequential, now confused. Just as the hero has apparently reached the apogée of the nightmare, uttering aloud a cry, "I no longer wish to leave!", his physician realizes that with the restoration of his speech there is hope for the dying man to be drawn out of the coma. In the end, reality and recovery return to the patient.

F. Maxims, Caricatures, and Satire

Maurois the short-story writer always behaves like Maurois the moralist. Even in his science-fiction he cannot free himself from an overriding concern for general human conduct. "La Machine à lire les pensées" deals not only with a strange sort of technological machine, but to a large extent also with the themes of sincerity and fidelity. This tale describes the relationship between our inner thoughts and feelings and our overt utterances and sentiments. As Maurois describes the eloquence of unspoken language, he intersperses many thought-provocative maxims among his accounts of the feats accomplished by the machine. For example: "Life has finally taught me that human beings, when they are not humiliated or offended, respond to confidence with more confidence" (*Les Mondes impossibles*, p. 151). In stories like "Raz de marée" and "Pauvre maman," he analyzes hypocrisy, contending that uninhibited sincerity is not necessarily a virtue. Gentle amounts of hypocrisy are even essential to preserve the fragile balance of happiness among human beings, especially between husband and wife.

One of his favored images in the short stories is that of the mask. All people must wear masks, if they are expected to adapt to the organized patterns of society: " 'To remove the mask?' said Bertrand Schmitt, 'Do you believe really that it might often be desirable to remove the mask? I believe on the contrary that, except for a few unusual and rare friendships, it is the masks, and they alone, which make the life of communities tolerable. . . . When circumstances arise which make one of us by chance reveal the truth only once to those from whom it has customarily been hidden, this person quickly repents for his mad sincerity' " (*Pour piano seul*, p. 275). The concept of the mask is an offshoot of the whole question of silence and "pudeur," a question that concerned him throughout his career. In the story "L'Escale," Maurois notes that "Most of the people do not say what they think. Behind their phrases, there is always a hidden thought. The idea which they express covers another idea which they wish to keep well concealed. . . . Or else they say any old thing, without thinking" (p. 65). In some cases, he demonstrates convincingly that silence is deliberate, while elsewhere—for example, his British heroes in *Les Silences du Colonel Bramble* and in "Le Peseur d'âmes"—his characters are simply incapable of vocalizing all of their thoughts and feelings. Instinctively they are hindered by "this impotence to express themselves."[20]

Like the other moralists in the French literary tradition, Maurois describes man's behavioral characteristics not only through maxims and aphorisms, but also by selecting a group of universal types of people, of whom he renders sharply delineated portraits. His short stories are liberally sprinkled with caricatures of the kinds of people he knew personally, and whose conduct he could observe at first hand. For example, some of his stories contain dozens of portraits based on the characters one habitually finds in the American academic scene: the president, the Nobel Prize physicist, the trustees, the clean-cut "jocks" and "preppies" and the not-so-well groomed "hip-type" college students, the usual varieties of babbling faculty wives (see, "Jeune fille dans la neige" and "La Machine à lire les pensées"). In other stories we find portraits of the impetuous politician (Victor Bertaut in "Toujours l'inattendu arrive"), the genius type of dramatist à la Jean-Louis Barrault (ibid.), the Maurois-type of writer (Bertrand Schmitt, especially in "Love in Exile"), the wealthy American patroness of the arts and her indulgent millionaire husband (the Robinsons in "Pour piano seul"), the enthusiastic Francophile Americans, who are more French than the French, in their love affair with Paris ("Le Dîner sous les marroniers"), the gracious land-owning gentry of the British aristocracy ("Biographie"), the intelligent bourgeoisie of Normandy and their leisurely upper-middle-class friends on the Côte d'Azur ("Bonsoir Chérie"). Indeed, Maurois's countless carciatures of British, American, and above all French types constitute a lively human comedy that is an important chapter in his overall fictional production.

Maurois the moralist excels in his depictions of characters in various stages of amorous involvement, from the initial stages of nascent love to the final lingering moments of a love that has spent itself. Often these romances consist of bittersweet skirmishes between hero and heroine. The playful tone of the language resembles the bantering we commonly associate with Marivaux and Musset. We discern this light touch in the following definition of love pronounced by Maurois's playwright-hero, Fabert:

> He explains willingly to his men that in the game of love as in the game of chess there is a small number of overtures, or of opening plays, classical steps which one must know by heart, each one being adapted to a definite type of woman. I do not remember his list exactly, but it is something like this: The available—or if you prefer, the accessible—woman can be divided into sensuous women, maternal women, and intellectual women. Each of these classes can be attacked differently. . . . ("Le Seigneur des ténèbres," *Pour piano seul*, p. 37)

Playing with each other's emotions, these leisurely characters resemble graceful mannequins of love who spend entire evenings flirting with one another on some fragrant terrace, under a romantic and star-studded sky. At times Maurois verbalizes types of *Fêtes galantes* in the manner of Watteau, as in the case below:

> The evening, on the terrace, was more beautiful than ever. The foliage of the trees did not stir. One heard only some rare far off noises: the call of a nocturnal bird, a dog barking in the distance in the village, the whistle of a

train in the valley. The guests of Saint-Arnoult had formed little groups and were speaking in low voices. As for me, I had remained alone, leaning back in my armchair and looking at the stars. The immensity of the world gave me the feeling of the vanity of our earthly agitations. Fabert had seated himself near Françoise and, leaning towards her, he spoke with animation. (Ibid., p. 40)

In a few of the stories, the sentimental complications become quite involved. "Les Ricochets," a three-page story, relates of Daniel, a properly married husband who prefers his mistress, Beatrice, to his wife, while the former prefers her other lover, Pierre Pradier, to Daniel. Other stories deal with the theme of nostalgia over a past love affair. Men and women, formerly in love with each other, marry other mates only to find many years later that, as their paths cross, the old smoldering flames have rekindled themselves perilously (see "Bonsoir Chérie"). In some of the selections the love is more sweet than bitter, and touching sentimentality leaves the reader with an irrepressible feeling of melancholy ("Toujours l'inattendu arrive," "Les Violettes du mercredi," "Fleurs de saison," etc.) Seldom do Maurois's sweethearts drift off into violent, tragic love affairs. His short stories contain relatively few deaths, suicides, or murders that result from fatal passion. Hardly ever is tragedy unavoidable. The one exception is "Tu ne commettras pas d'adultère," a work that revolves around the cruel dilemma of a Jewess hopelessly caught in the web of the Nazi occupation of Paris.

Maurois prefers to portray moderate, rational human beings who almost always possess the good sense and taste—not to mention the self-discipline—needed to avoid the pitfalls of blood-curdling tragedy. Not that these love affairs are superficial; the fact is that his heroes are endowed with the uncanny ability to analyze themselves and know just how far they can go before extricating themselves from an otherwise impossible situation. Essentially what Maurois has done in his novels he has done for his short stories.

Most of these characters are relatively idle people who have generous portions of free time available to frequent the literary and social salons of Paris and to indulge in a variety of amorous narcissistic pursuits. The largest single group of characters in Maurois's world is that of the writing profession. His sketches of playwrights, poets, novelists, and their wives and mistresses are especially felicitous. These are the people he knew most intimately. He treats them not as exceptional creative artists, but as frail human beings. In "Ariane, ma soeur," Jerome Vence is much weaker as a human being than as a writer: "The writer, in him, was admirable because of his talent as well as because of his conscience. Concerning the man, you have told the truth. No, Jerome was not an apostle . . ." (*Pour piano seul*, p. 49). Some writers are greater human beings than writers. One of the most pathetic figures created by Maurois is Chalonnes in "Une Carrière," who is the sad example of a would-be writer who talked and imagined a finer book than his meager talents permitted him to produce.

Maurois did more than forge character-studies of the creative artists. He utilized his stories to express his own personal literary theories. Apparently unable to write about creative artists without simultaneously diffusing his descriptions of them into his own artistic theories, he was more than a moralist and short-story narrator; he was also a literary critic. Falling back upon his author-characters, whom he used as spokesmen, Maurois expounded continually on his favorite topic, the relationships between art and life. To what extent, he asked, must a writer live a rich, exciting life in order to produce successful and vivid works? Can an author who has never experienced the tribulations of existence successfully formulate a masterful account of human pathos? According to Maurice Martin du Gard, this theme was a crucial one in Maurois's short fiction: "He studies the rapports between art and the life of the artist in his short stories."[21] In the fanciful "nouvelle" "Voyage au pays des articoles," Maurois compared the overly sheltered life of some artists with the sterility of their works: "The great weakness of the Articoles," he writes, "seems to me to be that they have lost contact with life. In a normal society, the artist must struggle, at least during his youth; he retains memories of it, loves, hatreds, finally vivid recollections" (pp. 75–76). It was inevitable for the biographer of Byron, Shelley, Hugo, Sand, and so many others to reflect lengthily on this question, and his short stories on literary life permitted him to permeate his prose with salon type of debates and maxims all dealing with literary criticism and the aesthetics of fiction. Many of his stories are laden with statements like these: "Force is one of the factors of aesthetic emotion, and because they are more than human the figures of the Sistine Chapel are not vulgar" (*Pour piano seul*, p. 161). Or: "The types of characters which the great writer sketches are those which an epoch desires, not those which it produces. . . . Art presents models, man realizes them . . ." (*Ibid.*, p. 188).

In some of his stories Maurois assumes the role of a satirist. Naturally, the first group to serve him as the target of his satire are the writers and creative artists. "Voyage au pays des articoles" is a far-fetched fantasy in which he pokes fun at his own friends of the now defunct group at Pontigny. Most of these shared what Maurois regarded as an exaggerated cult for intellectualized life. Such a cult, Maurois concludes, results inevitably in hollow, meaningless art. "Une Carrière" is an ironic tale of a writer lionized by literary and social circles more for the legend that surrounds his person than for the paucity and mediocrity of his published works. "La Naissance d'un maître" constitutes a satire of the frivolous world of the art galleries, phony critics, and snobbish fads. By far the most biting attack of all can be found in "La Vie des hommes," which treats of Man's incurable urge to embark upon destructive warfare. The tone of this work is similar to that of Anatole France's *L'Ile des pingouins* and Voltaire's *Candide.* Here is a typical passage:

That is nevertheless what happens on Earth. In a few years of observation, I have been able to observe sometimes in one corner, sometimes in another corner of this planet, compact masses of men who confront each other. Sometimes they combat under the open sky; sometimes, sheltered in tunnels, they try to demolish the tunnels of neighbors by sprinkling them with heavy masses of metal; sometimes they rig themselves out in rudimentary wings in order to drop on their enemies projectiles from the top of the sky. Note that at the same time they too are sprinkled in the same manner. It is a frightful and ridiculous spectacle. The scenes of horror which one witnesses then are such that, if these animals had the slightest memory, they would avoid repeating their mistakes, at least during several generations. But in the course of the lifetime of the same men, which is nonetheless so brief, one sees them twice or thrice throw themselves into the same murderous adventures. (*Pour piano seul,* pp. 350–52)

Even his children's tale, "Patapoufs et filifers," satirizes for the benefit of his juvenile and also adult readers the follies of war and of excessive nationalism (especially in the cases of France and Germany). The Patapoufs (the French) are fat, self-indulgent people who live for the sake of food and pleasure; the Filifers (the Germans) are thin, self-denying, regimented people who live for the pleasure of adhering to strict work schedules. "Le Pays des trente-six mille volontés" is a satirical tale concerning the French mania for individualism which, when exaggerated, leads to the worst kind of chaos and national folly.

G. A Diminutive Human Comedy

Whether this story consists of a single page or fifty pages, Maurois seems ever in control of his material. Perhaps it is a pity that he did not compose more very brief pieces of short fiction; this may well have been the forte of this author. In the opinion of the literary critic Edmond Jaloux, Maurois's genius was at its peak in his writing of short fiction. Maurois admitted that "Edmond Jaloux would often tell me that there [in tiny tales] was my true vocation. And it is a fact that I took great pleasure in composing them. But I have taken pleasure in doing so many things. . . ."[23] Taken as a whole, Maurois's stories, like his novels, form a diminutive world, a human comedy that possesses its own multiplicity of characters, themes, situations. The short stories form one of the most delightful parts of this urbane writer's many-sided career. Perhaps, along with the better-known biographies and *Climats,* it is the short stories that deserve most to endure for posterity.

Part V

The World of the Histories and Chronicles

Maurois as Historian and Chronicler of the Past and Present

When reading great books, we get the same impression of
oneness, not only in Space, but also in Time. Open Homer or
Plato, Goethe or Dickens, Tolstoy or Balzac, and you will
realize that human sentiments, fundamental passions and feelings changed very little in the course of three thousand years.
                Maurois, commencement address to
                University of Maryland
                graduating class, 1963

Maurois decided to expand his competence as a researcher in the archives of the
past from the domain of biography to that of history. One easily glides from
the life of a Lord Byron to that of a Disraeli, and from the biography of
Disraeli it is only a stone's throw to the History of England. Whereas biography is the history of an individual, history is the biography of a nation, a
civilization, or of a society. Both the biographer and historian must derive their
facts from a solid firmament of documentation. Both must interpret the available data with methodical rigor and be able to distinguish between legend and
fact. Both must transform chaotic piles of information into credible, orderly
accounts of past era. How could Maurois separate the history of French colo-
nialism in North Africa from the biography of the great soldier-hero, Marshal
Lyautey? How could he describe the career of Victor Hugo without examining
the historical evolution of nineteenth-century Europe?[1] Maurois's histories of
England, the United States, and France, like his biographies, are not only
reliable works; they are also effortless and enjoyable reading and remarkable
for their verbal polish and lucidity. These histories were composed by a creator
of novels and short stories. Maurois injected into his historical works every
stylistic device that he had learned to apply in his literary works. He really used
drama, pathos, tensions, and wit to make his histories come alive. Moreover,
his experience with short stories endowed him with a genuine ability to narrate
historical events quickly and compactly. The writer Abel Hermant complained
half seriously, half jestingly, that these histories were much too facile to read:
"one experiences also a strange feeling, a sort of badly defined feeling of shame,
at being able to read so easily a book which has cost so much research and

work, without any visible effort. . . ."[2] The tremendous behind-the-scenes labor expended by Maurois to document and to organize his facts is almost entirely obscured by the graceful flow of his sentences and by the simplicity with which he tells the story of a nation. Maurois had in his archives a private collection of testimonial letters written to him by eminent readers from around the world who reacted favorably to his histories. Clement Attlee, among the most appreciative admirers of his *History of England,* wrote: "It is delightful to read the old well-known story told again with such charm and insight. I am in danger of neglecting my work in order to continue the *History.* . . . I admire your power of selection and compression. I have long held that it should be a part of education to read our national history through the mind of another race, but other countries have not a Maurois."[3] The voice that mattered most to Maurois was of course that of his old teacher, Alain. The philosopher commented favorably on Maurois's *History of the United States:* "I reach another idea which interests me very much, and which is your *métier,* I mean the *récit* . . . but I found in your book, and more than once, an *epic movement* which corresponds, in my opinion, to the alexandrine verse-form and to the birth of the tragedian; a trait of the period is that it flies along while devouring time, with the sign of being irreparable. . . . I am full of enthusiasm when I see how a frail pen succeeds in sketching an entire world, and thousands of characters."[4]

A. The Extent of Maurois's Historical Production

The total historical production of André Maurois was immense, consisting not only of three major histories, those of England, the United States and France, but also of hundreds of articles and some smaller volumes. However, it was primarily his histories of these three major western countries that are his most significant contributions to the field.

The earliest work of the triology, the *Histoire d'Angleterre,* blossomed out of many fertile personal and scholarly contacts with the English people and their culture, dating back to World War I and continuing into the following decades. The twenty years following World War I may even be subtitled Maurois's English decades, for it was then that he was most preoccupied with things British. To these decades belong the *Bramble-O'Grady,* his biographies of Shelley, Lord Byron, Disraeli, King Edward VII, and numerous smaller essays and studies of Dickens, Cecil Rhodes, and the Entente Cordiale. Indeed, by 1937 he had accumulated such a rich collection of data on the English that it was only natural for him to crown this period with a conglomerate history of this gallant people. Published under the aegis of the Collection des Grandes Etudes Historiques of Arthème Fayard, the work was universally acclaimed by the general literary public and even by the more critical professional historians in England and France.

This first successful history was sufficient to give Maurois an appetite for still other successes in this field. During the years of exile in the United States, he encountered among his American friends so many persons who had misunderstood the reasons for France's sudden collapse in 1940, and so few who were willing to judge her sympathetically, that he undertook an ambitious project designed to explain historically how this once mighty nation had so depleted its resources that it could simply not withstand the destructive punch of the Nazi tidal wave. His two-volume *Histoire de la France*, probably his finest historical work, is the fruit of his desire to correct certain misconceptions concerning his native land in America.

But this was not the end of this historian's career as historian. He never ceased to be fascinated by the miraculous ascendancy to superpower status of the American people in less than two centuries. The miracle of America demanded an explanation, and he decided to write the story of this historical phenomenon: "for my own instruction and also in order to complete a trilogy of the three great liberal countries."[5] Out of this quest for knowledge came an eminently honest, readable, two-volume *Histoire des Etats-Unis*. But his fascination with America did not end there: in 1962 he wrote in conjunction with Louis Aragon a unique four-volume "parallel history" of the United States and the Soviet Union, from 1917 until 1960: *L'Histoire parallèlle des U.S.A. et L'U.R.S.S.* Maurois did the American sections, Aragon the Russian parts. Maurois's work, *From the New Freedom to New Frontier* (New York: McKay and Co., 1963) is the American translation of the first volume of this remarkable work.

B. *Maurois's Philosophy of History*

Fundamental to Maurois's conception of history was his conviction that history was little more than a world of human beings, all of whom the historian *arranges* into a chronological and social order. Maurois himself called his *History of France* a "continuous account of portraits."[6] He was especially fascinated by "the human side of history."[7] He agreed with Emerson's notion that there was really no history as such, only the collective biography of men and women. Throughout his historical tomes, what stand out most vividly are not the great battles, coronations, treaties, and congresses, but rather the actions of generals, kings and queens, prime ministers, presidents and parliamentarians. History, in the view of André Maurois, had little meaning except insofar as it represented the accomplishments of individual human beings. "This is why I took care to sow all of my histories with portraits of protagonists. . . . History is an infinite agglomeration of incoherent facts in which only man can establish directions and currents."[8]

Maurois's people are actors who seldom assume a passive attitude vis-à-vis the dynamic forces of destiny. On the contrary, people shape these forces themselves. History, for this student of Alain, does not make man. Rather, history is what man makes it. (So many men and women appear in his *History of France* that he deemed it necessary to include in the last edition published during his lifetime numerous genealogical tables and family trees illustrating the interrelationships of his figures, their ancestors, and their descendants.)[9]

Maurois believed in a second historical principle: namely, the history of a people is one of perpetual motion. Never do the wheels of change halt in their mobility. Wars glide into peace; peace glides into war. One reign or presidency leads to the next. Seldom does history contain abrupt abysses dividing one era from another. The story of a nation is that of a ceaseless flow of transformations. In contrast with so many histories that seem too neatly structured into sharp delineations, Maurois's histories contain few drastic lines of chronological demarcation. His sections blend into each other: "Well-cut periods are merely concepts of the historians. Always one finds at the two extremities of these periods fringes of interferences."[10] Almost the only factor distinguishing one period from another is the presence of a dominant hero in each epoch, as was the case, for instance, with King Edward VII: "The movement of ideas which gives its intellectual color to the Edwardian period begins in the last decades of the reign of Queen Victoria and continues up to the war, but the appearance of King Edward accelerated the rhythm of change."[11]

Just as Maurois believed chronological categorizations to be artificial props, so he insisted that there were no immutable laws, cyclic movements, or deterministic forces governing the drift of civilization. History is simply a perpetual motion of humanity. Maurois refused to believe in such eighteenth- and nineteenth-century doctrines as the inevitability of progress and the perfectibility of the human species. He held no illusions about the human race. Just as he described some of a nation's most majestic moments, he also gave equal attention and detail to some of the basest moments in the history of man. He knew how easily mobs could be incited to do both good and evil, how abusive majorities were apt to persecute minorities, and vice versa: "It is difficult to unite men for a constructive action and rather easy to league them against a minority."[12] Nevertheless, he did not view history as a justification for pessimism. All he was willing to accept was a vague philosophy of oscillations, coincidental repetitions, endless actions and reactions with no real patterns: "One ascertains [on examining history] oscillations, not a long ascending march."[13]

Although this historian would not color his historical works with particular points of view or make them bend submissively to the contours of his prejudices, it would be a mistake to regard his works as bland, uncritical, and amorphous. He preserved his histories from becoming colorless by larding them with vivid portraits. And though he sought to be as objective as possible, he never achieved unabashed neutrality. Frequently he even resorted to editorializing. The facts were presented in seemingly objective manner. But one cannot help but sense his subtle preferences for certain figures and his disdain for others. Though, in his preface to the *History of France,* Maurois claimed that "I attempted, through the length of the book not to deform the facts in order to bend them to my sentiments," he simply could not refrain from dropping little quips here and there that divulged his likes and dislikes. There is no mistaking his positive attitude toward Louis XVIII and Louis-Philippe, his unsympathetic reaction toward Louis-Napoleon, his mixed feelings concerning Thiers, and his solid admiration for Gambetta.[14]

Sometimes Maurois took delight in being an iconoclast or in debunking some of the hackneyed concepts of the professional historians. We learn not to be surprised by some of his unusual contentions. In his *History of England* he minimized the importance of Julius Caesar's victory in Britain (p. 26). He also negated the oversimplified myth that England had turned to Protestantism thanks to the personal life of its monarch Henry VIII. The reasons for the British Reformation were more complex: "The Reformation of England was not the caprice of a sovereign, but the religious form of an insular and linguistic nationalism" (p. 317). The historian in him imposed upon Maurois the obligation of presenting the facts as dispassionately as possible, but the artist in him stimulated him to interpret these facts in a personal manner. The resultant histories are not only faithful accounts of the events of the past; they are also, in a large measure, the subjective expression of an artist endowed with his own opinions and preferences.

If Maurois made no attempt to conceal his personal reactions, he always presented his opinions with modesty, even with humility. Obviously he did not expect to compete with men who had devoted their entire professional careers to history as an academic discipline. Hence he did not compose his works with the intention of writing definitive source-works. In essence, he intended his histories to be simplified, even vulgarized, but well-written, accurately documented, and interestingly told stories of a nation's past. Maurois humbly confessed that "I am not a historical researcher who seeks to find new things. My histories are attempts at explication."[15] This fact is clear from his subtitles in the History of France, all of which begin with the terms *How* and *Why*. His goal was simply to explain the motivations and manners of national behavior. An unpretentious clarifier with no claim to omniscience or completeness, he referred to his histories as mere sketches. In the preface to his two-volume *History of the United States,* he calls his work "a sketch of the development of a civilization and of a political system."

In his histories Maurois conceived of the nation-state not only in the political sense, but also in the social, economic, artistic, scientific, industrial, and educational sense. So, indeed, his works are the history of both a country and a civilization. For example, his chapters concerning the nineteen-twenties and thirties in France are almost *in toto* devoted to the state of banking, labor unionism, industrialization, agronomy, and other financial and social questions of the time. His discussion of Elizabethan England refers to the foods, customs, and dress of the era, while his early chapters on the origins of the English people are based in large part on his analysis of *Beowulf.* Never does Maurois allow us to forget that as a historian he was also an incurable novelist and an astute biographer.

C. History as a Means of Conciliation

Posterity may well consider one of Maurois's principal roles as a historian and essayist to have been that of a conciliator of nations, especially of England, the United States, and France. Enlightened conciliation was certainly one of the functions he assigned to himself. His three major histories served as a means of fulfilling this mission. The *History of England,* which incidentally was the first major history of that nation written by a Frenchman, is directed mainly to his contemporary French readers. At every juncture he explains, clarifies, justifies the intentions of England so that the French reader can better sympathize with the British point of view, especially when there existed divergences of policy between the two countries, as, for example, the Hundred Years War, Anglo-French rivalries in the New World, the Napoleonic period, the stresses and strains of the Entente Cordiale. The *History of France,* on the other hand, was directed both to his own compatriots and to his American readers. Continually he relied upon American points of reference to illustrate French history. In his *History of the United States,* written mainly for a French public, he explained events in American history through comparisons with similar events from the French past. Thus the French reader of Maurois's books on Anglo-American history sees these two nations in a more favorable light, while English and American readers of the French history adopt a more sympathetic attitude with respect to the often puzzling behavior of the French. Maurois the historian utilizes history as a tool to combat prejudices, ignorance, and fanaticism.

He summed up his life's work in behalf of mutual understanding among these three countries in an unpublished talk before a banquet of the New York City chapter of the Alliance Française on February 12, 1939 (a banquet that honored his election into the Académie Française): "Among France, England and the United States there are more things in common than things which divide them. . . . Among all of the joys which literary life has given me the greatest satisfaction is certainly that of having had the feeling of having contributed, in whatever feeble way it has been, to the rapprochement of these two countries [the U.S. and France]."

In France he quickly acquired the reputation as one of the most Anglophilic French authors. But in the British Isles, he incarnated the spirit of the typical Frenchman of letters. André Chevrillon stressed Maurois's role in the Anglo-French area: "To the intellectual entente, without which the alliance would be only a political combination, you have contributed greatly."[16] Louis Gillet also emphasized this Anglo-French theme in Maurois's work: "And for twenty years, Maurois continues to explicate to both nations those two mysteries which these two neighboring nations are, both of which are so similar and so close. He offers them a reciprocal course of psychology. He disentangles their 'complexes,' he dissipates their prejudices, he exposes to them their mutual reasons for esteeming and admiring each other. He has invented a kind of moral geography, a new notion. . . ."[17] However, Maurois's role as a conciliator is best summed up by himself:

England is the country which I know best and which I understand best, but I shall not go so far as to say it is a second native land for me. There are no second native lands. There is the native land, that is to say, the country in which one has been born, the country of one's language, the country of one's fathers. . . . I have esteem and affection for England and I desire her very close rapprochement with France. But in political matters nothing is transportable. Each nation is a living being who has lived for centuries. The millions of individuals who compose the nation have customs, ideas, and educational formations all their own and cannot resemble the millions of individuals of another nation. One can never bring peoples to resemble each other, but one can through explanation bring them to understand each other.[18]

Maurois's role in the sphere of international amity constitutes a crucial chapter in his career as historian and chronicler. More than a decade following World War II, which had firmly demonstrated the necessity for international cooperation, we find in his *Journal* (entry of April 8, 1957) the following remark that reveals his unrelenting conviction that his was a mission of conciliation between Great Britain and France: "More than ever the future of the world is going to depend upon the unity of the West. England remains the nation that is closest to us in civilization, common ideas, and finally age."[19]

Maurois's efforts in behalf of more intimate cultural and political rapport between the United States and France are somewhat less well understood than his Anglo-French activities. This may well be the case because he discovered America much later in his career and only after he had already been universally acclaimed for his efforts in behalf of Anglo-French cooperation. In his sole monograph on André Maurois, Jacques Suffel is among the few systematically to accentuate the American posture of Maurois, and he even writes an entire chapter aptly entitled "Amicus America." Prior to or soon after his publication of the *History of the United States* and the *Parallel History of the U.S.A. and U.S.S.R.,* Maurois had written a number of minor works all devoted to his fascination with contemporary American history. These chronicles include *L'Amérique inattendue (The Unexpected America)* (Paris: Mornay, 1931), *Chantiers américains (American Work Projects)* (Paris: Gallimard, 1933), two volumes of journals, *Etats-Unis 39, Journal d'un voyage en Amérique* (Paris: Editions de France, 1939) and *Journal Etas-Unis 1946* (Paris: Bateau ivre, 1946).

D. *The Works of History as Works of Literary Art*

The major histories of André Maurois should be treated as the product of an accomplished creative artist who applied to them his finest stylistic techniques and refined them until he considered them finished works of art. Maurois really wrote his histories not for the erudite specialist but rather for the non-specialized public-at-large. Nonetheless, distinguished scholars like Dean Christian Gauss of Princeton and Hamish Miles did indeed hold these histories in high esteem. Maurois believed that his readers could learn much from the facts of the past, provided that these facts were interestingly and clearly presented to them. Like another artist-historian, Voltaire, Maurois considered his function to be that of a vulgarizer, in the best sense of the term. To vulgarize the history of three major countries signified, in this case, the joy of simplifying, organizing, explicating, and dramatizing for a popular audience a vast collection of data that might otherwise be palatable only to a limited group of specialists. Accuracy is a *sine qua non* for the specialist historian, but in itself it is not sufficient to stimulate the interest of a lay public. The historian who wishes to communicate with a vast body of readers must go beyond the exigencies of accuracy and must incorporate the best characteristics of the teacher (clarity, order) and the literary artist (style, polish). Like Renan and Toqueville before him, André Maurois "knew how to unite learning and style."[20]

Maurois utilized every time-honored device of the pedagogue. For instance: rhetorical questions, outlines, and Cartesian classifications; illustrations of abstract concepts by utilizing concrete examples; statistics and graphs. But as an artist he also resorted to the more commonly accepted devices of literary art: concise narrative form; lively anecdotes and digressions of human interest; humor and wit; literary portraits and vignettes; metaphors and similes; dramatic visual scenes; wordplay; a rich and abundant use of adjectives; alliterative effects; antitheses; maxims; etymological references. The admixture of these devices seemed to enliven the readability of what otherwise might have resulted in a sequence of dull historical facts. Below are a few examples of what I mean. As an example of a visual scene, we "see" the aging Titan William Pitt appearing before Parliament to protest the Treaty of Paris of 1763: "He came himself to Parliament to protest. . . . Held up by his servants, leaning on crutches, his legs enveloped in flannel and hands in heavy gloves, he spoke for three hours, in spite of terrible suffering, claiming for his country the monopoly of world commerce, preaching hatred of the Bourbon House, predicting the impending grandeur of the House of Brandenburg." Maurois the dramatic painter in words concludes: "It was a tragic and grandiose scene . . ." (p. 553). As an example of Mauroisean humor we read: "Louis IX and his young wife, whose bedrooms were located on top of each other, were forced, in order to get around the surveillance of Blanche, Louis' overly domineering mother, to meet on the staircase, which did not prevent them from having eleven children." Here is an example of his human-interest anecdotes:

Here is placed a romantic and revealing episode of the mores of the time. Robert was in love with his cousin Berthe, daughter of the King of Burgundy; he detested his wife, who was much older than he, who was forced upon him, repudiated her, and as soon as he was made king, married Berthe. The Pope ordered the spouses and cousins to separate because they were relatives at a prohibited level. Robert was obstinate; the realm was placed under interdiction. In 1001, the excommunication triumphed over love. Robert left Berthe but, in 1011, unable to live without the woman he loved, he took a trip to Rome to implore the Pope. The latter was inflexible and Robert yielded.

Of course, these three humanized histories would be little more than a loose mosaic or string of portraits, if all they contained were portraits. But these are not stationary and unconnected images. Maurois makes his characters move and act in live fashion. As a novelist he was aware of how important it was to place his characters in dramatic situations. For his histories he did not have to invent dramatic incidents. The scenes from the lives of the crusader Saint Louis, the soldier-president Ulysses S. Grant, or the now-tempestuous, now-placid relationship between Queen Elizabeth and the Count of Essex were tailor-made for dramatic presentation.

E. The Distinguishing Qualities of Each of the Histories

Each of the three major histories of Maurois can claim certain distinguishing features that set it apart from the other two. Because *The History of England* was Maurois's first venture in the genre, he did not yet seem to realize the importance of well-documented footnotes and references. The scholarly reader cannot fail to be irritated by the absence of references in support of Maurois's abundant quotations. Despite the absence of footnotes, the quotations themselves are in almost every instance well selected and pertinent to the topic.

Maurois enumerates and reiterates certain basic constants that unify British history throughout the centuries. First, he stresses the insularity of the country; second, the fact that this insularity is attenuated by proximity to the nations of the continent; third, because of this geographical closeness, the British have always felt insecure as a result of the real and imagined threat of cultural and military invasion from the outside; fourth, Britain is a crossroads-nation for two principal cultures, Roman and Teutonic; fifth, Britain has set up a cult of the navy, which it regards as its principal defensive shield as well as its main instrument of imperialism and foreign trade; finally, Britain has utilized its navy successfully to transmit its highly developed culture to virtually every corner of our planet.

As for the *History of the United States,* Michel Droit set it apart from the other works for one reason: Maurois leaps from scene to scene in it with such titanic force that through his stylistic strength and speed he recaptures the energetic nature of the American people. Droit continues: "*L'Histoire des Etats-Unis,* constructed like a film scenario, develops with the overdriven rhythm which was that of the most extraordinary political and human blossoming of modern times."[21] Unlike the single-volume *History of England,* this work is comprised of two separate tomes, the first extending from Columbus's discovery of America in 1492 and ending with the opening of President Andrew Jackson's term in 1828; the second moving from 1828 until 1940 and the advent of World War II. Above all, we cannot overemphasize that this is the work of a Frenchman who writes mainly for French readers. Hence the historian refers constantly to French comparisons like these: "Lincoln, like Richelieu, had assured himself of the triumph of central power" (2:111). Or else: "The Reconstruction became a Revolution in which Stevens and his friends were the Jacobins" (2:126). Also, as a Frenchman, Maurois tended to stress the role played by the French in the colonization of the New World and above all in the American War of Independence. The author of *Adrienne ou la Vie de Madame de la Fayette* inserted into this text a complete chapter on the French Revolution and its relationship with American history. He saw the emergence of the American state as an outgrowth of various European phenomena; thus he devoted many pages on the Americans to events in Paris, London, Madrid, Amsterdam, and Lisbon, as he discussed the explorations and mercantile activities of the European nations in the western hemisphere. Stressing that Latin-American history was a part of United States history and vice-versa, he included many sections devoted to historical events in Venezuela, Chile, and along the river Plata (the exploits of San Martín, Bolivar, and O'Higgins). These he combined with parallel events of history in the northern half of the hemisphere (see vol. 1, secs. 5 and 6). Because he had no axe to grind—for he was both an Americanophile and an Anglophile—he confronted the American Revolution not as a biased partisan, but as someone who saw the justices and injustices committed by both parties. Maurois contended that, in general, "it [the Revolution] was an unfortunate affair in which the responsibilities were shared" (1:141) (see his summation of the British point of view, 1:136).

As a European he could be objective toward many of the not-always-altruistic activities of the American nation. Ideals like "Manifest Destiny," he demonstrated convincingly, were not so idealistic as they were expansionistic. Of the annexation of the lands north of the Rio Grande River he wrote: "It was not an annexation, but rather a forced sale" (2:49). Nonetheless, his overall view of the Americans was favorable. In his concluding note he confidently proclaimed that no nation had over the years served the cause of human justice so well as America.

Probably the most authoritative and most translated historical opus by André Maurois was his *History of France.* Nurtured since infancy on French history, he knew it best. In contrast with the Anglo-American histories, this one has a few footnotes, although not enough to satisfy his most erudite critics. Maurois quotes so extensively that it is indeed a pity that he did not demonstrate in his three histories the same scholarly meticulousness that is apparent in his greater postwar biographies. Yet the *History of France* gives every indication of solid erudition, and Michel Droit does well to state that ". . . his *Histoire de la France* is a patient search for the reasons for which through the centuries France became France and why the French have become what they are today: [This *History* is]a [carefully] thought out, impartial, and profound study."[22]

In reality, Maurois was a very partial historian; that is, he was very partial in behalf of France. Although he does not gloss over her mistakes of the past, there is no denying the fact that his French history is a work written by a fervent Frenchman proud of his nation's accomplishments.

The rhythm of this work is regrettably uneven: occasionally the author lingers too insistently over certain events, while at other times he dismisses whole epochs too summarily. For example, after an overly protracted description of Roman civilization, he leaps over the fall of Rome so quickly that we almost do not realize the importance of this momentous event (see 1:33).

He could not deal with the developments in the various arts with adequate detail and still do justice to the political history of the country. Thus, in a single ironic sentence, he covers all of mid-nineteenth-century French music—and Gounod and Berlioz: "In the world of music, Charles Gounod, a happy talent, triumphs with facility, but also with justice, whereas the great Hector Berlioz, overwhelmed by the ctitics, dies in 1869 without his genius being recognized" (2:221). In contrast, the section from which this overly brief citation is drawn, "Le Temps des Oscillations" ("The Time of Oscillations"), is a maze of minute political and social analysis.

One of the high points in his French history is Maurois's depiction of the Napoleonic era, which he presents almost as if it had been a five-act classical play, an incredible comedy (or tragedy?) that is stranger than fiction. Yet we cannot help regretting that Maurois stressed so much the international role Napoleon Bonaparte played—his battles, power politics, the kings he appointed, the victories and defeats—that he had little to say of Napoleon's achievements on the domestic scene. It is not until the very end of the section that he deals with Napoleon's contributions to the internal life of his nation. Had the historian synchronously combined both aspects, Napoleon might have appeared to his readers less as a comic figure and more as a complex, paradoxical character.

In the chapters concerning World War II, the discerning reader senses Maurois's personal involvement in the tragedy of the French defeat and his guarded hope that France would yet achieve a position of grandeur following Liberation. Because the history was written in America, it is obvious that he attempts to justify the French disaster in order to dispel misunderstandings held by his American readers over the reliability of their old ally. (see 2:322).

In most editions, Maurois's *Histoire de la France* is published in two volumes: the first, from prehistory until the Revolution; the second, from the Revolution of 1789 until the midway point of the twentieth century.

F. The Chronicles of Maurois's Own Period

Maurois's historical gaze moved both retrospectively into bygone eras and also across the decades of the age during which he lived. Continuously seeking to recapture contemporary events as they occurred from week to week, he analyzed, described, and evaluated in his daily writings the moments he himself had witnessed. His private papers contain numerous daily jottings, scribblings, and more formal entries that later figured in his journals, memoirs, and in syndicated columns scattered in dozens of newspapers in France and around the world. He was ever sensitive both to the most minute and also to the momentous happenings of his lifetime.

His commentaries on current events can logically be classified under the heading of "Chronicles," that is to say, the history of the contemporary scene. This aspect of his career belongs in the same category with his historical work, for it is really an extension into the present of his probings into the past. He wrote his chronicles from day to day as noteworthy events caught his interest or fancy. Newspaper deadlines and the swiftness with which he had to record what he saw did not permit the leisure needed for stylistic refinement. This branch of his writing belongs to the realm of historical journalism.

As in the case of the *Histoires*, most of his chronicles dealt with the three countries he knew most familiarly: England, the United States, France. His reactions to current events in these three nations were sought by the leading metropolitan dailies and periodicals on both sides of the Atlantic. André Maurois was commissioned to do an impressive number of articles, prefaces, and essays involving the events he had attended: for example, the spectacular pageantry of the state visit to France by King George VI and Queen Elizabeth in 1938 (whose festivities he reported on extensively in the *London Morning Post* of July 19, 1938, and for *Le Figaro* of the same date). One of his best chronicles in 1950, entitled "Le Vrai Truman," included eleven lengthy installments on the life and contributions of the often misunderstood and (at that time) underestimated American president, who, Maurois predicted, would occupy a place of first rank among United States chiefs of state of all history. This series, commissioned by the newspaper *France-Soir* for its issues between December 5 and 17 of that year, today represents a significant piece of writing on Truman's political philosophy. Maurois's lifelong fascination with the parliamentary traditions of Great Britain led him to record the period of British political history coinciding with the tenures of Prime Ministers Stanley Baldwin and Neville Chamberlain (see "Après la Retraite de Stanley Baldwin— Portrait d'un Homme d'Etat" in *Les Nouvelles Littéraires* of August 14, 1937, and "L'Angleterre de Neville Chamberlain in *La Gazette de Lausanne* of June 28, 1938).

While Maurois's position as a chronicler of his age reached its apex of activity during the thirties, even as a septuagenarian and as an octogenerian he was frequently asked to record his personal views of the world in which he lived.

In many ways the *Histoire parallèle des U.S.A. et de l'U.S.S.R.*, which Maurois co-authored with Louis Aragon, falls squarely within the realm of "chronicles" and not in the category of "histories." A large portion of the contents of this four-volume publication is devoted to events of the most recent historical vintage. The section entitled "Conversations with Several Eminent Americans" in volume 4 should be regarded as journalism in the strictest sense. Consisting of tape-recorded interviews between Maurois, on the one hand, and a large group of prominent Americans, on the other, made during December of 1960, the work offers a stimulating series of discussions on life in America in the mid-twentieth century.[23]

Several of Maurois's published volumes must be classified together with his hundreds of articles and prefaces as part of his collected body of chronicles. In future eras, when scholars and historians seek to trace the daily movements of life during the thirty-year span of 1920–1950, they will be well advised to consult Maurois's *Livres de circonstance,* all of which form a valuable collection of source-documents on our contemporary society. The American journals previously referred to are key documents on the New World. We relive whole years of the author's life. Through his eyes we perceive the excitement of the Bikini atomic tests, the effects of the Constellation airplane that had just been ordered grounded because of minor structural defects, and the impression on American theater audiences made by *Henry V* as performed by Lawrence Olivier.

World War II was indisputably the greatest human drama Maurois the chronicler had recorded for posterity. Aside from his articles and prefaces, we see this catastrophe best in his book-length publications dramatizing the holocaust in his own inimitable manner. If we were to arrange these volumes in their chronological order, we would have a complete and systematic chronicle of the period, starting with the prewar epoch through the aftermath. Maurois analyzes the background leading up to the war in *Les Origines de la guerre de 1939 (The Origins of the War of 1939)* (Paris: Gallimard, 1939). His most poignant pages are reserved for his description of the fall of France in June of 1940: *Tragédie en France (Tragedy in France)* (New York: Editions de la Maison française, 1947). The postwar years of Liberation and rebirth are reached when this chronicler recorded the impressive moral and material regeneration of France during the decade following the termination of hostilities; see *Portrait de la France et des Français (Portrait of France and of the French)* (Hachette, 1955) and *La France change de visage (France Changes Faces)* (Gallimard, 1956). It is in this latter work, especially, that one recognizes in Maurois a truly well-informed observer of French industry, education, urban renewal, unionism, agriculture, and the postal and railway systems. A sleeping giant, Maurois noted, has arisen and has rebounded with unprecedented vigor. Yet he remains only cautiously optimistic; he knew that many of the key human and national problems still remained to be resolved.

Two of Maurois's best-written works are documentary chronicles on the city in which he received his education, Rouen. They deserve to be categorized both with his most serious works of literary art and with his documentary almanacs of contemporary history. Together *Rouen* (Paris: Gallimard, 1929) and *Rouen dévasté* (Paris: Nagel, 1948) form a bipartite testimonial to a town that he knew and loved intimately.

After describing the Rouen of his childhood, he donned the hat of a "war correspondent" and utilized every trick he had learned in his other literary genres; familiar enumerative series abound everywhere: "The ramp was very quickly located, marked, attached, pounded, annihilated." Then there are his figures of speech; the destroyed Rouen he characterizes as a theater whose "gaping face let us see, as in the decor of a theater, beds, toilets, privies, an entire pitiless intimacy which was perched on a high place" (p. 18). His prose assumes some of the tensions and repetitious sounds we associate with the finest poetry of Charles Péguy:

> Prudent city. Wise city. City which, with Strasbourg, is in all of France the one which best preserved a thirteenth-century quarter intact. City which, with Marseille and Le Havre, knew how best of all to become a twentieth-century port. City with a hundred bell-towers and a hundred chimneys. City of the countryside and of industry; city-capital and city-museum; river city and ocean city. Complete city. (Pp. 138–39)

All of which reminds us that Maurois the journalist-chronicler-historian and Maurois the literary artist were quite often one and the same man. Maurois was essentially a poetic being.

Rouen was not the only city Maurois loved so intensely and whose modern life he recorded. He had composed several excellent guidebooks in which he used to advantage his experience as a chronicler who was sensitive to the ceaseless changes going on in various parts of the world. He described the historical changes of New York City.[24] Demonstrating that he knew Manhattan well, he spoke authoritatively not only of the midtown distrinct in which he lived but also of Harlem, the lower East Side, Westchester, Brooklyn, and the New Jersey suburbs. Similarly, his guide to London is a substantial chronicle of that ancient city's urban transformation.

G. *Conclusion*

Maurois's contributions as a historian-chronicler ought not to be compared to those of the lifelong professionals or academicians in the field. Rather should we regard him as a novelist and short-story writer who used his cumulative experiences as a biographer and moralist to create some of the most readable and lucidly organized histories ever written by an author who was first and foremost a leading literary artist. That his histories manifest both his finest traits as a verbal artist and an impressive degree of factual authenticity is a point worth noting here. Future assessors of the literary life of twentieth-century France may find that, among the bellettrists of our era, Maurois the historian and chronicler may rank with very few other authors in a highly select circle.

Part VI
The World of Maurois's Criticism and Literary Philosophy

7
Maurois as Critic: His Philosophy of Art

Art brings remedy.
Maurois, in radio address from Lausanne Switzerland

André Maurois was the fruitful writer incarnate. His energies were so entirely consumed by the creation of novels, stories, biographies, essays, memoirs, and histories that he could scarcely find the time to write about the art of creation itself. Not once did he produce a book-length, systematic exposé of his philosophy of writing. Temperamentally, Maurois was a doer, not a theorizer or speculator.

To understand Maurois's aesthetics we have no choice but to turn to his short pronouncements diffused haphazardly throughout his large bibliography. In no single work did he sum up his views of the art of literary creation. But he often utilized his fictional alter egos, especially Bertrand Schmitt and Christian Ménétrier, to divulge some of his literary concepts. Also, in his critiques of the works of others, he revealed his own attitudes. Especially is this true in his biographies of literary figures. Additionally, one finds examples of literary self-analysis in his journals and memoirs. Book-length essays like *Un Art de vivre*, *Dialogues sur le commandement*, and *Alain* also contain occasional expressions of Maurois's philosophy of literary art.

A. Art and Life

Maurois's aesthetic philosophy is built around one constant proposition: namely, artistic creation is little more than the external manifestation of the thoughts, dreams, emotions, and experiences of the artist. Because of peculiar circumstances of life—perhaps resulting from some physical weakness, monetary impediment, or psychological maladjustment—the artist seeks to express himself through writing. In books, symphonies, or paintings artists find refuge from the cares of their daily life. The artist might have preferred to travel to distant lands, to enjoy the ecstasies of fulfilled love, or to derive pleasure from the ownership of material objects; however, various obstacles of life prevent the realization of these preferences. If he is a vigorous person, endowed with the talent and energies needed to translate his frustrations into concrete form, he may indeed succeed in producing a book or picture. Art can thus be considered as an outlet for pent-up feelings. It serves as a remedy.

Maurois remembered dreaming about becoming a writer since the earliest days of his childhood, when he first became conscious of the significance of literature. He assumed that other writers entertained similar dreams during their youth: "At the beginning of any writer's life, there is a vocation. A child experiences the need to express through words the sentiments and ideas which people and things inspire in him."[1] Maurois then develops the notion that those who become literary artists do so to compensate for some personal or physical handicap: "In general . . . the need to express oneself in literary form is born from a certain inadaptation to life, or from an inner conflict which the adolescent (or the man) cannot resolve through action."[2] The term *inadaptation* is inherent in Maurois's conception of the artist. If the writer had not been an "inadapté," he would probably have been content to adjust to the normal activities of life. In *Prometheus or the Life of Balzac,* Maurois restates the same idea: "Only the artist creates in a universe of which he is the God; as soon as he finds himself at grips with obstacles and hazards that he himself cannot master, he flees into his work, where the worst failures become his finest subjects."[3]

In evaluating Maurois's own personal experience, we note that he did not opt for a literary career because of failure to adapt himself to the nonliterary world. On the contrary, his successes in the military and as an executive in the world of business are impressive facts of his life. Voluntarily he renounced the normal life of action in his wool mill to seek in literature the personal gratification that he felt he could derive only from self-realization as a writer.

Maurois believed that the artist must live and suffer like all human beings. Unless he lived and suffered he would possess no substance with which to construct his works of art. Art necessarily reflects the lived experiences of human existence; otherwise it becomes hollow and meaningless. As Maurois put it, "It is then necessary that outside of his technical work (and in this respect he differs from the artisan) that the artist live or rather it is important for him to have lived."[4] Elsewhere he develops the same line of thought: "We note then that the life of the artist must be composed of at least three parts: one part of human, carnal, sentimental life, which alone is capable of teaching the poet the understanding of man; one part of meditation and solitary revery (the artist is a ruminator who must ceaselessly re-chew his past in order to digest it and transform it into artistic matter); and finally, one part of technical work."[5] The "technical work" is of course essential if the artist is to convert the raw materials from his life into literary form. In fact, the artist is a magician who must skillfully transform one kind of matter into another. The image of the creative artist as a magician runs through many of Maurois's writings and is most clearly enunciated in *In Search of Marcel Proust,* where Maurois demonstrated how Proust took the raw material of his life and, thanks to his magical powers, subjected it to a complete metamorphosis: "But the real objects of his loves, objects of delight and disgust, were these young unknown men who, by the charms of the magician, one day were to become metamorphosed into

Albertine."[6] Similarly André Maurois transformed Emile Herzog into fictional characters like Antoine Quesnay, Philippe Marcenat, and Bertrand Schmitt.

Is art a refuge into which the writer escapes from the cares of daily life in order to hide in some sort of ivory tower? Can the writer isolate himself hermetically from the frustrations of life? Or rather are art and life really indivisible? At first glance, Maurois's response might appear to be dichotomous. On the one hand, he acknowledged his escape into the artistic realm in search of greater satisfaction through fiction: "I discovered the joys of the author: to compose, arrange, especially to find refuge in a world created by him."[7] But this statement should not be interpreted too narrowly. While he did find certain joys in literary creation, joys that either circumstantially or physically he could not experience in daily living, he knew that what he had to say in his literary productions would have to reflect the experiences of his extraliterary career. To withdraw completely into artistic creation would seal him off from the most interesting subjects needed as the very basis of his artistic content. His novelette *Voyage to the Land of the Articoles* satirizes those artists whose lives consist only of art, men who have no other life outside of their books. In fact, Maurois gave would-be writers the following advice: "It is necessary that writing not make you forget to live. Style does not breathe in a vacuum."[8] Maurois's biographies reflect his own predilection for individuals who were energetic actors on the stage of life as well as in the wings of art: Byron, Hugo, Sand, Chateaubriand, Dumas père. One of the men of his own era whom Maurois esteemed most deeply was Romain Rolland. During two world upheavals, he refused to escape from the mêlées of men, even when he appeared to have assumed an unpopular position. Maurois applauded the author of *Jean Christophe* for being "full of scorn for the false brave men who waged war in the pages of the newspapers. . . ."[9]

Once, only once during his lifetime, when his friend the critic Charles Du Bos introduced him to the intellectual circle at Pontigny, did Maurois ever associate himself as a participant on a full-time basis with a literary group. Maurois's *Voyage to the Land of the Articoles* depicts this group of extremists in an openly condemnatory and satirical manner: "The great weakness of the Articoles seems to me to be that they have lost contact with life. In a normal society an artist must struggle, at least during his youth; he retains memories of it, loves, hatreds, finally some intense feelings."[10] Repeatedly, Maurois employs the term "contact with life" as a basic prescription for the would-be man of letters.

He realized that once the writer had embarked upon his formal career, the formulation of his books would almost inevitably become a full-time habit of existence, with little leisure left him for nonliterary life. Therefore Maurois hoped that at least the writer as a young man would enjoy a rich existence: "First a long preparatory contact with real life," he adds; "then a very large effort of work!"[11]

But the artist may necessarily need to express in literary form these rich experiences at some later interval in life, an interval that will enable him to view them from an appropriate distance in time and place ("recul"). He can then describe them with detachment and with objectivity. Maurois clarified his position on the relationship between art and life: "The only real paradises are the paradises which one has lost. The possibilities of the hours, which are so full and so beautiful, of childhood will never be reborn, except for a few brief love affairs, which bring back enthusiasm and innocence to us for a time. But in order to discover the magical world of childhood, in order to paint it, in order to transform it into fictional matter, it is necessary to remove oneself from it, and that is what Proust could not do, so long as his parents were alive."[12] If the artist tries to copy what he has lived during the act of living, he runs the risk of copying it too closely and with an excess of photographic precision. And art is not a mere copy of life; it is really a transformation or an interpretation of it.

B. Art as the Action of Life

André Maurois, a fundamentally intellectual human being, sought to eradicate from his texts a purely cerebral approach to literature. He held the conviction that such an approach stifled the glow of human warmth on the pages of a text.

Only sincerity and sentiment can enflame the otherwise icy pages of books. He cites as the most serious defect in American literary criticism its over-intellectualization of artistic questions. The new American literary critics, Maurois asserted, diminished their creative warmth out of fear of revealing their personal emotions and by not admiring works of art that reflected the heart as well as the mind: "Cocteau understood the weakness of American criticism which almost always deceives itself because it is afraid of deceiving itself, and which prevents one of the best publics in the world, one of the most sensitive, from abandoning itself innocently to its tastes and its passions. . . . At a time of cynicism, it can be an audacity to dare to show oneself to be sentimental."[13] Excessive intellectualization of the arts leads ultimately as Michel Droit voiced it—in reference to Maurois's *Voyage to the Land of the Articoles,* to a "hyper-intellectualisme," to a kind of "préciosité" in its worst form.[14] As a critic, Maurois did all he could to avoid these pitfalls. Purposefully he selected a nontechnical vocabulary. Purposefully he blended lucid analyses concerning the techniques of art with subjective and sincere impressions. Purposefully he addressed himself to the broadly educated public of nonspecialists, for nothing was more useless for the large body of cultured people, he believed, than criticism by specialists aimed at other specialists. Nothing annoyed him more than pedantry. Often he amused himself by pointing out in the monographs of even the most erudite scholars errors of fact.[15] Pedants and extremists concern themselves so much with technical jargon that they forget the more fundamental need for verity and sincerity: "Pedantry, which is always dull, becomes unpardonable when the pedant is not even well informed."[16]

Throughout his career Maurois placed his total faith in the following principle: An artist works of necessity. He cannot stop for too long a period of time to analyze what he wishes to do because analysis may prevent him from completing his grand design and may even lead him astray. Nor should the artist halt too lengthily in the process of creation to analyze what he is in the act of doing. The mere act of creation is so all-engulfing that the artist cannot possibly disengage himself from the total process of art without seriously endangering its fulfillment. Maurois was visibly unhappy when asked to discuss works in progress. In his *Balzac* he wrote that "a great artist does not know how he works. He tries to understand it by contemplating the finished work; he attempts to explain, through a system, the unity that is due to a temperament" (p. 448). In the same biography he explained further that: "Works are born, like institutions, like children, not out of a series of conscious acts, but out of the play of uncontrollable forces" (p. 265). It is in this statement that Maurois seemed to have come closest to a definition of the phenomenon of inspiration. Once the artist responded to the overriding call from within, he simply *acted.*

On the other hand, Maurois, who valued willpower so dearly, knew how paramount was the power of deliberate volition in defining the contours of a work once it had been started. He recognized the unavoidable necessity for the artist to make corrections, to control the steadiness of his hand, to make sound decisions. In the end, only after the author judges his work to be in as perfect a state as he can humanly compose it, is it ready for public release. Even then Maurois, speaking through the voice of Aurelle in the *Bramble-O'Grady* series, cautions the public to learn to appreciate the work without intellectualizing too intricately on its technical substance: "Ah! you see, Doctor, you must not talk of the arts; you have to observe and listen. I have always admired this saying of the old Renoir: 'Don't ask me to be objective or subjective, I shall confess to you that all of that makes no difference to me.'" And Aurelle's interlocutor, Doctor O'Grady, who seldom agrees with him, shouts out: "Ah! Messiou, how right that gentleman was!"[17]

C. The Living Artist and the Heritage of the Past

Maurois wisely recognized the inadequacy of instinct and inspiration as the sole sources of artistic creation. Only after a writer has been inculcated with a profound and broad knowledge of the masters of the past, only after he has comprehended the reasons for their successful accomplishments and failures, only then should he risk venturing forth on his own. "The style of the masters, once it has been studied over a long time, will give him [the new author] the instinct for language."[18] Perhaps the greatest criticism that can be leveled against Maurois's own novels is that in the matter of form they follow too closely some of the patterns of fiction evolving out of the French, Russian, and English novels of the past. He loudly proclaimed that "in literature we are always the son of someone."[19]

He insisted that many of the so-called innovations, the blatantly experimental phenomenon we call *Nouveau Roman*, or *Nouveau Nouveau Roman*, for example, were not so original as some of the vociferous exponents of novelty would have us believe. Merely because sentence and paragraph structures, the layout of chapters, unusual typographies, and uncommon uses of personal pronouns, catch our eye, deeply hidden beneath all of these superficial trappings we find in the newest novels the traditional attempt of writers of fiction to tell a story, to develop and study human psychology, to transport the reader into a different world of reality. Speaking of one of Michel Butor's novels, he jestingly wrote that "Certain critics state: 'It is a new form of the novel.' Not at all. The length of sentences, paragraphs without capitals are only accessories. The content remains the essential basis for the novel."[20] The conservative author of *Cercle de famille* did admit that "here is [Butor] one of the important authors of tomorrow—and of today," but precisely because this *Nouveau Romancier* belongs to the tradition of Balzac and Flaubert and Proust. In all likelihood, Butor, himself a specialist of Balzac, would readily agree with Maurois's line of reasoning. Maurois would be the last to discourage younger authors from producing new forms of expression. In most of his essays on contemporary literature, he praised originality and innovative style wherever he perceived their existence—in moderate dosages. But he was openly hostile to those who carried original effects to the point of excess.

In his lifelong campaign against the philosophy of newness for the sake of newness (he knew that in art total newness was an impossibility), Maurois warned us not to confuse deliberate complexity or "préciosité" with authentic originality. He may have been thinking of those critics who exaggerated the novelties of the Nouveau Roman and the so-called *Théâtre de l' Absurde*.

Maurois knew that younger readers, in particular, are more apt to be attracted to those aspects of art that *seem* fresh and entirely novel. Too often young readers prefer books composed by one of their chronological peers, believing that they have more in common with young authors than with men from preceding generations. Nevertheless, Maurois was confident that older men who kept abreast of the changing times could continue to hold a salutary influence over a public of youthful readers: "Pleasing youth, when one has oneself attained old age, is not impossible. Claudel is the proof of this. . . . A man lasts because he has expressed lasting sentiments. 'What ages most quickly is novelty,' Valéry used to say. That which by definition does not grow old is the eternal. Things that are sublime and natural do not have any age."[21]

D. Maurois's Method of Creation

Maurois revealed his method of writing during a personal interview with the well-known art critic René Huyghe:

The first image of a work, he [the author] catches a glimpse of in a burst of lightning. Then he tries to make a plan, a sketch. As soon as he begins his real work, he is led to tumble the plan upside down, to flow beyond the limits of the sketch. What has already been done is used as a model and as a priming for what is going to come. In my case, it often happens that I begin an article without any plan. *I know approximately what I wish to say. I have a title. I depart in search of discovery.* ("Journal," in *Carrefour*, March 28, 1956; my italics)

First, the need to create imposed itself upon the artist. In response to this impulse he begins to work. He acts. He creates. One act leads to the next act: "Once again the work engenders itself, what is done commands and calls forth what remains to be done."[22]

Artistic creation is a single, unified, and integral process and cannot be subdivided into such separate stages as inspiration, desire to create, composition, correction, and final realization of the project. Nor should one subdivide the substance from the author's life and personality into distinct components. Intuition, physical instincts, emotions, intellectual experiences, dreams, and muscular activity all form a single, indivisible phenomenon of writing. Maurois's philosopher, in his *Dialogues on Command*, suggests with exaggerated simplicity a view that will later be attenuated in subsequent works:

the movement of a thought at the moment of the decision is made by a thrust of the body, I have noticed it very clearly in artistic creation. There is nothing more beautiful than the avid glance, one that is almost ravenous, through which a great painter seems to take possession of his model. The great writer, in the confused mass of his notes, his filing cards, his memories, catches a sudden glimpse of his subject in a sort of flash of lightning.[23]

It follows that artistic creation represents the fusion of emotional and corporal (or muscular) gestures, on the one hand, with mental and intuitive activity, on the other. Nevertheless, this insistence on the suddenness of the "éclair"—the flash of lightning—combined with spontaneous action somehow does not truly conform to all of Maurois's creative processes, especially in his long biographies and major histories. He once avowed that even some of his short stories did not emerge with an immediate burst (see *Portrait of an Artist Whose Name is Me*, p. 83). It is true that the final completion of a short story was accomplished in a brief space of time, perhaps a week at his country retreat, but the theme for some of these stories he had been nurturing within him for a long time before. In the case of the longer works, the creative procedures are very different. His biographies of Balzac, Hugo, or Chateaubriand were the realization of years of dreams and meditations. Nor could he write his longer histories in flashlike bursts of muscular activity. Large-scaled works normally proceeded along deliberate and even arbitrary lines, and called for slow, methodical stages of work. These longer works conform to the order imposed upon the writer by the basic laws of chronology, if nothing else.

Because Maurois was a most deliberate artist, he designed his extra-creative experiences and his participation in the world around him so they might be built around his need to write texts. Maurois wrote not when the "éclair" of inspiration illuminated his creative faculties, but rather because and when he had planned his time to permit himself many unbroken hours of writing.

The composition of books Maurois transformed into a serious routine of life, even a daily habit: "No day is there without me trying to write at least a few lines. . . . The habit of writing is healthy if one imposes upon oneself the need to say exactly what one means without abandoning oneself to the facility of the cliché."[24] Hence, every morning at an early hour Maurois would seat himself in his sunlit study before the manuscript left unfinished the previous day and *tried* to write. When his spirit was charged with the fire of inspiration, he managed to write several pages in a brief period of time. When obstacles of expression and content asserted themselves, he wrote little, even though he had available to him several uninterrupted hours. What really mattered was that every morning Maurois the artist made an effort to create.

During these morning rites of artistic creation, he composed each sentence slowly, carefully; he reread his paragraphs, making corrections in them, changing terminology, punctuation, or phraseology. He literally struggled to write with precision and stylistic polish. Despite his innate facility, writing demanded arduous attention.

His manuscripts, even those written for the most trivial newspaper article—and above all for the major biographies and novels—reveal the unrelenting labors of a writer who spared no effort to correct his works and bring them to a point of perfection. His apparently easy flow of prose is illusory. His abundance is equally illusory. After all, after six decades of uninterrupted writing, it is natural to expect an abundance of texts. A glance at any page among his manuscripts will demonstrate the difficulty and care with which he formulated his thoughts and feelings on paper.[25]

An examination of his manuscripts divulges the following categories of alterations: A. Those which lent greater rapidity to the movement of the action; B. Elimination of redundancies and repetitious elements; C. The addition of precise descriptive adjectives and adverbs for greater specificity; D. The elimination of sentences and clauses in order to make room for ellipses; E. The insertion of proper names, possessive adjectives, and pronouns to clarify confused incidents and to eradicate vagueness; F. The insertion of whole sections to make the descriptions more colorful.

E. Traits of Maurois's Style

But all of the above discussion of Maurois's philosophy of the creative process is useless if it does not lead to a discussion of the author's own stylistic achievements. "Le style c'est l'homme." This celebrated remark, attributed in its somewhat modified form to Buffon, is one of the most famous slogans of French literary history. A man's style is the faithful exteriorization of his most intimate being, for in his style one has the right to search for the vibrant soul of the artist. Maurois illustrated this principle in one of his novels, when his fictional heroine Denise Herpain studies the text of one of her writer-friends in search of the presence of his personality in the very lines of the book: "She tried to find again, through the characters and the sentences, the man who had been her friend. This search was difficult. Denise recognized several elements, some names from Rouen, some sentences of Royer, but they were bathed in a richer paste that was formed by new acquisitions of life. Bertrand, since the war, had been writing and living in Paris."[26] Style necessarily reflects the events of an artist's life: the places he visited and knew, the people with whom he associated, the foods he ate, the objects he possessed, the personality that was his, the dreams he dreamt. The writer may wish to transpose the proper names he uses, so as not to identify too pointedly the real people and places he knew. He may also wish to make the physical trappings of his existence undergo a literary metamorphosis so that they do not too obviously reveal his own environment. On searching deeply within the layers of the "paste," we inevitably find certain recurring terms and traits that we soon learn to regard as cognates or constants of a particular artist's style. These are uniquely his own and can belong to no other writer. Individually some of these traits may be shared with other artists, but collectively they form the manner of expression of one unique creative being.

In the case of André Maurois, some critics felt that there was no need to analyze something that was already so clear. Maurois's obsession with simplicity and translucence seems to make analysis unnecessary. Some critics consider Maurois an author who left no mysteries to be solved. And critics thrive on mysteries! It is often most interesting for the scholar to launch a search for solutions to riddles erected by hermetic artists who cultivate obscurity. But Maurois's famous clarity is deceptive; as Robert Kemp metaphorically put it: "The luminous pages propose enigmas: this stream of pure water glides over a depth of algae and sand; we run the risk of being caught in it or being engulfed there."[27]

Maurois's works conform perfectly to the general patterns of traditional French literature. In his view, the finest, most characteristic French works of art do not stand out for their dramatic pathos, tear-jerking sentimentality, melodrama, inordinate or overwhelming force. Rather they are quiet, simple, restrained, refined, and solidly crafted: "It is the perfection of simple things which in France makes life worthy of being lived and which constitutes at the same time the culture of our country and its salvation."[28] He once pointed out to a midwestern American audience that the essential features of French music ("even in the depiction of the liveliest feelings") consisted of "order, simplicity, sensuality, no excess or emphasis whatsoever."[29] Certainly the style of André Maurois is an example of all of the foregoing elements.

During a moment of auto-analysis he outlined the most consistent features found in his writings. First, he maintained that there were in his texts no clichés or facile formulae. Second, he stated that he suppressed, as much as was feasible, conjunctive and connective terms (like "donc," "car," "mais,") and thus he could leap from section to section with little transition. Third, he avowed making heavy use of the "precision of scientific language," a language consisting of direct references, a minimum of indirect figurative expressions, and a modest-sized vocabulary limited to specific and concrete terms. Finally, he admitted his preference for condensation, brevity, compactness, above all for sledge-hammer endings ("end with a punch"). ". . . I like to end a chapter with a jolt or with a concrete detail, one that is a bit strange, which leaves the reader in a state of suspension and surprise." Then Maurois quoted from Alain, who had advised him to "reduce the preparatory passages to the minimum." Maurois added, "It is rare that a beginning is as abrupt as it should be." The author, he believed, ought to waste no time on nonessentials. Style should be reduced to its most skeletal necessities. On summing up his other stylistic predilections, Maurois noted his tendency to write clear, crisp, and vivid dialogues. He emphasized also his indebtedness to music, from which he learned to insert musical imagery into his prose and to use counterpoint, that is to say, the art of interlacing themes and leitmotifs. Finally, everything he did stylistically reflects his thirst for lucidity: "I have attached a capital importance to clarity," he announced.[30]

The book that most closely typifies his art is neither one of his novels nor one of his biographies. Rather it is *Choses nues (Bare Things)*, a work written when he was nearly an octogenarian. Not only does the title reflect the cardinal trait of his style—nudity—but this journalistic mosaic of tiny sketches, miniature scenes, bare outlines, and sparse portraits forms the literary testament of one man's lived experiences, thoughts, and reactions to the world around him. In *Choses nues* we confront the real André Maurois through the style of the man. In clear and terse style, with luminous sentences, Maurois recaptured his most unforgettable moments and emotions when he came in contact with some of the great intellectual and political leaders of his time: for example, Valéry, Pirandello, Churchill, Aristide Briand, Berthelot, Anatole France, Charles Du Bos. However, his narration transcends pure journalism, for he had had time (three decades!) to reflect upon the meaning of these events and to describe them in his own personal literary style.

F. The Algae and Sands of Overabundance

The sheer quantity of Maurois's works makes critics wince. Even experts have been put off by the sheer numbers of titles that Maurois produced. This colossal production may well be the product of the most fertile pen in twentieth-century French literature. Maurois had simply produced too much and interested himself in too many subjects to fit into the time available to most specialists. The author himself acknowledged his overabundance, which he described in the following metaphoric manner:

> The voyage towards posterity must be undertaken with light baggage. . . .
> Alas! I present myself at the customs office of criticism with an excess of
> baggage that is contrary to the regulations. At least, if these pieces of baggage
> were all of the same type, recognizable by some painted mark, by some giant
> and metaphysical sticker, it might be possible to gather them together. But
> no. . . . In reality, it is despairing to abandon this abounding disorder, in
> favor of some aggressively obscure and sterile author. And yet . . .[31]

This overabundant biographer was drawn to do the biographies of writers who were equally overabundant because he understood them so well. It is a fact that he produced no biographies of authors who wrote sparingly: Fromentin, Baudelaire, Mallarmé, Madame de La Fayette. Instead, he felt strong affinities for the titans of literature who poured forth incredible quantities of pages: Voltaire, Balzac, Byron, Hugo, Dumas père, Chateaubriand, George Sand. Of Dumas père's too great fertility Maurois wrote the following few lines that one is tempted to apply to the biographer as well! "It is astonishing to realize what this inexhaustible verve, this torrential cascade gives to the reader; this man who fills volumes as others fill pages. . . ."[32]

Did Maurois produce too many minor, frivolous titles which, by their astronomical numbers, are capable of submerging his more substantial literary monuments in their incessant tides? Some of Maurois's closest friends have often wondered why he wrote so profusely. Dr. Albert Delaunay once asked him: "Why do you work so much? . . . The books, I understand, but why all of these articles?" Here was Maurois's response: "The answer is simple:—Because it is my pleasure. Writing is, for me, a hygiene of the mind. I know that the books are essential, but they take a long time to terminate. An article is a brief flash of thought; I enjoy seeing it finished, cleaning it up, polishing it."[33]

In a personal interview with Maurois at his Paris home (on February 11, 1964), I rephrased the question of Dr. Albert Delaunay. I too was disturbed by his overabundance. I too suspected that out of Maurois's immense productive force there emerged minor articles that were not always equal to his finest compositions. He replied emphatically that there were in his literary career two completely different categories of writings: First, the writing that he wanted to produce. This writing, an integral part of his intimate self, yielded the great biographies and histories, the major works of fiction, the finest essays. Then there was a second category of work, obviously one that the author did not esteem so highly as the first, namely, the works forced upon him by external circumstances: the articles, prefaces, series for journalistic syndicates. Maurois mentioned his moral obligations to friends and his duty to write in behalf of certain causes in which he believed; he also mentioned his contractual obligations. Here one cannot overstress one aspect of Maurois's character—his acute sense of moral obligation to people and causes.

Was it a disgrace to write short works dictated by external necessities of one sort or another? In twentieth-century French literature, there is no more exalted writer than Paul Valéry. Yet Valéry composed some of his most successful works under the duress of a commitment to some outside party. In *Choses nues* (p. 189), Maurois defended "the literature of circumstance" as a legitimate concern of the artist. He emphasized that "Valéry loved to do commissioned works. Every constraint sustains the artist."

It is a fact that Maurois did yield much too often to pressures to write prefaces and introductory comments that today fill the pages of dozens of heterogeneous volumes and are scattered in all sorts of periodicals. Occasionally regretting his excessive generosity, he wrote: "I reproach myself for not having said *No* more often to those who asked me for a useless article, speech, or interview."[34]

If Maurois did indeed write too much, he did so because he had so many interests and such a broad range of curiosity, both literary and extra-literary. He wished to express his views on such subjects as cinema, politics, fashion, education, marriage, literary prizes, industry, science, war, and peace. He wrote a commentary entitled "The Art of Working," dealing with the fecundity of the painter Whistler. He may well have been thinking of his own personal example:

> Naturally, after this long research, the artist acquires an experience, a sureness of hand and style, which allow him, at certain moments and when he is perfectly aware of what he wishes to represent, to do it with a rapidity, with an immediate success that seem to the layman to be miraculous. Whistler made fun of those who reproached him for having painted a certain canvas in one hour. He could paint it in one hour because he had painted it during his entire life.[35]

What Maurois wrote during a single morning also often reflected what he had been writing and meditating during his entire existence.

T. The Writer and His Public

André Maurois was haunted by the question of relationship between the literary artist and the public for which he wrote. Maurois once composed a lengthy article on these question entitled, "The Writer and His Public" (in the *Gazette de Lausanne*, March 29, 1935), in which he maintained the position that the creative artist can consciously create for only one audience: himself. He further affirmed that the moment the writer consciously sought to write for a particular audience, he ceased to be faithful to himself and risked compromising the integrity of his position as an artist. In the same statement he stated flatly that the artist wrote "not because he thinks of reaching a public, but because he experiences the need to write."

After the manuscript has been converted into a published volume in the hands of an anonymous reader, it would be foolish for this reader to try to associate himself too closely with the man who had envisioned and formulated the work. The public must remember that a book represents in the life of an author but one brief moment out of a long sequence of many other lived moments. Like all men, the artist of today is not exactly the same artist who wrote the book yesterday. He moves on from one event in life to the next, undergoes transformations and fluctuations, and, in so doing, also moves on from one manuscript to the next. It is naive to assume that the Lamartine of "le Lac" was the identical human being who produced *L'Histoire des Girondins.* Similarly, we cannot expect the young André Maurois, who wrote the biography of Shelley, to write another similar biography thirty or forty years later in his life. Maurois once underscored this paradox of literary life: "For the works remain and man changes. The writer whom you meet is not the one whom you have read."[36] Thus, on launching his book, the writer disengages himself from it, leaving his audience free to interpret it as it sees fit. The author simply moves forward in life to the following assignment: his next book.

Maurois classified his readers into three categories: First, he distinguished those who would immediately reject his works: "There are people who ought not to read any of my writings, because they are not capable of loving them." These are the readers who would reject his books because of their clarity, simplicity, and unaffected style. Second: "At the other extreme, I can see my ideal reader, the one who, going beyond my hopes, is interested in everything I write, ardently devours my novels, biographies, essays; collects the slightest articles and knows my thought better than I myself. I experience in his behalf a natural and affectionate sympathy, but do not draw from his predilection any pride whatsoever. Every human being needs a certain spiritual nourishment. It just happens that to certain people I furnish the ingredients that are suitable for them." He recognized a third and larger category of readers, "an entire world of readers of good will who have no prejudices for or against a work which they do not know well or do not know at all."[37] This last group constitutes the greatest challenge for the literary artist.

This writer reflected seriously on the responsibility of the creative artists as a collective body vis-à-vis the public of laymen, which constituted another collective body. Although he tried to eliminate from his thoughts all concern for public reaction, he did sincerely believe in the obligation of the artist to uplift, to enrich, to improve the lives of his readers. He opposed those writers whose works appealed most directly to the lascivious appetites of a small segment of the reading public. Furthermore, he opposed the utilization of art for purposes of preaching, moralizing, and sermonizing: "The role of art," he wrote, "is to permit a disinterested contemplation. If the author preaches and blames, the work loses its beauty; if the author adopts distances, the reader is moved and understands."[38] Maurois believed that one could write constructively, and with edification, without necessarily having to preach the virtuous life. On the other hand, he averred that certain writers went too far in a negative direction; that is, they created universes comprised almost exclusively of monstrous types. He considered Tennessee Williams to be such an author:

> I must recognize it: Tennessee Williams is not an author with whom I get along. Too many monsters; too many storms in the air. I understand very well that there are, on this planet, tempests, but one cannot live in a state of perpetual electric boosting. There are quarrels, there are impotent types, there are alcoholics, but there are also the smiles of virile men and moderate drinkers. The danger of this infernal art is that it gives to many young people the impression that life is like this."[39]

Maurois was no puritanical writer who confined his presentation of the world to the angelic types. Many of his own fictional characters were far from being pure. And certainly his depictions of Hugo, George Sand, Chateaubriand, and Shelley paint these heroic figures in all sorts of sordid experiences. But the biographer demonstrated that these heroic people were also capable of rising to the loftiest summits of human behavior. At the end of his life Maurois restated his conviction that art must not always be all black, that the artist must paint much more than the bleak aspects of human life, that great art was imperishable because it contained moral values:

> The danger of our time, is not that one finds a few amoral beings, a few adventurers, bandits and scoundrels. This mire has always existed on the margin of our civilization. Our particular danger is that some writers believe in good faith that it is courageous to justify amoralism, the law of the jungle, and formless art. I am certain that they are mistaken. The great works of art, from Homer to Shakespeare, from Balzac to Proust, have always been impregnated with high moral values *which they suggested without expressing them.* It was like this at the beginning and it will be like this until the end.[40]

We should note in the citation above that Maurois does make a distinction between expressing a lofty moral lesson openly (in which case, literature degenerates into propaganda) and conversely suggesting the same lesson through indirect means (in which case the integrity of art has not been violated.)

However, in *Choses nues* Maurois unwittingly divulged his belief that there must be a limit to uncommitted art. When the artist's civilization is threatened, he must place himself at the service of his nation. He quoted Winston Churchill, who had once told him: "For your country and mine are running the risk of dying. . . . Culture, literature, that is very nice, but culture without strength soon ceases to be a living culture." We do not know what Maurois replied to Churchill at the time, but, in a post-scriptum, he disclosed the following meaningful reaction to Churchill's statement: "I never wrote, out of modesty and incompetence, the articles which Churchill has asked me to write, and I have never ceased to regret this."[41] In a sense, Maurois did contribute, in his own indirect and subtle manner, to the strength of western civilization. In effect, audiences may long consider his *History of France,* some of his biographies, a few of his critical essays on French literature, two or three of his novels, several of his short stories, as works written by an artist deeply aware of the dignity of art. These works form some of the most solid pillars supporting the French wing of the edifice we call Western Civilization. And what would that edifice be without its French literary wing?

Part VII
Summary and Conclusion

8
André Maurois and Posterity—A Personal Assessment

We might think that such universal spirits are not profound in any subject, and that in the act of vulgarizing, there is the idea of vulgar, but even that is not a very profound thought. It is certainly necessary from time to time, that syntheses be made and that there be writers who chew up again and again for the masses, the work done by the specialists. Without this effort an insurmountable breach would develop between the technicians and the man on the street, all of which would lead to great disorder.

Maurois, *Voltaire*

The works of creative artists can be thought of as monuments of sorts. In contrast with their original solidity, some of these monuments eventually decay with the passage of the years. Others, barely noticeable during the artist's lifetime, assume in the eyes of posterity a stark prominence. A few of the artist's monuments continue to resist the corrosive forces of time and the whims of an unpredictable posterity. It is appropriate now to pose one of the central questions about André Maurois: Where will the literary monuments that he so conscientiously constructed during his lifetime stand in the eyes of the posthumous public?

Ranking among our century's most productive literary artists, Maurois produced a most abundant and varied array of literary monuments. Unlike certain writers who deliberately sought to limit their productivity, Maurois, for his part, broadcast a bit too generously the seeds of his literary activity over the terrain of his epoch. After six fruitful decades of writing and armed with a remarkable stamina for work, he was able to write so many books that they do not readily lend themselves to reduced categorizations. The idle literary voyager is repelled by the vast reaches of Maurois's prose. His work defies easy negotiation. But for the dedicated and patient reader, contact with Maurois's books can be a most rewarding adventure.

It is now time to confront the totality of Maurois's literature. It is time also to measure its virtues and some of its limitations. Despite the enormity and variety of Maurois's productivity, the underlying architecture of his literary edifices does not lack either a sense of unity or an element of cohesiveness. In the first place, his works are held together by a restricted number of recurrent themes or leitmotifs: that is, "pudeur" or discretion, fidelity to one's friends and associates, the attainment of happiness through love, the cult for action, reconciliation among people and nations, the adaptation by individuals to the surrounding cosmos, respect for tradition and order, a strong sense of cosmopolitanism attenuated by patriotism. Maurois's works are further buttressed by an underlying similarity of tones: for example, his need for moderation, his horror of violence, his gentility and intellectuality, and his rational, analytical approach to the problems of the world. One is also impressed by his unquenchable drive to transform the mysteries of the universe into lucid and comprehensible formulae. Maurois's works, furthermore, bear the imprint of his personal literary style: his clear language, his simple elegance and elegant simplicity, his special kinds of sentences and word-order, his private reservoir of vocabulary. His fiction and even his biographies are also cemented together by his own repertory of faces, places, and atmospheres. We see in his prose fiction the recurrent scenes of the Dordogne and Normandy countrysides; we hear there the throbbing pulsebeat of Paris's glittering salons; we feel the reverberations of the English and American landscapes. His life of George Sand contains many of the same characters from his lives of Dumas père, Victor Hugo, and even Tourguéniev. Maurois's literary environment is his alone and that of no one else.

Essentially an autonomous, almost isolated figure, Maurois associated his name with none of the myriad "isms" clogging the horizons of twentieth-century literature. He could not subordinate his own intellectual freedom to the requirements of a single doctrine, creed, or party. Interested in philosophical dialogues, he belonged to no philosophical school. In a century replete with so many literary fads, André Maurois worked as an independent artist concerned only with writing the best possible prose that he was capable of producing. It did not disturb him that his own approach to artistic excellence did not relate to the movements that formed the rage of his lifetime.

Where will posterity position this author in the general scheme of French literary history? Will there be a permanent niche reserved for him in the rich web of his country's ongoing literary heritage? Maurois was the first to insist that no artist toiled in a historical vacuum. Thus he believed that through his pen he continued the work of a great many of his precursors. Rooted in the conventions of the past, he was reluctant, especially in the domain of prose fiction, to break ties with the conventions of yesteryear. Literary history he held in the highest reverence. He believed that textual criticism and the history of literature were inextricably intertwined. This is a natural position for a literary biographer to assume. In many ways Maurois the twentieth-century novelist perpetuated the proven narrative traditions of Madame de La Fayette, Stendhal, Balzac, and Flaubert. As a moralist, Maurois is yet another link in the brilliant chain of French moralists that includes Montaigne, La Bruyère,

Joubert, Vauvenargues, Renan, and Alain. As a biographer, historian, and critic, he injected into his writings many of the ingredients from the biographies, histories, and critical essays of Voltaire, Sainte-Beuve, Taine, and Faguet. More a preserver of the values of the past than a zealous practitioner of innovation for the sake of innovation, Maurois did, nonetheless, add new dimensions of his own to the literary treasure chest he inherited from the past. Especially noteworthy were both his receptivity to liberal tendencies on the part of other writers and the encouragement he gave to promising young talent. Although he himself scarcely indulged in bold experimentaions of form, he appreciated the inventiveness of others. In the tradition-bound Académie Française, André Maurois represented a hospitable and liberal voice that defended the originality, novelty, and bold creativity of many of the newest movements of the century.

I personally perceive Maurois as a kind of eighteenth-century *philosophe* who has undergone reincarnation in the nuclear age. He reminds me of Voltaire, the subject of one of his most delightful and underestimated biographies. Like the author of *Candide*, Maurois was one of the important vulgarizers of his age. He was a vulgarizer in the best sense of the term; I mean that he assumed for himself the mission of digesting, interpreting, and transmitting to the broadest possible international public highly sophisticated and complex knowledge. And he did so in strikingly clear language. Maurois can also be thought of as a reductionist of information. Not that he reduced information to simplistic terms! Rather, with impressive literary artistry, he reduced complexity to a distilled essence of comprehensibility. In a word, he replaced obscurity with transparency.

The histories of England, the United States, and France; the scientific probings of Sir Alexander Fleming; the creative processes of Olympian and Promethean giants like Balzac, Hugo, Byron, and Proust; the subtle political temperaments of Disraeli, Lyautey, and Edward VII—these were the vital human experiences which, when interpreted by the logical mind and lucid pen of an André Maurois, were transported into the range of understanding of many reading publics scattered around the world. Did not Voltaire perform similar miracles in his histories, essays, and letters?

But Maurois was more than a modern-day version of Voltaire; he was also something of a twentieth-century Diderot. Like the eighteenth-century Encyclopedist, he manifested an insatiable curiosity about an infinite repertory of subjects. The mind of André Maurois, like that of Denis Diderot, touched on many spheres of human interest. Maurois's medley of interests included among others the following: the psychology of love, the political systems of nations, the processes of international diplomacy, contemporary industrial and financial issues, age-old metaphysical problems, the arts, sciences, and literatures of many lands and historic periods. Like Diderot, Maurois expressed his alter ego through the medium of dialogues rich in paradoxes and ironies. Like Diderot too he scattered the pollen of his talent in a great many (possibly too many) articles and genres. As with Diderot, Maurois scholars will keep discovering, for the next hundred years, previously unknown little gems: prefaces, micro-essays, newspaper articles, sketches, aphorisms, and letters. Maurois's literary corpus will continue to offer the literary prospector a virtually inexhaustible supply of surprises.

I cannot help ranking Maurois among the best storytellers of the twentieth century. By his clarity, wit, satirical tendencies, and lightness of touch, he reminds us once again of Voltaire, possibly also of Mérimée, and most as-suredly of Anatole France. Maurois mastered the art of condensation by saturating his prose with sprightly dialogues, rapidly paced plots, and carefully selected vocabulary. Louis Chaigne predicted that the formal perfection of Maurois's short stories will place him within the "classical heritage [of short fiction]." R. M. Albérès expressed wonderment at these "rapid tales, master-pieces in a few pages," and asked if anyone during our century would ever be capable of replacing André Maurois in his domain. François Mauriac enter-tained no doubt about the permanence of Maurois's stature as a short-story writer and expressed warm admiration for "cet art, le mieux fait, à mon avis pour durer" ("This art, the best one made, in my opinion, to endure."). Ed-mond Jaloux predicted that one day Maurois's unique stories would rank alongside those of Mérimée and even Maupassant; he foresaw the day when these works would be included in the future anthologies of the best-written short stories. Jaloux's prediction had already been largely realized during Maurois's lifetime, for the latter's short stories were already commonly in-cluded in the textbooks of many countries' educational systems.[1]

Maurois's consummate talent as a storyteller transcended the genre of the short story; his longest and densest volumes of biography and history have been so readable largely because of his ability to recount the events in them with vividness and verve. The same can be said for his novels. As a novelist, he occupies a certain place among the writers of his century. His early "metaphys-ical" novels, *Les Silences du Colonel Bramble* and *Les Discours du Docteur O'Grady* have continued to charm readers during more than half a century following their initial appearance. The characters "Bramble" and "O'Grady" have already joined the living mythology of modern fiction. *Climats,* one of the most personal and beautifully written novels produced during the first half of the twentieth century, although not the success in the Anglo-American world that it was in the Latin countries, may well be regarded as a potential French classic. Works like *Terre promise* and *Cercle de famille* have been read by hundreds of thousands of persons in dozens of countries. Though Maurois's novels are not dramatic works dealing with earth-shattering problems of the human condition, they encourage the reader to float in a world of vaporous climates, lacy style, lingering moods, and shimmering experiences. His fictional works lack a certain brooding quality. Unlike a Franz Kafka, for example, he did not change the world's consciousness of literature. There is a universally acknowledged term, *"Kafkaësque,"* to denote a special kind of awareness of contemporary human experience. No such new awareness derives from the literary works of André Maurois. Instead of adding his own original literary dimensions, Maurois excelled at interpreting and explicating the literary contributions of writers like Kafka and Camus. As an interpreter, as an explicator, he had few peers!

In an age of violence, terrorism, and blatant crudeness, how comforting it is to escape into the pleasant atmosphere of Maurois's novels! Whereas the modern reader has learned to accommodate himself to a literary style that is at once immediate, spontaneous, even in some cases totally incoherent or deliberately perplexing, Maurois's prose has always been carefully constructed and phrased in tightly controlled paragraphs and sentences. In fact, it is a relief sometimes to escape from the tons of amorphous and instant expressionism pouring forth from so many of today's most respected authors and enjoy the rational, well-organized, and lucid prose style of an André Maurois.

If all of Maurois's novels were read during a single segment of time, they would form an intertwining Human Comedy—a small-scaled Human Comedy when compared to that of Balzac, to be sure, but not an insignificant one! Like the contrapuntal melodies in a symphony, Maurois's characters, landscapes, and episodes crisscross from novel to novel. The lives of his fictional offspring, starting during the first decades of our century, halt abruptly with the advent of World War II. But Maurois's Human Comedy was not intended to end there. On August 12, 1964, the octogenarian Maurois once confided as follows:

> The novel that I needed to compose, that novel required that I take all the people of the society I had created; I need to show what they did in 1938—then during the war—and then show that after the war their destiny had changed. But unfortunately I am perhaps too old. But I must, nevertheless, begin and stop en route, if necessary.[2]

Destiny granted Maurois the time to travel along his route long enough to fulfill his dream, at least partially. Before his death he had come close to completing a collection of short stories entitled "Les Retours." This collection ought to be regarded as the coda to Maurois's symphonic cycle of fiction. For the sake of expedience, he decided in 1966, just before his death, not to try to write a single novel combining his characters, generations, and milieux into a unified world; instead, it seemed easier for him to write a series of short stories in which he could delineate the final stages in the lives of his novelistic figures. In "Les Retours" Bertrand Schmitt has finally been accepted into the French Academy. Denise Herpain Holmann has married off her daughter. Like Maurois's own wool mill of Fraenkel et Herzog in Elbeuf, the textile empire of the Quesnay family has been effaced by the vicissitudes of World War II. The aging Academician, Guillaume Fontane, is left with little more than some nostalgic reminiscences about his exciting love affairs of yesteryear. One by one, each of these characters made his or her final bow on the proscenium of Maurois's private Comédie Française.

If Maurois's novels lack the transcendental anguish or tragedy that we have come to associate with the greatest novels of all time, his biographies, on the other hand, depict some of the most dramatic examples of human triumph and tragedy experienced by men and women of any age. It is hard to imagine existences that are more impressive than those lived by a Shelley, a Byron, an Alexandre Dumas père, or a George Sand! It is as a biographer that Maurois's contribution has been most widely recognized. His supremacy as the "Prince of Biographers" of the twentieth century is almost a fact of literary life. This image is the one that Maurois will probably project most distinctively in the eyes of posterity. He possessed that special blend of literary style and scholarly competence needed to illuminate the lives of his writers, statesmen, and other historical figures. Thanks to Maurois's biographies, these figures have acquired a special glow that will not easily be extinguished. Out of the murky windows of the past, Maurois's biographical heroes surge forth in rugged relief. Their "exemplary destinies" assume additional dimensions of vividness. It is no mere coincidence that the first major posthumous monograph to appear on Maurois was Judith Kaufmann's *Aspects d' André Maurois Biographe* (Paris: Diffusion Ophrys, 1980). Mrs. Kaufmann, an Israeli scholar, aptly stresses that Maurois's cumulative biographical work "has no other model in France" and that in the realm of biographies Maurois enjoys "a place of first rank among the writers who practice the genre." She even refers to Maurois's biographies as the "apotheosis" of this field of literature (see p. 198). Nor is it surprising that Maurice Druon compared Maurois's achievements as a biographer to Balzac's successes as a novelist. Druon, in effect, referred to Maurois's collection of biographies as "la Comédie humaine des génies" ("The Human Comedy of Geniuses").[3]

Maurois's historical works are more difficult to evaluate. When compared with some of the greatest histories written by professional historians, they appear somewhat superficial or even frothy. The fact is that one reads them with much too much effortlessness. There is in these histories a facile veneer that tempts the reader to regard them with less gravity than they deserve. In truth, let us recall that these were books written by a nonspecialist historian who addressed not the professional historical community but rather the broad marketplace of nonspecialists and literary laymen. Let us not dismiss Maurois's histories with too much levity, for the truth of the matter is that some very reputable historians have considered them to be works of high caliber. Professor H. L. Fisher of Oxford University once wrote that "this at last is History large and sweeping." Professor Madelin of the Sorbonne declared that "I read you [Maurois's histories] with a great deal of suspicion—but I found explanations."[4] The fact that this nonspecialist belletrist should have attempted to write at least three major historical treatises, and the fact that he succeeded in all three cases in producing highly readable, informative, and accurate works—these facts of life cannot go unnoticed by posterity.

The thousands of minor writings of André Maurois, dispersed in myriads of magazines and newspapers throughout the globe, will continue to serve as a backdrop against which this author's more imposing titles must be evaluated. There were some critics who considered it a fault for Maurois to have diffused his talents so profusely. The noted literary historian François Porché warned Maurois as early as 1935 against the pitfalls of excessive productivity: "We would like him not to be a dupe of his own kindness, which gives him the inclination, without doubt, to yield too easily to solicitations. . . . We beg him to believe that the combination of his critical faculties, content and form, lucidity, sensitivity, style, constitutes a veritable power, an exceptional force, and that this imposes upon him the duty not to disperse himself in minor works."[5] Maurois never heeded Porché's advice and continued to compose all sorts of prefaces, minor essays, newspaper chronicles, and advice to the lovelorn. He felt that by working in a large spectrum of circumstantial literature, he could combat within his personal life his tendency to lead a cloistered, insular literary existence. When one writes regularly for such publications as *Elle, Esquire,* and *Pour vous madame,* it is hard to remain isolated from the mainstream of human life. What really matters is that Maurois's self-imposed discipline, his incredible work ethic, his herculean regimen of daily toil, and his personal talents were always adequate for him to create *both* the minor works and the major literary monuments. And it is the latter titles which in themselves suffice to preserve for André Maurois a position of importance in the future histories of twentieth-century French letters. For every several dozen articles Maurois wrote in some popular journal, he leaves us at least one *Prométhée ou la Vie de Balzac.*

Maurois championed the cause of his former teacher Alain. For this he will be remembered. None advocated this cause with greater devotion than did the author of *Climats.* Eventually the disciple's steadfast struggle yielded positive results for Alain. Maurois once predicted that Alain would, in the eyes of the next century, be regarded as the Montaigne of his age. This lofty prediction is not altogether farfetched, for the teachings of this wise philosopher have become the object of increasingly sympathetic attention. In fact, Maurois lived long enough to see the partial fulfillment of this mission in his life; *The Propos* are being read by more and more readers.

There is another dimension in Maurois's life that must be mentioned here. He was one of those literary artists who did not restrict his activities to the hermetic fortress of literature. Instead, he committed much of his life to preaching rapprochement among men and nations. Especially did he promote amity among the French people for those of Anglo-America. In England and the New World Maurois was accepted as the most articulate Ambassador of French Culture, while in France he enjoyed a reputation as one of the most important interpreters of the values of art and life shared by the English-speaking peoples. Much of what cultured readers have come to know of each other on both sides of the Atlantic derives directly or indirectly from the influence Maurois once had exerted as a reconciler of nations.

Let us not forget also that if Maurois promulgated the cause of international interdependence and intercultural communications, he also supported—and he did so with equal zeal—the cause of French culture as a vital force within western civilization. Maurois was at once a sincere patriot and an incurable cosmopolitan!

The personal philosophy of life of André Maurois is adequate proof that one can forge an outlook of optimism about the ultimate fate of the human race and still protect oneself against the perils of foolish illusion. In men and women Maurois saw true grandeur. He knew that there was a special dignity in human life. But he realized that human beings were inevitably endowed with serious frailties and limitations. This philosophy of disabused optimism remains as one of the most enduring of all of Maurois's lessons for those of us who continue to read his works after his death. He taught that happiness was within the reach of the human race. But we must have the *will* to translate our desire for happiness into a reality of life. Toward the end of his career André Maurois published a book on the theme of will and action: *Au commencement était l'action* (Paris: Plon, 1966) *(In the Beginning was Action)*. If a slogan were ever devised to summarize Maurois's philosophy of life, it would necessarily include the words *volonté* (will) and *action*. Actually, as a disciple of Descartes, he summed up his life's slogan himself: namely, "Je veux, donc je suis." ("I wish, therefore I am").[6]

Maurois's career represented a continuous search for self-knowledge. As he lived his daily routine, he placed himself in symbiotic relationships with his fictional and biographical characters. Through them he hoped to comprehend himself better as well as to impart some of the lessons he had learned about himself to his millions of readers scattered around the earth and throughout the decades of time. As I personally observed him during the autumnal years of his life—he was already an octogenarian!—I saw in him a man with a restless soul still groping for additional knowledge and always interested in being informed of the most exciting events of his day. On one of his final birthdays he wrote the following: "My birthday, I neither rejoice nor am I sad. Brother, you have to grow old. So far the pain of growing old is limited: a few rheumatic aches, a bit hard of hearing. For an 1885 motor, the pick-up is still fairly good."[7] This calm, light-hearted and sprightly message is one that posterity might well ponder.

Posterity is unpredictable. During the years following his death, Maurois continues to linger in the same kind of purgatory to which so many major authors have been relegated. Relatively few readers have been attracted during the nineteen eighties to reading the works of a Paul Valéry, an André Gide, or an André Maurois. Even the number of experts studying Camus has declined. How long this purgatory will last is difficult to gauge. In October of 1977 the Bibliothèque Nationale, seeking to resurrect Maurois from what was hoped was but temporary oblivion, scheduled a major exposition and colloquium in his honor to commemorate the tenth anniversary of his death. Despite the uniform excellence of the papers delivered by scholars and authors from around the world, despite the high quality of the memorabilia in the exhibit, despite the superb job done by the Bibliothèque in publishing a major catalogue of the event, despite the large attendance, and despite the enormous coverage given to these events by the press and electronic media, Maurois's books continue to be largely neglected by the younger readers of the last decade or so.

Personally, I regard the rather dramatic decline of Maurois's popularity as a temporary phenomenon. I continue to be impressed, even at times stunned, by the sheer immensity of these collected works. I am equally impressed by their literary and aesthetic caliber. Maurois may not have been a "superstar" of his age, as Marcel Proust, Albert Camus, or Jean-Paul Sartre seem to have been. But during his lifetime he was read by a vast audience. In fact, he probably enjoyed vaster audiences than most of the superstars. He helped millions of readers around the world to formulate their clearest perceptions about the universe. As such he was part of the backbone of French literature. Without a backbone a literature cannot live. André Maurois's works form, in my judgment, a significant massif on the literary horizon of the twentieth century. I do not believe that this massif will evaporate into permanent oblivion. The time then may not be distant when the literary worlds of André Maurois will once again serve as a beacon for the future. The human race needs to be comforted from time to time. In their on-again, off-again quest for clarity, lucidity, moderation, sanity, and urbanity, people may yet one day return to Maurois. Of this I am almost convinced. At the very least, I am hopeful.

And now it is time for us to return to *Climats, Les Nouveaux Discours du Docteur O'Grady,* and some of the other important books from the worlds of André Maurois.[8]

Appendixes

86, BOULEVARD MAURICE BARRÈS

NEUILLY-SUR-SEINE

·T· MAILLOT 24-84

Le 15 Décembre 1964

Mon cher ami, .

      Oui, vous avez raison : nous sommes sur le point d'aller à Essendiéras, et ma femme travaille depuis longtemps à préparer son Arbre de Noël.

      Je suis très heureux de savoir, et de constater par les articles que vous m'envoyez, que vos étudiants s'intéressent à vos cours sur moi. Quant au livre, il se fera, et je l'attends avec impatience.

      Je réponds à vos questions :

A/ J'appelle "conte" ce que vous avez appelé en Amérique "a short, short story", un simple récit des faits, sans effort pour analyser les personnages.

      Une "nouvelle" est pour moi comme l'amorce d'un roman; elle est plus courte que le roman lui-même, mais relève un peu de la même technique.

      Quant au "récit", c'est un terme très général qui peut aussi bien s'appliquer à un conte qu'à un roman, pourvu qu'il s'agisse d'une histoire racontée par l'un des personnages.

B/ Je n'ai pas le temps aujourd'hui de remplir le questionnaire de PROUST, mais je le ferai à Essendiéras et je vous l'enverrai.

C/ Vous me demandez s'il y a un moment qui a déterminé pour moi le choix de la carrière d'écrivain : c'est probable mais cela s'est passé si tôt dans mon enfance que je m'en souviens à peine. Je crois que ce qui a été déterminant, c'est le fait que ma mère nous lisait beaucoup de vers et de grands auteurs, et je crois que c'est un jour, en entendant un poème de Victor Hugo, que je me dis : "Comme je serais heureux si je pouvais écrire!" C'est un fait qu'à 10 ou 11 ans j'avais écrit une tragédie en cinq actes et en vers, fort mauvaise bien sûr!

      Je continue à espérer que le BALZAC sera prêt fin Février. Quant à votre article pour La Revue de Paris, Isabelle s'en occupe.

      Dites nos amitiés à votre femme et à votre fils.

      Mille affections de tous deux à tous deux.

Le Professeur Jack KOLBERT
6645 Lanview Road
PITTSBURGH 17, Pa.

André Maurois

Letter from André Maurois to Jack Kolbert, explaining certain aspects of his short fiction. Jack Kolbert Archives. (Courtesy, Estate of André Maurois.)

86, Boulevard Maurice Barrès
Neuilly-Sur-Seine
Maillot 24-84

Le 15 Décembre 1964

Mon cher ami,

Oui, vous avez raison: nous sommes sur le point d'aller à Essendiéras, et ma femme travaille depuis longtemps à préparer son Arbre de Noël.

Je suis très heureux de savoir, et de constater par les articles que vous m'envoyez, que vos étudiants s'intéressent à vos cours sur moi. Quant au livre, il se fera, et je l'attends avec impatience.

Je réponds à vos questions:

A/ J'appelle "conte" ce que vous avez appelé en Amérique "a short, short story", un simple récit des faits, sans effort pour analyser les personnages.

Une "nouvelle" est pour moi comme l'*amorce* d'un roman; elle est plus courte que le roman lui-même, mais relève un peu de la même technique.

Quant au "récit", c'est un terme très général qui peut aussi bien s'appliquer à un conte qu'à un roman, pourvu qu'il s'agisse d'une histoire racontée par l'un des personnages.

B/ Je n'ai pas le temps aujourd'hui de remplir le questionnaire de Proust, mais je le ferai à Essendiéras et je vous l'enverrai.

C/ Vous me demandez s'il y a un moment qui a déterminé pour moi le choix de la carrière d'écrivain: c'est probable mais cela s'est passé si tôt dans mon enfance que je m'en souviens à peine. Je crois que ce qui a été déterminant, c'est le fait que ma mère nous lisait beaucoup de vers et de grands auteurs, et je crois que c'est un jour, en entendant un poème de Victor Hugo, que je me dis: "Comme je serais heureux si je pouvais écrire!" C'est un fait qu'à 10 ou 11 ans j'avais écrit une tragédie en cinq actes et en vers, fort mauvaise bien sûr!

Je continue à espérer que le *Balzac* sera prêt fin Février. Quant à votre article pour *La Revue de Paris*, Isabelle s'en occupe.

Dites nos amitiés à votre femme et à votre fils.

Mille affections de nous deux à vous deux.

Le Professeur Jack KOLBERT
6645 Landview Road
Pittsburgh 17, Pa.

André Maurois

86, Maurice Barrès Boulevard
Neuilly-sur-Seine
Phone: Maillot 24-84

December 15, 1964

My dear friend,

Yes, you are right: we are on the verge of going to Essendiéras, and my wife has been working for a long time in preparing her Christmas tree.

I am very happy to know, and to learn from the articles that you have sent me, that your students are interested in your courses on me. As for the book, it will be completed, and I await it with impatience.

I am responding to your questions:

A/ I call "conte" what you in America have called "a short, short story," a simple account of facts, without any effort to analyze the characters.

A "nouvelle" for me is the "primer" for a novel; it is shorter than the novel itself, but depends a bit on the same technique.

As for the "récit," it is a very general term that might be applied as well to a short story or to a novel, provided that it is a question of a story related by one of the characters.

B/ I have not yet had the time to fill out the Proust questionnaire, but I shall do it at Essendieras and I will send it to you.

C/ You ask me if there was a moment that determined for me the choice of a career as writer: there probably was one, but it occurred so early in my childhood that I scarcely remember when. I believe that what was a determining factor is the fact that my mother used to read us many verses and some of the major authors, and I believe that it was one day when I heard a poem of Victor Hugo that I told myself: "How happy I might be if I could write!" It is a fact that at 10 or 11 years of age I had written a tragedy in five acts and in verse form, something quite bad, to be sure!

I continue to hope that the *Balzac* will be ready at the end of February. As for your article for the *Revue de Paris,* Isabelle (de la Rochefoucauld) is taking care of it.

Give my regards to your wife and son.

A thousand affections to both of you from both of us.

Le Professeur Jack Kolbert
6645 Landview Road
PITTSBURGH 17, Pa.

André Maurois

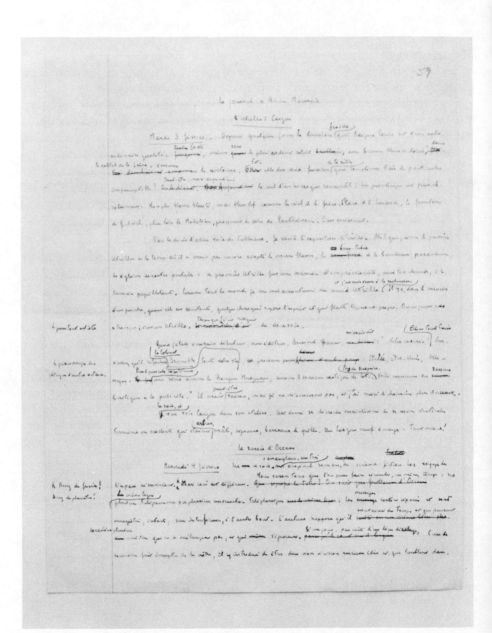

Manuscript pages from Maurois's Journal. From Jack Kolbert Archives. (Courtesy, Estate of André Maurois.)

gouverner le fonctionnement de sa société. J. H. Rosny avait jadis imaginé de [...] les [...] le désire, qui entrerait dans sa maison, dans notre chambre, mais ne nous serait pas perceptible, parce que leur [...] ne correspondraient pas à nos sens.

Le roman anglais est très bien fait, parce que l'appareil scientifique qui supporte la fiction ne montre aucune faille. Et pourquoi si peu étrange ? Vous savez (ou ne savez pas) que Guillaume d'Occam était un philosophe théologien du XIVᵉ siècle qui enseignait la loi de parcimonie : "[...] Elle ne faut pas multiplier les [...] au delà de ce qui est nécessaire." Or le système que, dans ce roman, [...] contre [...] [...] l'intelligence de deux univers, [...] telle expérience sur la loi de parcimonie. Il [...] [...] [...] de ces [...] comme l'enfant le retour irrationnel, d'où la suite... Mai liKing.

Vocabulaire

Jeudi 5 Février. — Dans une de ses savoureuses chroniques du Mercure de France, Nicole Vedrès raconte qu'elle a entendue devant le palais de l'Élysée une dame demander à son mari :

— Qu'est-ce que ça veut dire : Otan ?
C'est le mot anglais
— C'est [...] pour OTAN, a répondu le mari.

C'est drôle, mais c'est aussi singulier, car ce compte rôti. En Octobre 489 un mot avait conquis par le même : Veto, [...] [...] la monarchie.

André Maurois

RÉPONSES APRÈS MARCEL PROUST

Quel est, pour vous, le comble de la misère ? *Ne pas être aimé*

Où aimeriez-vous vivre ? *Où je vis.*

Votre idéal de bonheur terrestre ? *Beaucoup de travail, une femme aimée, des amis fidèles.*

Pour quelles fautes avez-vous le plus d'indulgence ? *Pour celles de ceux qui sont intelligents.*

Quels sont les héros de roman que vous préférez ? *Le prince André (Guerre et Paix), Fabrice del Dongo.*

Quel est votre personnage historique favori ? *Périclès.*

Vos héroïnes favorites dans la vie réelle ? *Adrienne de Lafayette, Juliette Drouet, Julie Talma.*

Vos héroïnes dans la fiction ? *La duchesse Sanseverina, Natacha Rostov, Henriette de Mortsauf*

Votre peintre favori ? *Vermeer*

Votre musicien favori ? *Beethoven*

Votre qualité préférée chez l'homme ? *La loyauté.*

Votre qualité préférée chez la femme ? *La tendresse.*

Votre vertu préférée ? *La bonté.*

Votre occupation préférée ? *Écrire*

Qui auriez-vous aimé être ? *Alain .*

Le principal trait de mon caractère ? *Le besoin d'agir, de créer.*

Ce que j'apprécie le plus chez mes amis ? *Un mélange d'intelligence et de bonté*

Mon principal défaut ? *L'impatience*

Proust Questionnaire prepared expressly in manuscript form for Jack Kolbert Archives. (Courtesy, Estate of André Maurois.)

Mon rêve de bonheur ? *Je ne le rêve pas, je le vis.*

Quel serait mon plus grand malheur ? *L'exil*

Ce que je voudrais être ? *Ce que je suis : un écrivain français. J'aurais aussi aimé être Premier Ministre.*

La couleur que je préfère ? *Le bleu des ciels de Paris*

La fleur que j'aime ? *Le glaïeul*

L'oiseau que je préfère ? *L'oiseau magique, l'alouette*

Mes auteurs favoris en prose ? *Retz, Saint-Simon, Proust, Bossuet.*

Mes poètes préférés ? *Du Bellay, Baudelaire, Verlaine, Hugo, Shakespeare*

Mes héros dans la vie réelle ? *Alain, Spinoza, Lincoln, Descartes*

Mes héroïnes dans l'histoire ? *Jeanne d'Arc. (Oui, homme même ?)*

Mes noms favoris ? *Nicole, Dominique, Isabelle, Odile.*

Ce que je déteste par dessus tout ? *La méchanceté*

Caractères historiques que je méprise le plus ? *Le mépris n'est pas mon fort*

Le fait militaire que j'admire le plus ? *La Marne, la bataille d'Angleterre*

La réforme que j'admire le plus ? *La déclaration des Droits de l'homme*

Le don de la nature que je voudrais avoir ? *Le génie*

Comment j'aimerais mourir ? *A ma table de travail, au milieu d'une phrase*

État présent de mon esprit ? *Sérénité*

Ma devise ? *Je sers, donc je suis.*

Signature :

André Maurois

Questions	*Maurois' Responses*
What is, for you, the height of misery?	Not to be loved.
Where would you like to live?	Where I live (now).
Your ideal of earthly happiness?	A great deal of work, a woman you love, faithful friends.
For which faults do you have the greatest amount of indulgence?	For those of the people who are indulgent (themselves).
Who are the novelistic heroes whom you prefer?	Prince Andrew (War and Peace), *Fabrice del Dongo (Stendhal)*
Who is your favorite historical character?	Pericles
Your favorite heroines in real life?	Adrienne de Lafayette, Juliette Drouet, Henriette de Morsauf
Your favorite painter?	Vermeer
Your favorite musician?	Beethoven
The virtue you prefer in men?	Loyalty.
The virtue you prefer in women?	Tenderness.
The virtue you prefer?	Kindness.
Your preferred occupation?	Writing.
Whom would you have liked to be?	Alain.
The principal trait of my character?	The need to act, to create.
What I appreciate the most in my friends?	A mixture of intelligence and kindness.
My principal fault?	Impatience.
My dream of happiness?	I do not dream it. I live it.
What might my greatest misfortune be?	Exile.
What would I like to be?	What I am: a French writer. I might also have liked to be Prime Minister.
The color I prefer?	The blue of the Paris skies.
The flower I like?	The gladiola.
The bird I prefer?	The swallow.
My favorite prose authors?	Retz, Saint Simon, Proust, Bossuet [Maurois crosses him out].
My preferred poets?	DuBellay, Baudelaire, Verlaine, Hugo, Shakespeare
My heroes in real life?	Alain, Spinoza, Disraeli [Maurois then crosses him out], Descartes.
My heroines in history?	Joan of Arc (Where can you find anyone better?)
My favorite names?	Nicole, Dominique, Isabelle, Odile.
What I detest above all	Wickedness.
Historical characters whom I scorn the most?	Scorn is not my forte.
The military feat that I admire the most?	The Marne, the Battle of England.

The reform that I admire the most?	The Declaration of the Rights of Men
The gift of nature that I would like to possess?	Genius
How I would like to die?	At my work-table, in the middle of a sentence
The present state of my mind?	Serenity.
My slogan?	Never explain, never complain [which he strikes out and instead writes the following] I want, therefore I am.

[Signature]
André Maurois

Appendix D: Maurois's French Titles and Their Literal English Translations

In my text I have generally used my own literal English translations for Maurois's French titles. Occasionally, I mention only the original French, and in a few cases I have included both the English and the French. Below is a systematic list of the French titles and the exact English translations thereof. The reader should note that in many of the commercial translations of Maurois's works, the publishers have created a loose approximation of the French title, or else they have invented titles that have little relation to the original. The list below follows the order in which these titles appear in my bibliography.

Portrait d'un ami qui s'appelait moi	*Portrait of a Friend Whose Name Was Me*
Ariel ou la Vie de Shelley	*Ariel or the Life of Shelley*
Don Juan ou la Vie de Byron	*Don Juan or the Life of Byron*
Tourguéniev	*Turgenev or Turgenieff or Tourgueniev*
Lyautey	*Lyautey* (also known as *The Life of Lyautey*)
Voltaire	*Voltaire*
Edouard VII et son temps	*Edward VII and his Time*
René ou la Vie de Chateaubriand	*René or the Life of Chateaubriand*
A la recherche de Marcel Proust	*In Search of Marcel Proust*
Lélia ou la Vie de George Sand	*Lelia or the Life of George Sand*
Olympio ou la Vie de Victor Hugo	*Olympio or the Life of Victor Hugo*
Robert et Elizabeth Browning	*Robert and Elizabeth Browning*
Les Trois Dumas	*The Three Dumas*
Le Vie de Sir Alexander Fleming	*The Life of Sir Alexander Fleming*
Adrienne ou la Vie de Madame de Lafayette	*Adrienne or the Life of Madame de Lafayette*
Prométhée ou la Vie de Balzac	*Prometheus or the Life of Balzac*

Dialogues sur le commandement	*Dialogues on Commanding*
Conseils à un jeune Français partant pour L'Angleterre	*Advice to a Young Frenchman Leaving for England*
Etudes anglaises	*Studies on the English*
La Conversation	*Conversation*
Rouen	*Rouen*
Un Essai sur Dickens	*An Essay on Dickens*
Aspects de la biographie	*Aspects of Biography*
Le Côté de Chelsea	*Chelsea Way*
L'Amérique inattendue	*Unexpected America*
Proust et Ruskin	*Proust and Ruskin*
Chantiers Américains	*American Workyards*
Byron et les femmes	*Byron and Women*
Magiciens et logiciens	*Magicians and Logicians*
Malte	*Malta*
Les Origines de la guerre de 1939	*The Origins of the War of 1939*
Un Art de vivre	*An Art of Life*
Tragédie en France	*Tragedy in France*
Etudes littéraires	*Literary Studies*
Espoirs et souvenirs	*Hopes and Memories*
Etudes littéraires, vol. 2	Literary Studies, vol. 2
Franklin	*Franklin*
Eisenhower	*Eisenhower*
Conseils à un jeune Français partant pour les Etats-Unis	*Advice to a Young Frenchman leaving for the United States*
Alain	*Alain*
Ce que je crois	*What I Believe*
Cours de bonheur conjugal	*A Course on Marital Happiness*
Destins exemplaires	*Exemplary Destinies*
Discours prononcé à l'Académie française pour la réception de Jean Cocteau	*Discourse Presented at the French Academy for Jean Cocteau's Reception*
Hollande	*Holland*
Périgord	*Perigord*
Portrait de la France et des Français	*Portrait of France and the French*
La France change de visage	*France Changes Faces*
De La Bruyère à Proust (Lecture, mon doux plaisir)	*From La Bruyère to Proust (Reading, My Sweet Pleasure)*
Dialogues des vivants	*Dialogues of the Living*
Le Monde de Marcel Proust	*The World of Marcel Proust*
Paris	*Paris*
De Proust à Camus	*From Proust to Camus*
De Gide à Sartre	*From Gide to Sartre*

Au commencement était l'action	*At the Beginning was Action*
Lettre ouverte à un jeune homme	*Open Letter to a Young Man*
Les Illusions	*Illusions*
Le Chapitre suivant	*The Next Chapter*
Les Silences du Colonel Bramble	*The Silences of Colonel Bramble*
Ni ange, ni bête	*Neither Angel nor Beast*
Les Discours du docteur O'Grady	*The Discourses of Doctor O'Grady*
Bernard Quesnay	*Bernard Quesnay*
Climats	*Climates*
Le Cercle de famille	*Family Circle*
L'Instinct du bonheur	*The Instinct for Happiness*
Terre promise	*Promised Land*
Nouveaux Discours du docteur O'Grady	*New Discourses of Doctor O'Grady*
Les Roses de septembre	*September Roses*
Romans	*Novels*
Pays des trente-six volontés	*Land of the Thirty-six Wills*
Voyage au pays des articoles	*Trip to the Land of the Articoles*
Les Mondes imaginaires	*Imaginary Worlds*
Le Peseur d'âmes	*The Weigher of Souls*
Patapoufs et filifers	*Patapoufs and Filifers*
Premiers Contes	*First Short Stories*
La Machine à lire les pensées	*The Thought-reading Machine*
Toujours l'inattendu arrive	*Always Does the Unexpected Occur*
Tu ne commettras d'adultère	*Thou Shalt Not Commit Adultery*
Aux Innocents les mains pleines	*For the Innocent the Hands are Full*
Pour piano seul	*For Unaccompanied Piano*
Fragments d'un journal de vacances	*Fragments from a Vacation Journal*
En Amérique	*In America*
Discours de Réception de M. André Maurois à l'Académie Française et réponse de M. André Chevrillon	*Discourse of the Reception of Mr. André Maurois at the French Academy and Response of Mr. André Chevrillon*
Etats Unis 39, Journal d'un voyage en Amérique	*United States 1939, Journal of a Trip to America*
Mémoires	*Memoirs* (known in America as *I Remember, I Remember*)
Etudes Américaines	*Studies on America*
Retour en France	*Return to France*
Journal Etats-Unis 1946	*Journal, The United States—1946*
Journal d'un tour en l'Amérique latine	*Journal of a Tour in Latin America*
Journal d'un tour en Suisse	*Journal of a Tour in Switzerland*
Choses nues	*Nude Things* or *Bare Facts*
Mémoires (II)	*Memoirs II*

Histoire d'Angleterre	*History of England*
La Monarchie anglaise de Victoria à George VI	*The English Monarchy from Victoria to George VI*
Histoire des Etats-Unis	*History of the United States*
Histoire de la France	*History of France*
Louis XIV à Versailles	*Louis XIV at Versailles*
Histoire parallèle: Histoire des Etats-Unis de 1917 à 1961	*Parallel History: History of the United States from 1917 to 1961* (includes also Louis Aragon's *History of the Soviet Union from 1917 to 1961*)
Napléoon	*Napoleon*
Histoire d'Allemagne	*History of Germany*

Notes

Preface

1. "Prèlerinages littéraires," *Le Journal de Rouen* (August 1937).
2. The book in which he wrote this inscription was *De La Bruyère à Proust* (Paris: Fayard, 1964).
3. Robert Kemp, Preface to Michael Droit, *André Maurois* (Paris: Editions Universitaires, 1953), p. 11.

Chapter 1. Maurois's Eight Decades

1. André Maurois (hereafter referred to in all notes as AM), "Self-Portrait," *Portraits and Self-Portraits*, ed. George Schreiber (Boston: Houghton-Mifflin, 1936), pp. 99–101.
2. Quoted with permission from the manuscripts in the archives of the Collection of Simone André-Maurois.

AM's *Mémoires* were originally published in New York City in 1942 by the Editions de la Maison Française in two volumes: Vol. 1, *Les Années d'apprentissage*, and Vol. 2, *Les Années de travail*. In 1948, because the New York edition was so hard to find in France, Flammarion reissued an abridged, one-volume edition. The British version, *Call No Man Happy*, and the American, *I Remember, I Remember*, have been widely sold.

3. The entire saga of the move of the Herzogs, Fraenckels, and other Alsatian families from Alsace to Normandy is dramatically related by Georges Delahache in his volume *De Bischwiller à Elbeuf* (Paris: Hachette, n.d.).
4. Marguerite Herzog later married the writer Jean-Richard Bloch (1884–1947). Germaine Herzog married a maritime engineer, David Wolkovitch, a graduate of the famed Ecole Polytechnique. She died in 1964. Marguerite Herzog lived from 1886 until 1975.
5. AM, *Mémoires*, 1:14.
6. AM, *Portrait d'un ami qui s'appelait moi* (Namur: Wesmael-Charlier, 1959), p. 16.
7. Ibid.
8. AM, *Rouen* (Paris: Gallimard, 1928), p. 8.
9. Ibid.
10. AM, *Portrait d'un ami qui s'appelait moi*, p. 18.
11. This incident is related by Amélie Fillon in *André Maurois Romancier* (Paris: Société française d'éditions littéraires et techniques, 1937), pp. 36–37.
12. AM, *Mémoires*, 1:65 for the details of this grueling success.
13. Ibid., p. 63.
14. Ibid., p. 99.
15. Ibid. See chapter entitled "Ecole de Campagne" ("Country School").
16. Ibid. p. 167.
17. Ibid., pp. 171–72 *passim*.
18. Ibid., p. 189.
19. Ibid., p. 200.
20. Ibid., p. 212.

21. AM, *René ou la Vie de Chateaubriand* (Paris: Grasset, 1938, p. 69.
22. AM, *Portrait d'un ami qui s'appelait moi*, pp. 25–26.
23. AM, *Mémoires*, 1:250–51.
24. AM in *The Listener* of London, February 1, 1940.
25. AM, *Portrait d'un ami qui s'appelait moi*, p. 28.
26. AM, *Mémoires*, 1:259.
27. AM, *Portrait d'un ami qui s'appelait moi*, p. 30.
28. AM, *Mémoires*, 2:22.
29. Ibid., pp. 13–15.
30. Simone de Caillavet had been taught by a remarkable private tutor from Britain named Annie Lavinia Varley, who had been closely associated with her from 1907 until 1939. Miss Varley taught her fluent English and served as a model for the typical English nanny and tutor in Maurois's novel *Terre promise*.
31. AM, *Portrait d'un ami qui s'appelait moi*, p. 38.
32. An explanation of some vital statistics concerning Maurois's second spouse may be useful at this point in my biography of the author. To begin with, Simone Maurois and her first husband, the Rumanian diplomat Georges Stoïcesco, were first married in a civil ceremony on February 2, 1920, in Paris and three days later in a religious ceremony in Cannes. Despite the fact that Simone successfully obtained an annulment from the Vatican, her brief marriage (and ironically, according to the ecclesiastical annulment, her nonmarriage) produced a daughter, Françoise-Georgina Stoïcesco, who was born on November 23, 1920. For the sake of completeness, I note too the biographical dates of Simone Maurois's most important antecedents. Her grandfather, Albert Arman de Caillavet, was born in 1840 and died in 1919; his wife, the former Léontine-Charlotte Lippman (1844–1910) won international notoriety as the celebrated "égerie" of Anatole France. Madame Maurois's father Gaston Arman de Caillavet, was born in 1869 and died in 1915. Her mother, Jeanne Pouquet, on the other hand, lived from 1874 to 1961. Following Gaston's death (in 1915) she married a first cousin, Maurice Pouquet (1883–1956), and thus reassumed her maiden name. Simone de Caillavet was born in 1893.

As for Simone de Caillavet Maurois herself, she had been something of a productive authoress in her own right. Her literary roots she disclosed quite candidly in the following preface:

I have lived in the world of the theater as much as, if not more so than in the real world. I was a daughter of a dramatic author, since my father, Gaston de Caillavet, was the author of the *Roi*, the *Habit vert*, of *Primerose* and of twenty other plays; I was the ward of a dramatic author, since Robert de Flers, a constant collaborator and fraternal friend of my father became, after the death of the latter my legal guardian; I was niece of a dramatic author since Alexandre Dumas fils was my great uncle. Add to this that Victorien Sardou was the father of Geneviève de Flers, wife of my guardian, that this illustrious old man treated me a bit as if he were my grandfather and that all of the dramatic authors of that time came ceaselessly into the home of my parents.

She further refers to [Anatole France] as "another old childhood friend.

Among the many literary anecdotes recounted frequently by Simone was one concerning a salon evening at her avenue Hoche *hôtel particulier*. Her illustrious guests were performing a "comédie de salon." Robert de Flers and Georges Feydeau played the leading male roles; her mother, Jeanne Pouquet, the main feminine part; and Proust that of the "intermittent prompter." On another evening she remembered Anatole France producing a one-act play for a special series called "Au Petit Bonheur," and Maurice Donnay produced his celebrated play "Amants." Of Simone de Caillavet as a young girl, Anatole France has left a charming verbal portrait: "Simone was able to wish to do things. She was born a person of the will; that was obvious from her well framed mouth, her strong chin, her head which she carried in an upright fashion, and in her decisive mannerisms" (printed in the preface to his *Les Heures latines* and cited by Maurois in *Mémoires*, 2:19). Proust reincarnated her in the guise of the youthful Mlle de Saint-Loup and later used her as the culminating figure in *Le Temps retrouvé:* "I found her most beautiful: full of hopes . . . Laughing, formed by the years I had lost, she resembled my youth" (see Maurois's *Mémoires,* 2:16).

33. Michel Droit, *André Maurois* (Paris: Editions Universitaires, 1953), p. 34.

34. One of her important publications is the volume-length study, *Miss Howard and the Emperor,* the story of the relationship between Napoleon III and his British mistress (London: Collins, 1957).

35. All of these and subsequent personal inscriptions are quoted with the permission of M. and Mme A. Maurois, permission that they granted me prior to their deaths. From the Collection Simone André-Maurois.

36. AM, *Un Art de vivre* (Paris: Plon, 1939), p. 75. "Tout travail fait avec amour est délicieux, mais l'amour mêlé au travail est ce qu'il y a au monde de plus délicieux. Ainsi naissent ces merveilleux ménages de savants, d'artistes, d'apôtres, qui sont à la fois un couple et une équipe."

37. Information gleaned from a private conversation with the late Mme Maurois on March 19, 1964.

38. Originally acquired by Antoine Pouquet (1757–1833), a royal notary under King Louis XVI, this lordly manor was bequeathed to his eldest son, Pierre-Chéri Pouquet (1799–1877), who in turn transmitted it to his son, Eugène Pouquet (1844–1919), a stockbroker attached to the Paris Bourse. His daughter, Jeanne Pouquet, Madame Maurois's mother, inherited the estate upon the death of her father and left it to her only daughter, Simone. Jeanne Pouquet authored an important volume that reveals the nature of the relationships between her mother, Madame Arman de Caillavet, and Antole France, Proust, Jules Lemaitre, and other writers. See Jeanne Maurice Pouquet, *Le Salon de Madame Arman de Caillavet* (Paris: Hachette, 1926).

39. His first major decoration was bestowed upon him in 1916 by the British Military Command: The D.C.M. (Distinguished Conduct Medal).

40. According to Professor Emeritus Coindreau, in an interview with me at his Paris apartment on January 11, 1964.

41. Jean-Albert Bédé wrote an important article on Maurois in which he sums up his successful first contact with the academic world: "Ariel Professeur," *Les Nouvelles Littéraires,* November 29, 1930.

42. AM, *Mémoires,* 2:117.

43. See Maurois's chronicle of these episodes in *Choses nues,* p. 71.

44. Ibid., pp. 149–50.

45. Initiations into the Académie Française are most colorful and pompous ceremonies. First one hears the penetrating martial drumroll of the Gardes Républicaines attired in full-dress regalia, and then comes the processional entry under the imposing rotunda of the Immortals themselves, many of them outfitted in their splendid academic trappings. Around them the semicircular rows of benches are overflowing with the upper echelons of Paris's social, intellectual, political, diplomatic, and artistic elite. The ubiquitous journalists and media people were flashing their cameras.

The creator of the Bramble-O'Grady myth enjoyed a particularly brilliant Academic ceremony. The critic André Thérive ecstatically described the inflections in Maurois's voice as he delivered his address: "What a delightful discourse it was! Pronounced by this voice, which is clear and witty, impeccable and captivating, a voice which had made of him our most famous lecturer." Years of public lectures were paying off for Maurois; in contrast to most Academicians, who excelled more in the finesse of their pen than in that of their oral delivery, André Maurois demonstrated convincingly that he was not only an experienced author but also an accomplished orator.

The two "parrains" (sponsor-ushers) escorting Maurois to his place under the Dome were Georges Lecomte and Abel Hermant. The honorary delegation, outfitted in the traditional academic gilt, included writers Mauriac, Lacretelle, Bérard, and Pesquidoux. The initiate bore the traditional Academic sword, long a symbol of the lengthy history of the famed house. *His* sword, however, was a sight to behold! Designed especially for him by the internationally famous jeweler Cartier, its handle, constructed of layers of ivory and vermillion, was covered with symbols evoking Alsace (the source-place of Maurois's family), Elbeuf (where he himself had been born), Périgord (the site of his vacations), the Entente Cordiale (Maurois's lifelong mission to unite the English and the French), and the army (symbolic of his military service between 1914–1948; all of this adornment was crowned by a massive star representing the glory of literary achievements. The resplendent ceremony was tinged with international overtones: many diplomats crowded the hall, led by the British Ambassador, Sir Eric Phipps, and by many other American and British celebrities who came to see the initiation of this friend of the English-speaking world.

After all of the pomp and martial drumrolls have faded away and the colorful robes and swords have been packed away, what remains for posterity out of an Academy initiation are the discourses of the new member and by the Academician selected to respond on behalf of the members of the company. By all accounts, Maurois's was a successful discourse. Customarily, the new member pays homage to the achievements of his illustrious predecessor. The basic disparities between Maurois and Doumic, however, made this task especially arduous. The former's easy-flowing style betrays some effort to paint a warm portrait of a man whose traits contrasted diametrically with his own. Maurois, the supple, tolerant moderate, vaunted the inflexible and traditionalist traits of Doumic. Yet, the successor did manage to convey his appreciation of the qualities of his predecessor. After all, both men were products of a solid classical education. Both prided themselves on their style of cartesian limpidity. Both consciously avoided complexity for the sake of complexity. Both, in their systematic perception of literature might have been excellent pedagogues. Both were fervent patriots, imbued with a sincere love of things French and above all of the literature of their country. But the biographer of Tourguéniev and Disraeli was far more cosmopolitan than the editor of *La Revue des Deux Mondes.* Maurois had nourished his spirit with the great writers of England, America, and Russia. Doumic could scarcely see beyond the virtues of Racine and Molière, his great heroes. The crux of Doumic's career—his action as editor of the celebrated *Revue*—Maurois characterized in the following laudatory way:

> Entrusted with the task of satisfying the intellectual needs of the lettered middle class—that is to say the readers who possessed, as he did, a taste for the classics, respect for a traditional morality, and love of their country and its history—all he had to do to satisfy them was to abandon himself to his own tastes. . . . He painted the general and durable content of human nature and respected certain sympathies, affections, and decencies, without which there are no societies. (Discours de l'Académie, pp. 50–51).

46. *Discours de l'Académie,* p. 82.

47. *Discours prononcés a L'Académie française pour la réception de Jean Cocteau et Réponse de M. André Maurois* (Paris: Didot, 1955), p. 72.

48. AM, "Preface," *Paris* (Paris: Fernand Nathan, 1951), p. 14.

49. "The Forty Immortals," *Holiday Magazine* (April 1957), pp. 74 et seq.

50. See Maurois's article in *Le Figaro,* September 14, 1939, and September 21, 1939.

51. AM, *Portrait d'un ami qui s'appelait moi,* p. 35.

52. "En juillet 1940 arriva aux Etats-Unis l'écrivain français André Maurois. Bien qu'il fût très malheureux, ayant tout perdu, son pays, sa maison, ses livres, il fut si courageusement aidé par sa femme qui se fit à la fois épouse, secrétaire, amie, collaboratrice, housekeeper, qu'il reprit rapidement confiance et travailla mieux que jamais." *Ex libris* Simone André-Maurois.

53. AM, *Espoirs et souvenirs* (New York: Editions de la Maison Française, 1943), pp. 27–28, 42.

54. Ibid.

55. AM, *Journal-Etats-Unis-1946* (Paris: Editions du bateau ivre, 1946), p. 181.

56. "Scanning the Arts," *The Kansas City Star,* November 21, 1965.

57. AM, *Mémoires,* 2: 290.

58. Ibid.

59. Ibid.

60. See AM's entry concerning Pope Pius XII in "Journal," *Carrefour,* October 15, 1958.

61. The text of this address has been reprinted in *Les Nouvelles Littéraires,* July 21, 1949.

62. See Françoise Giroud's account of this radio series in "Maurois a attendu ses noces d'argent pour donner des cours de mariage (par sans fil)" in France-Dimanche, March 11, 1950.

63. AM, *Portrait d'un ami qui s'appelait moi*, p. 41.

64. Ibid., and "Sur la tombe d'Alain," *Combat*, June 7, 1951.

65. The entire text of Maurois's allocution is printed in *Notre Bordeaux*, "Hebdomadaire Régional," May 23, 1953, no. 73.

66. AM, "Journal," *Carrefour*, August 4, 1954.

67. According to AM, "IXmes Rencontres Internationales," *La Tribune de Genève*, September 10, 1954.

68. AM, *Aux innocents les mains pleines* (Paris: La Table Ronde, 1955).

69. Francis Steegmuller, Review of AM's *Prométhée ou la Vie de Balzac*, lead article, cover page *New York Times Book Review Magazine*, May 22, 1966, sec. 7, pp. 1 and 22.

70. For complete accounts of AM's participation in the World Congress, see "L'Oggi," in *Il Resto del Carlino*, June 21, 1962, and Marcello Lucini, "Il Compito dello Scrittore Moderno," in *Il Tempo*, June 21, 1962.

71. From the unpublished texts of the proceedings of 1963 commencement of the University of Maryland's European division.

72. Ibid.

73. AM, "Mes Vacances Périgourdines," *L'Aurore*, August 16, 1949. All quotations in this paragraph are from this article.

74. AM, "Choses Nues," *Les Nouvelles Littéraires*, August 20, 1964, p. 10.

75. Ibid., July 23, 1964, p. 10.

76. *Les Illusions*, preface by Jean Mistler (Paris: Hachette, 1968). English trans. New York: Columbia University Press, 1968. Foreward by Edouard Morot-Sir.

77. I have translated Maurois's text freely. "Compagnon de route" actually means "fellow traveler," but because of the special connotation of this label in English, I prefer "life companion."

78. For important accounts of the death of Simone André-Maurois, see Anon., "Mort à Neuilly de Mme André-Maurois," *France-Amerique*, January 2, 1969; Jacques Suffel, "Simone André-Maurois n'est plus," *Les Nouvelles Littéraires*, January 2, 1969, p. 2; Gilbert Cesbron, "Adieu à une Dame," *Les Nouvelles Littéraires*, January 2, 1969; Anon., "Mrs. André-Maurois, 75, Husband's Collaborator," *New York Times* (obituary page), December 28, 1968, p. 27; Danielle Dordet, "Une Grande Dame Disparue: Simone André-Maurois," *Périgord Magazine* (January 1969).

79. Cited in "Cactus Académiques," *Le Figaro*, April 25, 1969.

Chapter 2. André Maurois in Search of a Genre—Biography

1. Pierre de Boisdeffre, "Balzac et Maurois," *Les Nouvelles Littéraires*, April 8, 1965, p. 5.

2. *Das Schönste*, November 11, 1957, pp. 32–33.

3. Fanny Butcher, "Review of *Les Trois Dumas*, *Chicago Sunday Tribune Magazine of Books*, February 9, 1958, pt. 4.

4. Cyril Connolly, Review of *The Life of Sir Alexander Fleming*, *London Sunday Times*, May 3, 1959.

5. Michel Droit, personal interview with me at his offices at *Le Figaro Littéraire*, February 21, 1964. Translated from his French.

6. Jacques Suffel, *André Maurois* (Paris: Flammarion, 1963), pp. 80 and 93.

7. Jean Dutourd, personal interview with me at his office in the Gallimard headquarters, January 28, 1964.

8. AM, *Alain* (Paris: Gallimard, 1963), pp. 97–98.

9. André Billy, "Les Livres," *Le Figaro*, April 7, 1954, no. 2979.

10. Marcel Thiébaut, "André Maurois," *Entre les lignes* (Paris: Hachette, 1962), pp. 208–9.

11. AM, *Mémoires* (New York: Editions de la Maison Française, 1942), 2:83–84.

12. The text of this lecture has been reprinted in its entirety. See Simone André-Maurois, "La Femme de l'écrivain," *Les Annales* (Paris: March 1956), no. 65, pp. 23–28.

13. Simone Maurois also served as a vital critical reader, who checked his manuscripts for scholarly precision and possible vagueness. For example, in the *Balzac* manuscript he wrote: "Mme de Berry était morte le 17 juillet." But in her typed version of this page she inserted the year 1836 after 17 juillet. On another page he wrote: "Chagrins de famille: un fils de famille. . . ." In red letters, in her handwriting, she asks: "Est-ce Alfred OU Alphonse de Montzaigle?" In the end, Maurois decided whether clarification was needed and whether or not to follow her suggestions.

14. "L'Art de la biographie," inédit, published at end of Michel Droit, *André Maurois* (Paris: Editions Universitaires, 1953), p. 138.

15. AM, *Les Trois Dumas* (Paris: Hachette, 1957), p. 7.

16. AM, in a personal interview with me at his Neuilly home, February 15, 1964.

17. During the preparation of *Tourguéniev* he was in close contact with the Tourguéniev descendents in France. The Russian's grandchild was so enthusiastic about the biography that he wrote Maurois in the following complimentary terms: "Thanks to the nobility of your character, to your beautiful and courageous loyalty, my grandfather will at long last have a historiographer worthy of him. Your lectures will be a novelized life but also the very expression of truth." In an unpublished letter by I. Tourguénieff to A. Maurois, dated June 1, 1930, Collection Simone André-Maurois.

18. AM, *Les Trois Dumas*, p. 459.

19. AM, Préface, Simone André-Maurois, *George Sand-Marie Dorval Correspondance inédite* (Paris: Gallimard, 1953), p. 9.

20. René Lalou, Préface, AM, *Disraeli* (Extraits) (Paris: Classiques Larousse, 1955), p. 10.

21. AM, Préface, *Ariel ou La Vie de Shelley, Oeuvres Complètes* (Paris: Arthème Fayard, 1953), 15:i.

22. Ibid., p. ii.

23. Louis Chaigne, "André Maurois," *Vie et Oeuvres d'Ecrivains* (Paris: Pierre Bossuet, n.d.), p. 168.

24. André Chevrillon et André Maurois: *Discours de Reception á l'Académie Française* (Paris: Didot, 1939), pp. 106–7.

25. *La Vie de Disraeli* in its American edition was a selection of the Book of the Month Club. This automatically assured it an immense number of readers. *Climats* has appeared in pocket book form in several languages, and *Disraeli* in a Classique Larousse edition.

26. AM, *Mémoires*, 2:41.

27. François Mauriac, in a personal interview with me at his Auteuil home, February 13, 1964.

28. André Maurois, in a personal interview with me at his Neuilly home, November 18, 1963.

29. Michel Droit, *André Maurois*, p. 82.

30. AM, *Les Trois Dumas*, p. 11.

31. AM, *Adrienne ou La Vie de Madame de la Fayette* (Paris: Hachette, 1960), p. 9.

32. Droit quotes Desmond MacCarthy in his book on Maurois, p. 35.

33. Marshal Lyautey, in unpublished letter to Maurois, dated November 27, 1933, Collection Simone André-Maurois. "Avec vous, qui êtes pour moi dans les meilleurs entre les meilleurs, je me débonde."

34. *Ex libris* Simone André-Maurois.

35. King Albert I, in an unpublished letter to Maurois, dated November 10, 1933, Collection Simone André-Maurois. "Ce livre est un chef d'oeuvre. Il ajoute une documentation de tout premier ordre et des aperçus originaux à l'histoire contemporaine, toujours la moins connue."

36. AM, *René ou La Vie de Chateaubriand* (Paris: Grasset, 1938), p. 409.

37. Ibid., p. 461.

38. Ibid., p. 237.

39. Ibid., p. 463.

40. AM, "L'Art de la biographie," at the end of Droit, *André Maurois*, p. 137.

41. Nevertheless, many eminent French literary authorities seem to prefer the great lives of the English figures, which for them are more interesting. Disraeli the man is relatively unknown in France, and the French reader has the satisfaction of meeting someone new. The lives of Sand and Hugo, on the other hand, are much better known by even the French nonexpert in literature.

42. Emile Henriot, "La Vie littéraire," *Le Monde,* April 27, 1949.

43. AM, *A la recherche de Marcel Proust* (Paris: Hachette, 1949), p. 331.

44. AM, *Portrait d'un ami qui s'appelait moi* (Namur: Wesmael-Charlier, 1959), p. 89.

45. Robert Kemp, "La Vie des livres," *Les Nouvelles Littéraires,* February 14, 1952.

46. Even in the shorter life of the more introspective Proust, Maurois manages to inject the names of some five-hundred persons, many of whom he knew personally; e.g., Edmond Jaloux, Vaudoyer, Jeanne Pouquet, Robert de Flers, etc.

47. In contrast with Gide's sigh of "hélas" at the thought that Hugo was France's greatest poet, Maurois opined: "Victor Hugo est notre plus grand poète, heureusement!" in a "Soirée Littéraire," Comédie Française (Salle Richelieu), January 13, 1964.

48. See, for example, for some of the best: AM, *Olympio ou la Vie de Victor Hugo,* (Paris: Hachette, 1954), pp. 136–37, p. 209, and p. 425.

49. Anon., "Portrait Gallery," *London Sunday Times,* November 23, 1958.

50. *The Life of Sir Alexander Fleming* (London: Penguin Books, 1963), p. 11.

51. Dr. Albert Delaunay, "Qui est Fleming," *Les Nouvelles Littéraires,* March 19, 1959.

52. Harold Nicolson, "The Discoverer of Penicillin," *The Observer,* May 3, 1959.

53. As an item of curiosity, Maurois's longest citation (13 pages long) appears in *Adrienne.* He quotes from Gilbert's description of his wife's death scene.

54. Pierre Audiat, "Femmes dans la révolution," *Le Figaro Littéraire,* April 22, 1961.

55. In *France Nouvelle,* February 11, 1960.

56. Thiébaut, pp. 202–3. (See Note 10, Chapt. 2)

57. Henri Bergson, in an unpublished letter to Maurois, dated November 7, 1933, Collection Simone André-Maurois. "Il faut que je vous dise avec quel plaisir et quel intérêt je viens de lire "Edouard VII at son temps." C'est un vrai tour de force que d'avoir rendu aussi un livre aussi instructif. Comment faites vous pour donner à une très exacte histoire le charme d'un roman—le charme d'un de vos romans?"

58. Jean Rostand, in unpublished letter to Maurois, dated May 17, 1950, Collection Simone André-Maurois. "Une fois de plus, par ce livre fort ravissant, vous donnez une leçon à ceux qui l'ignorent que la profondeur peut être transparente et que le sérieux peut être souriant."

59. AM, *Portrait d'un ami qui s'appelait moi,* p. 61.

60. Robert Kemp, Préface to Michel Droit, *André Maurois,* p. 13.

Chapter 3. André Maurois's Aesthetics of Biography

1. AM, Préface, Robert Sencourt, *La Vie de Meredith* (Paris: Gallimard, 1931), p. 7.

2. Michel Droit, *André Maurois* (Paris: Editions Universitaires, 1953), p. 64.

3. AM, "L'Homme et l'Oeuvre," *Les Nouvelles Littéraires,* June 10, 1954, p. 4.

4. Ibid.

5. Edmond Jaloux, "L'Esprit des Livres," *Les Nouvelles Littéraires,* June 4, 1938, p. 4.

6. AM, "L'Homme et l'Oeuvre," *Les Nouvelles Littéraires,* June 10, 1954, p. 4.

7. Ibid.

8. AM, *Choses nues* (Paris: Gallimard, 1963), pp. 199–200.

9. AM, *Tourguéniev* (Paris: Grasset, 1931), p. 211.

10. AM, *Byron* (Paris: Grasset, 1930), 2:72.

11. Ibid., 1:161.

12. Luc Estang, "Hugo l'Olympien," *La Croix,* n.d. no. 21791.

13. AM, *Lélia ou la Vie de George Sand* (Paris: Hachette, 1952), p. 12.

14. AM, *René ou la Vie de Chateaubriand* (Paris: Grasset, 1938), p. 53.

15. AM, *Adrienne ou la Vie de Madame de La Fayette* (Paris: Hachette, 1960), p. 20.

16. AM, *Portrait d'un ami qui s'appelait moi* (Namur: Wesmael-Charlier, 1959), pp. 63–64.

17. His histories are also influenced by his biographies, since they form a vast collection of shorter biographies of historical figures. As Maurois introduces each of the characters in the historical works, he does so with concise portraits and lives of them.

18. AM, *Portrait d'un ami*, p. 65.

19. Ibid., pp. 65–66.

20. Ibid.

21. Droit, *André Maurois*, p. 70.

22. AM, *Aspects de la biographie* (Paris: Au sens pareil, 1928), p. 20.

23. Ibid., p. 42.

24. Ibid., p. 51.

25. Ibid., p. 63.

26. AM, *Les Trois Dumas* (Paris: Hachette, 1957), p. 125.

27. AM, *Tourguéniev*, p. 199.

28. AM, *Portrait d'un ami*, p. 72.

29. AM, "l'Oeuvre et son Créateur," *Les Nouvelles Littéraires*, January 31, 1952.

30. Alain, in an unpublished letter to André Maurois, dated December 18, 1949, Collection Simone André-Maurois.

31. AM, *Etudes Littéraires 1* (Paris: Sfelt, 1947), p. 150.

32. Alain letter, see n. 30. "A chaque fois, j'ai mieux compris ma propre pensée . . . Réellement je me suis instruit sur moi-même en lisant votre *Alain*. Comme Gabrielle [Alain's wife] l'a dit sans hésiter, 'cela est écrit avec amour.' Je découvre aussi ce point de doctrine, c'est qu'on ne peut comprendre que ce qu'on aime. Eh bien! J'admets. Je me mets à l'école, je prends leçon à mon tour, mon semblable (mon autre) me devait bien cela. Qu'est-ce que penser? C'est penser comme l'autre. Cela j'y suis arrivé; je ne me laisserai plus déplacer. *Je serai humain*. C'est un grand drame que j'ai joué avec vous, mon Hamlet, ce n'est pas peu . . . Ce que je trouve admirable, c'est que vous avez donné à cet élève, qui enseigne, une sorte d'autorité grave, qui ne va pas sans gaîté. Vous avez saisi jusqu'à mon style; c'est merveilleux. Bref, jamais auteur ne fut lu comme je le fus par vous, mon seul ami . . ."

33. Jeanine Delpech, "Maurois a ressuscité George Sand," *Carrefour*, No. 387 (February 13, 1952).

34. AM, *Les Trois Dumas*, p. 14.

35. AM, *Byron*, 2:130.

36. René Lalou, Préface to *Disraeli* (Paris: Classiques Larousse, n.d.), p. 9.

37. André Chevrillon and André Maurois, *Discours de reception à l'Académie Française* (Paris: Didot, 1939), p. 111.

38. AM, *A la recherche de Marcel Proust* (Paris: Hachette, 1949), pp. 10–11.

39. Ibid., p. 13.

40. AM, *Aspects de la biographie*, p. 110.

41. AM, "Dickens," *Etudes Anglaises* (Paris: Grasset, 1927). See especially p. 38.

42. AM, *Les Trois Dumas*, p. 420.

43. AM, *A la recherche de Marcel Proust*, p. 267.

44. AM, *Aspects de la Biographie*, p. 52.

45. Chevrillon, *Discours*, p. 104.

46. AM, *The Life of Sir Alexander Fleming* (London: Penquin Books, 1963), p. 12.

47. Droit, *André Maurois*, p. 46.

48. AM, *Aspects de la biographie*, p. 62.

49. Ibid., p. 46. See also p. 52.

50. The most important exception is in his life of Proust, in which he pauses in the biographical account to devote three major sections to the analysis of Proust's themes. The unique relationship between Proust's life and work fully justifies this approach.

51. Commencement Address delivered by André Maurois at the University of Heidelberg Grand Auditorium, Sunday, June 2, 1963, as part of the graduation ceremonies of the University of Maryland's European Division.

52. AM, "Première Rencontre avec Virginia Woolf," *Les Nouvelles Littéraires*, January 15, 1929.

53. AM, "L'Homme et l'oeuvre," *Les Nouvelles Littéraires*, June 10, 1954, p. 4.

54. AM, "A nos jeunes camarades," *Discours* printed in pamphlet, *Lycée Corneille de Rouen* (Rouen: Lecerf, 1953), pp. 9–10.

55. AM, *Destins exemplaires* (Paris: Plon, 1952), Preface.

56. AM, *Lélia*, p. 222.

57. AM, *Aspects de la biographie*, p. 128.

58. AM, *Destins exemplaires*, p. i.

59. AM, "L'Art de la biographie," in Droit, *André Maurois*, p. 139.

60. AM, *Voltaire* (Paris: Gallimard, 1935), p. 103.

61. AM, *Portrait d'un ami*, p. 71. Actually, on second thought, Maurois (in a personal interview with me at his Neuilly home, May 31, 1964) had some reservations about this statement. As an artist, he still derived profound satisfaction from pure fiction. It would, it seems, be a mistake then to take this statement too literally.

Chapter 4. Themes and Variations—Novel by Novel

1. AM, *Discours prononcé pour la réception de Jean Cocteau à l'Académie Française* (Paris: Didot, 1955), p. 103.

2. André Chevrillon, *Discours de réception de M. André Maurois à l'Académie Française* (Paris: Didot, 1939), p. 89.

3. AM, *Mémoires* (New York: Editions de la Maison Française, 1942), 1:230. All quotations in my text from the novels of Maurois are from *Romans* (Paris: Gallimard, 1961).

4. Michel Droit, in *André Maurois* (Paris: Editions Universitaires, 1953), p. 29, insists on this tripartite approach and very aptly calls the book "a metaphysical novel."

5. AM, preface to *Ni ange ni bête* in *Oeuvres complètes* (Paris: Arthème Fayard, 1950), 1:387. All pagination in this chapter referring to this novel is from this edition.

6. AM, *Etudes anglaises* (Paris: Grasset, 1927), p. 224.

7. Miguel Pérez Ferrero, *ABC* (Madrid), May 1, 1949.

8. See Droit, *André Maurois*, p. 97.

9. Amélie Fillon discusses the question of the multilevel nature of this novel in *André Maurois, romancier* (Paris: Société Française d'éditions littéraires et techniques, 1937), p. 71.

10. AM, *Mémoires*, 2:39–40.

11. Edmond Jaloux, "Climats," *Perspectives et Personnages—L'Esprit des livres* (Paris: Plon, 1931), sér. 3, p. 240.

12. Chevrillon, *Discours*, p. 93.

13. See AM, *Mémoires*, 2:79 ff.

14. Jean Paulhan, unpublished letter to André Maurois, dated November 20 (probably 1928) in Collection Simone André-Maurois.

15. J. Tharaud, unpublished letter to André Maurois (dated only "mardi"), in Collection Simone André-Maurois.

16. Paul Desjardins, unpublished letter to André Maurois, dated November 29 (probably 1928), in Collection Simone André-Maurois.

17. Collection Simone André-Maurois.

18. Edmond Jaloux, "Climats." See note 11.

19. Louis Chaigne, "André Maurois," *Vie et oeuvres d'ecrivains* (Paris: Pierre Bossuet, n.d.), p. 176.

20. AM, *Romancier*, pp. 76–77 ff.

21. See AM, *Portrait d'un ami qui s'appelait moi* (Namur: Wesmael-Charlier, 1959), p. 74.

22. Jacques Suffel: *André Maurois* (Paris: Flammarion, 1963), p. 43.

23. AM, *Portrait d'un ami qui s'appelait moi,* p. 78.

24. Chaigne, "André Maurois," p. 160.

25. AM, in a personal interview with me, at the Château d'Essendiéras on August 9, 1964. Here is exactly what he told me: "Le Roman qu'il fallait faire—c'est de prendre tous les gens de la société que j'avais créée, c'est de montrer ce qu'ils ont fait en 1938, ensuite pendant la guerre, et de montrer qu'après la guerre tout leur destin avait changé. Mais malheureusement, je suis peut-être trop vieux. Mais il faut commencer quand même et s'arrêter en route—si nécessaire."

26. Alain in a personal and unpublished letter to André Maurois, dated January 3, 1929, in Collection Simone-André Maurois.

27. Michel Droit, *André Maurois* (Paris: Editions Universitaires, 1953), p. 39. The italics are by M. Droit and designate a quotation by Maurois himself.

28. AM, in an untitled and unpublished statement of his convictions, delivered over Radio Lausanne (Poste de Sottens) in Switzerland. Quotation is from p. 115 of the text.

29. AM, *Prométhée ou la Vie de Balzac,* p. 393.

30. AM, *Portrait d'un ami qui s'appelait moi,* pp. 79–80.

31. AM, "Examen," *Les Nouvelles Littéraires,* March 1, 1951.

32. AM, *Prométhée ou la Vie de Balzac,* p. 389.

33. AM, Préface, Tolstoi's *Anna Karénine* (Paris: Stock, 1960), p. v.

34. Ibid., pp. v–vi.

35. AM, "Examen," *Les Nouvelles Littéraires,* March 1, 1951.

36. AM, Préface, George Markow-Totevy: *Henry James* (Paris: Editions Universitaires, 1958), p. 9.

37. AM, *Tourguéniev* (Paris: Grasset, 1931), p. 59.

38. AM, "Préface," Pierre de Boisdeffre: *Métamorphose de la littérature de Barrès à Malraux* (Paris: Editions Alsatia, 1950), p. 11.

39. AM, "Dialogues des Vivants," *Les Nouvelles Littéraires,* July 10, 1958.

40. AM, in a private conversation with me at Château d'Essendiéras, December 23, 1963. "J'aime beaucoup les petits détails concrets qui font revivre le personnage et replonge le lecteur dans la réalité."

41. AM, *A la recherche de Marcel Proust* (Paris: Hachette, 1949), p. 150.

42. Henri Clouard, *Histoire de la littérature française du symbolisme à nos jours* (Paris: Albin Michel, 1962), 2:318–19.

Chapter 5. *André Maurois as a Writer of Short Stories*

1. AM, "Leur Premier livre, une enquête," *Candide,* September 13, 1934.

2. Among his best-known stories, which originally appeared as "nouvelles inédites" in the periodicals and were later published in volumes are: "Biographie," *Candide,* August 1, 1935; "Après dix ans," *Candide,* November 29, 1935; "Jeune Fille dans la neige," *Candide,* June 27, 1935; "Le Lingot," *Paris-Soir,* June 9, 1937; "Thanatos-Palace Hotel," *Candide,* December 16, 1937; "Toujours l'inattendu arrive," *Candide,* November 16, 1938; "Pour piano seul," *Réalités,* June 1951; "Un Amour secret de Byron," *Marie-Claire,* no. 5 (March 1956); "La Naissance d'un maître," *Courrier Frigidaire* (the trade journal of General Motors of France), January 23, 1957; "Le Coucou," *Le Soir,* December 26, 1958; "L'Ange gardien," *Lectures pour tous* (September 1959); "Trois actes," *Marie-Claire* no. 64 (February 1960); "L'Escale," *Pour vous madame* (October 1960); "Raz de marée," *Pour vous madame* (July–August 1961).

3. To these two titles let me add the tales Maurois included entirely within the framework of certain longer volumes: for example, *Les Nouveaux Discours du Docteur O'Grady* contains the delightful "Voyage au pays des Erophages," a work reminiscent of *Voyage au pays des Articoles,*

and also "Fragments d'une histoire universelle publiée en 1992 par l'université de . . . ," The *Journal-Etats-Unis-1946* contains his nightmarish tale, "Le Départ."

4. AM, *Les Mondes impossibles* (Paris: Gallimard, 1947), p. 84.

5. Once at his Château d'Essendiéras, during a conversation on scientific progress with my teen-age son and nephew, Maurois suddenly left the room to go upstairs. A moment later he returned holding a highly technical volume on electronics that he happened to be reading at the time and wished to discuss with the boys.

6. AM and Frédéric Lefèvre, "Propos sur le conte philosophique," *Les Nouvelles Littéraires,* November 13, 1937.

7. Jacques Suffel, *André Maurois* (Paris: Flammarion, 1963), p. 62.

8. Even Alfred Hitchcock, the master of Hollywood "thrillers," judged one of Maurois's stories to be sufficiently spine-tingling as a source for one of his productions on his television series "Alfred Hitchcock Presents." During the winter of 1965 he did present on his national television series the story of "Thanatos-Place Hôtel," which he scarcely revised for the screen.

9. AM in an unpublished personal letter to me, dated December 15, 1964, at Neuilly-sur-Seine. Permission to quote granted by the author before his death.

10. Henri de Régnier: "La Vie littéraire," *Le Figaro,* November 30, 1935.

11. AM, *Tourguéniev* (Paris: Grasset, 1931), p. 202.

12. Thomas Mann, Bruno Frank, John Erskine, André Maurois et al; *Les Dix Commandements* (Paris: Albin Michel, 1944). Maurois's story concerns the sin of adultery and the treatment of the Jews by the Nazis in Paris.

13. See the excellent example of the first type of discussion in *Toujours l'inattendu arrive,* p. 119; as a sample of the second type see the discussion between the poet and the dramatist, *Pour piano seul,* pp. 73–74.

14. William Bridges, "Thinks We Still Need Balzac," *New York Sun,* November 18, 1930, p. 8.

15. AM, *Portrait d'un ami qui s'appelait moi,* p. 116.

16. AM, *Choses nues* (Paris: Gallimard, 1963), p. 7. "Its nudity will be its only adornment."

17. AM, *Mémoires* (New York: Editions de la maison française, 1942), 1:87.

18. Those who had been familiar with this author's daily domestic life know how much his most fantastic tales were laden with the tiniest objects from his own personal world. Such sundries as the table mats customarily used on his own table were astonishingly similar to those described in "Le Pays des trente-six mille volontés." (See *Les Mondes impossibles,* p. 241).

19. Maurois was quoted in the Suffel book, n. 8.

20. *Les Mondes impossibles,* pp. 48–49.

21. Maurice Martin du Gard, "André Maurois," *Les Nouvelles Littéraires,* January 10, 1925.

22. AM, Préface, *Oeuvres complètes* (Paris: Artheme Fayard, 1951), 4:v.

Chapter 6. Maurois As Historian and Chronicler of the Past and Present

1. See AM's *Napoléon, A Pictorial Biography* (London: Thames Hudson, 1963). According to the author, it was commissioned directly by the British publisher. This lavishly illustrated work had later been issued in a French edition published by Hachette in 1964. In this work Victor Hugo is depicted as a principal actor in the history of the Napoleonic era.

2. Abel Hermant, "M. André Maurois et l'histoire," *Marianne,* March 17, 1937. Hermant reviewed Maurois's *Histoire d'Angleterre.*

3. Clement Attlee, in an unpublished letter addressed to André Maurois, dated London, March 1, 1937, in Collection Simone André-Maurois.

4. Alain, in an unpublished letter to André Maurois, dated May 17, 1947 in Collection Simone André-Maurois.

5. AM, *Portrait d'un ami qui s'appelait moi*(Namur: Wesmael-Charlier, 1959), p. 60. AM also

hastily wrote the text for a lavishly illustrated history of Germany. He never took this work seriously, and, in effect, this work does not at all deserve to be considered among his major histories of England, the United States, and France. See AM, *Histoire de l'Allemagne* (Paris: Hachette-Beaux Livres Series, 1965).

6. AM, Preface to *Histoire de la France* (Paris: Editions Albin Michel; new ed., 1958), 1:8.

7. AM, *Rouen* (Paris: Gallimard, 1929), p. 25.

8. AM's comments on "L'Oeuvre historique" in Jacques Suffel, *André Maurois* (Paris: Flammarion, 1963), p. 116.

9. See, for example, the superb table that illustrates graphically the entire political situation in Europe during the first half of the nineteenth century. *Histoire de la France,* 2:108. One can speculate that his wife, Simone André-Maurois, must have played an important part in the composition of these tables for she had consistently demonstrated a flair for family trees. Of her role, Maurois wrote: "My wife has been, more than ever, narrowly and constantly associated with my work." *Histoire de la France,* 1:9.

10. AM, *Edouard VII et son temps* (Paris: Flammarion, 1949), p. 216.

11. Ibid.

12. AM, *Histoire d'Angleterre* (Paris: Fayard, 1937), p. 627.

13. AM's comments in Suffel, *André Maurois,* p. 113.

14. Here are a few samples of Maurois's discreet use of quips and short words to divulge his true attitude: ". . . and the Senate, which was composed of one hundred and fifty members named to life-terms by the President and acting as guardians of the Constitution. Guardians who were *hardly* vigilant with virtue that was hardly *fierce.*" (Italics are my own. Maurois uses the term *peu,* which I have translated as "hardly."). *Histoire de la France,* 1:189. "Liberty, said Louis-Napoléon, has never helped establish a lasting political edifice; it crowns it when time has consolidated the edifice." Then Maurois adds this quip: "Without doubt he has never read the history of the United States" (ibid., 2:190). And speaking of Louis-Napoléon he wrote: "He would, in all sincerity, have wanted to be a good tyrant." Then Maurois adds this little remark that shatters the position of this character: "The unhappy thing is that there are no good tyrants" (ibid., 2:191).

15. AM, in a personal interview with me at his home in Neuilly-sur-Seine on October 14, 1965. His exact words: "Je ne suis pas un chercheur historique qui cherche à trouver des choses nouvelles. Mes histoires sont des essais d'explication."

16. André Chevrillon, *Discours de réception à l'Académie Française de M. André Maurois* (Paris: Didot, 1939), p. 131.

17. Louis Gillet: "Notre Ami André Maurois de l'Académie Française," *Paris-Soir,* June 23, 1939.

18. According to a personal interview with me in the Château d'Essendiéras in Périgord on August 5, 1964. In the same interview he contended that the French could learn from the Americans the art of warm and sincere hospitality and open friendliness, as well as the respect for one's civic duties.

19. AM quoted in Anon., "M. André Maurois," *Les Nouvelles Littéraires,* November 6, 1937.

20. AM, *Histoire de la France,* 2:220.

21. Michel Droit: *André Maurois* (Paris: Editions Universitaires, 1953), p. 84.

22. Ibid., p. 84.

23. With John Galbraith and Eugene Black, Maurois discussed economics; with James Conant and Fred M. Hechinger he touched upon education; with Professors Whipple and I. Rabi he dealt with astrophysics and physics respectively; Professor T. Dobzhanski and he talked about biology; Roy Wilkins covered the area of civil rights; James Sweeny and Leonard Bernstein held forth on the arts; Sig Michelson on television and information media; Jacob Potofsky on the union movement in America; Arthur F. Burns on agriculture; Charles Abrams and Aaron Fleisher on urbanism; Howard Rusk on medicine; and Howard Mumford Jones and Bruce Caton on America's historical heritage. With all of these specialists the urbane and eclectic André Maurois spoke knowledgeably and did so on a high level of sophistication.

24. AM, Préface, *Le Guide Bleu: New York et ses environs* (Paris: Hachette, 1954), pp. 17–22.

Chapter 7. *Maurois as Critic: His Philosophy of Art*

1. AM, "Comment devenir écrivain," *Lecture pour tous* (April 1961), no. 88.
2. Ibid.
3. AM, *Prométhée ou la vie de Balzac* (Paris: Hachette, 1965), p. 306.
4. AM, *Un Art de vivre* (Paris: Plon, 1939), p. 131.
5. Ibid., p. 131.
6. AM, *A la recherche de Marcel Proust* (Paris: Hachette, 1949), p. 116.
7. AM, from text of radio address delivered in Lansanne, Switzerland. Unpublished. N.D.
8. AM, "Comment devenir écrivain." See n. 1 above.
9. AM, Préface to *Ces Jours lointains—Alphonse Séché et Romain Rolland* (Cahiers Romain Rolland, Cahiers 13) (Paris: Albin Michel), p. 9.
10. AM, *Voyage au pays des Articoles* (Paris: Gallimard, 1928), pp. 75–76.
11. AM, "Leur Premier Livre," *Candide*, September 13, 1934, no. 548.
12. AM, *A la recherche de Marcel Proust*, p. 123.
13. AM, "Les Propos littéraires d'André Maurois: Vues sur les Amériques," *Opéra*, May 11, 1949.
14. Michel Droit, *André Maurois* (Paris: Editions Universitaires, 1953), p. 27.
15. During various personal discussions with him on the status of university scholarship. For example, he appeared to take no small satisfaction in demonstrating a very obvious factual mistake in a "scholarly" work on Proust written by an internationally known Proustian authority.
16. AM, *Choses nues* (Paris: Gallimard, 1963), p. 174.
17. AM, *Les Discours du Docteur O'Grady, Romans* (Paris: Gallimard, 1961), p. 992.
18. AM, *Un Art de vivre*, p. 41.
19. AM, *Comment devenir écrivain.* See n. 2 above.
20. AM, "L'Ecrivain et ses lecteurs", *Les Nouvelles Littéraires*, August 19, 1954, no. 1407.
21. AM, *Portrait d'un ami qui s'appelait moi* (Namur: Wesmal-Charlier, 1959), p. 61.
22. AM, *Dialogues sur le commandement* (Paris: Grasset, 1925), pp. 103–4.
23. AM, "Comment devenir écrivain." See n. 1 above.
24. Ibid.
25. On glancing at the page of a manuscript from his popular novel *Terre promise*, for example, we note instantly the multitudinous array of changes on the paper. On page 1 he has crossed out "il fallait encore quelques minutes" ("several minutes were still needed") and replaced it by a more generalized statement "il fallait un peu de temps" ("a bit of time was needed"). Instead of "Et si elle déchiffrait les inscriptions," ("And if she could decipher the inscriptions"), he modified the tense and thus made the sentence more vivid: "Et dès qu'elle avait pu déchiffrer les inscriptions," etc. (p. 5) ("And as soon as she had succeeded in deciphering the inscriptions"). Often Maurois added an adjective to fortify his text: "la maîtresse" ("the mistress") became in the final version "la pauvre maîtresse" ("The poor mistress") (p. 6). Occasionally he wished to make his story move more quickly, so he eliminated whole lines of text and created a brisk transition from one part to another. On page 9 of the manuscript he made so many changes, crossed out so many lines, that the successive versions are illegible. Most of the corrections stemmed from his concern for heightened vividness: "Claire eut alors plus que jamais l'impression d'être la plus malheureuse des enfants" ("Claire had more than ever the impression of being the unhappiest of children") was changed first to "Claire eut alors plus que jamais le sentiment d'être la plus malheureuse des enfants" ("Claire then had more than ever the impression of being the unhappiest of children"). Then he changed to a third version: "Cet épisode confirma Claire dans l'idée qu'elle était la plus malhaureuse des enfants" (p. 13) ("This episode confirmed to Claire the idea that she was the unhappiest of children"). The insertion of "Cet épisode" serves as a link with the preceding section. And certainly "confirma Claire dans l'idée" is a much more precise wording than "eut . . . le sentiment." Maurois often deemed his sentences to be too lengthy, too complex, so that he quite commonly split a long sentence into several shorter units by inserting words like "Mais" or "Cependant" at the beginning of dependent clauses, making them independent, but more concise sentences.

26. AM, *Le Cercle de famille* in *Romans,* p. 359.

27. Robert Kemp, Préface to Michel Droit's *André Maurois,* p. 12.

28. AM, "La Vraie France," *Samedi soir,* September 20–26, 1952, no. 377.

29. AM, according to his entry of January 23, *Journal-Etats-Unis-1946* (Paris: Edition du Bateau ivre, 1946), pp. 48–49.

30. All of the short quotations and stylistic qualities in the above paragraph are taken from AM, *Portrait d'un ami qui s'appelait moi,* pp. 101–7 *passim.*

31. Ibid., pp. 43–45 *passim.*

32. AM, *Préface, Alexandre Dumas, Voyage en Russie* (Paris: Hermann, 1960), p. 1.

33. AM, "Le Journal," *Carrefour,* March 9, 1960, no. 808.

34. AM, "Je n'ai pas dit assez souvent: Non," *Panorama Chrétien* (November 1957), no. 9.

35. AM, "L'Art de Travailler," *Un Art de vivre,* p. 130.

36. AM, Preface to Arnold Bennett's *Escalier de Riceyman* (Paris: Stock, 1929), p. xi.

37. AM, *Portrait d'un ami qui s'appelait moi,* p. 118.

38.p AM, *Prométhée,* p. 442.

39. AM, "Le Journal," *Carrefour,* January 23, 1957, no. 654.

40. AM, manuscript essay, "Les Dangers de notre temps," intended for publication in *Les Nouvelles Littéraires.*

41. AM, *Choses nues,* p. 109.

Chapter 8. *André Maurois and Posterity—A Personal Assessment*

1. My references by Chaigne, Albérès, Mauriac, and Jaloux are taken from a circular of critical evaluations of Maurois's short fiction printed by Flammarion in conjunction with the publication of Maurois's *Pour piano seul.* Maurois's role in education is not limited to textbooks. In the well-known and sometimes infamous national examinations for competition of June 1966, one of Maurois's most penetrating statements on the characters of the novel was a statement in which students throughout France were instructed to write their principal literary composition.

2. In a personal interview with me on July 19, 1966, at his Neuilly home.

3. Maurice Druon, "Une Volonté pour vingt destins," *Livres de France,* no. 6 (June–July 1965), p. 7.

4. In an interview with Maurois at Essendiéras on July 17, 1966, the latter shared this information with me. Professor Madelin wrote: "Je vous ai lu avec méfiance—mais j'ai trouvé des explications."

5. François Porché, "La Vie littéraire," *Le Figaro,* November 3, 1935.

6. Part of his "Réponses après Marcel Proust" composed expressly at my request. See appendix, where I have included the text of this entire questionnaire.

7. AM, *Choses nues* (Paris: Gallimard, 1963), p. 24.

8. On July 9, 1966, during the course of a chat with André Maurois in his study at Essendiéras, I read an early version of this concluding section to him. He seemed to object to it, saying that it was too "élogieux" ("laudatory"). I believe nevertheless that he deserves this conclusion as a fitting culmination for my monograph.

Select Bibliography

Special Note

No bibliography dealing with André Maurois's total production can really be complete. His book-length works were translated into the major languages of the world. These translations pose a problem for the bibliographer. Moreover, Maurois added or subtracted chapters in some of his works and often changed their titles in later editions. A large number of his books were later reissued by different publishing houses. The more popular titles appeared in both bound and paperback editions. His thousands of articles were published in newspapers, literary magazines, and trade journals. Moreover, his syndicated columns, book reviews, and limited-edition pamphlets are so numerous as to be almost unclassifiable. For these reasons it would be difficult to compile a satisfactory and lacuna-free list that includes both the more substantial books and the more ephemeral or shorter works.

It would be presumptuous for me to claim that the ensuing bibliography is an all-comprehensive one. Even if I were so rash as to seek to make an effort at completeness, the resulting bibliography might be longer than this entire monograph. I have therefore decided to be selective. Below I include those titles which, in my view, will be most useful for the reader who wishes to explore Maurois more fully. Also I include those titles which were most helpful to me in my own research. Because of their sheer numbers, this bibliography includes no articles by or on Maurois, many of which are itemized in the notes.

As an aid to the scholar, I have selected several bibliographies in which the chapters on André Maurois are particularly useful. These chapters will serve as a launching pad for further exploration of Maurois's vast production. Since my work is intended for both English and French readers, I shall list both the French titles and also a select number of English-language translations.

A. Useful Bibliographies

Alden, Douglas W. and Richard A. Brooks. *A Critical Bibliography of French Literature*, Vol. 6: The Twentieth Century. Syracuse: Syracuse University Press, 1980. See especially pp. 1408–10; Vol. 6, pt. 2, prepared by Jack Kolbert. Stresses mainly works about Maurois.

Bibliothèque Nationale. *André Maurois*. Paris: Bibliothèque Nationale, 1977. Catalogue listing the works of and items dealing with Maurois on exhibition in the events at the Bibliothèque Nationale marking the tenth anniversary of Maurois's death.

Kauffmann, Judith. *Aspects d'André Maurois biographe*. Paris: Diffusion Ophrys, 1980. See specially pp. 201–7. Highlights Maurois's biographical production.

Keating, L. Clark. *André Maurois*. New York: Twayne Publishers, 1969. See pp. 159–66. Professor Keating has prepared what is possibly the best English-language bibliography on Maurois. His lists of English-language translations of Maurois's works are especially useful.

Lemaître, Georges. *André Maurois*. Palo Alto: Stanford University Press, 1939. See pp. 120–24 for the Bibliographical Section, which is particularly useful for English translations prior to 1939.

Maurois, André, *Portrait d'un ami qui s'appelait moi*. Paris and Namur: Wesmael-Charlier, 1959. See pp. 6–10 for a chronological enumeration of Maurois's French-language works from 1918–1959.

Talvart et Place. *Bibliographie des Auteurs modernes de langue française*, 1801–1958, Vol. 14. Article on André Maurois. The most complete bibliography on Maurois until 1958. Since Maurois contined to produce actively from 1958 until his death in 1967, almost a decade of his works are of course not included here.

B. *Maurois's Collected Works*

Oeuvres complètes. 16 vols. Paris: Grasset, 1950–1956. The most complete edition of Maurois's works, this superb collection does not contain many of the shorter works by this author prior to 1956 nor does it contain some of the titles that he did not regard as being significant. The edition was halted in 1956 and therefore does not contain Maurois's many works written between 1956 and 1967, the year of his death.

C. *Maurois's Biographies* (in chronological order)

Ariel ou la Vie de Shelley. Paris: Grasset, 1923

Don Juan ou la Vie de Byron. Paris: Grasset, 1930.

Tourguéniev. Paris: Grasset, 1931.

Lyautey. Paris: Plon, 1931.

Voltaire. London: Peter Davies, 1932, and Paris: Gallimard, 1935.

Edouard VII et son temps. Paris: Editions de France, 1933.

René ou la Vie de Chateaubriand. Paris: Grasset, 1938.

A la recherche de Marcel Proust. Paris: Hachette, 1949.

Lélia ou la Vie de George Sand. Paris: Hachette, 1952.

Olympio ou la Vie de Victor Hugo. Paris: Hachette, 1954.

Robert et Elizabeth Browning. Paris: Grasset, 1955.

Les Trois Dumas. Paris: Hachette, 1957.

La Vie de Sir Alexander Fleming. Paris: Hachette, 1959.

Adrienne ou la Vie de Madame de Lafayette. Paris: Hachette, 1961.

Prométhée ou la Vie de Balzac. Paris: Hachette, 1965.

D. *Maurois's Essays, Criticism, and Nonfictional Works*

Dialogues sur le Commandement. Paris: Grasset, 1924.

Conseils à un jeune Français partant pour l'Angleterre. Abbéville, 1927.

Etudes anglaises. Paris: Grasset, 1927. (On Dickens, Walpole, Ruskin, Wilde, and others).

La Conversation. Paris: Hachette, 1927.

Rouen. Paris: Emile-Paul, 1927.

Un Essai sur Dickens. Paris: Grasset, 1927.

Aspects de la biographie. Paris: Au Sans Pareil, 1928.

Le Côté de Chelsea. Paris: Editions du Trianon, 1929. (Pastiche on Marcel Proust's style)

L'Amérique inattendue. Paris: Mornay, 1931.

Proust et Ruskin. Oxford: Essays and Studies by Members of the English Association, 1932.

Chantiers Américains. Paris: Nouvelle Revue Française, 1933.

Byron et les femmes. Paris: Flammarion, 1934.

Magiciens et Logiciens. Paris: Grasset, 1935.

Malte. Paris, Editions Alpina, 1935.

Les Origines de la guerre de 1939. Paris: Gallimard, 1939.

Un Art de Vivre. Paris: Plon, 1939.

Tragédie en France. New York: Editions de la Maison Française, 1940.

Etudes littéraires. New York: Editions de la Maison Française, 1941, and Paris: Editions S.F.E.L.T., 1947.

Espoirs et Souvenirs. New York: Editions de la Maison Française, 1943.

Etudes littéraires. vol. 2. New York: Editions de la Maison Française, 1944, and Paris: S.F.E.L.T., 1947.

Franklin. Paris: Fayard, 1945.

Eisenhower. Paris: Fayard, 1945.

Conseils à un jeune Français partant pour les Etats Unis. Paris: Editions de la Jeune Parque, 1947.

Alain. Paris: Domat, 1950.

Ce que je crois. Paris: Grasset, 1951.

Cours de bonheur conjugal. Paris: Hachette, 1951.

Destins exemplaires. Paris: Plon, 1952.

Discours prononcé à l'Académie française pour la réception de Jean Cocteau. Paris: Didot, 1955.

Hollande. (with photographs by Gérald Maurois) Paris: Hachette, 1955.

Périgord (photographs by Hughes O'Heguerty). Paris: Hachette, 1955.

Portrait de la France et des Français. Paris: Hachette, 1955.

Robert et Elizabeth Browning. Paris: Grasset, 1955. (Followed by portraits of Emily Dickinson, Kleist, Gogol, James Boswell, Alain, Hemingway, Sainte-Beuve)

La France change de visage. Paris: Gallimard, 1956.

De La Bruyère à Proust. (Lecture, mon doux plaisir). Paris: Fayard, 1957.

Dialogues des Vivants. Paris: Fayard, 1959.

Le Monde de Marcel Proust. Paris: Hachette, 1960.

Paris. Paris: Fernand Nathan, 1960. (Travel book, copiously illustrated).

De Proust à Camus. Paris: Perrin, 1963.

De Gide à Sartre. Paris: Perrin, 1965.

Au Commencement était l'action. Paris: Plon, 1966.

Lettre ouverte à un jeune homme. Paris: Editions: Albin Michel, 1966.

Les Illusions. Paris: Hachette, 1968.

Le Chapitre suivant. Paris, 1979.

E. Maurois's Novels (in chronological order)

Les Silences du Colonel Bramble. Paris: Grasset, 1918.

Ni ange, ni bête. Paris: Grasset, 1919.

Les Discours du docteur O'Grady. Paris: Grasset, 1922.

Bernard Quesnay. Paris: Nouvelle Revue Française, 1926; revised, 1928.

Climats. Paris: Grasset, 1928.

Le Cercle de famille. Paris: Grasset, 1932.

L'Instinct du bonheur. Paris: Grasset, 1934.

Terre promise. New York: Editions de la Maison Française, 1945; revised 1947.

Nouveaux Discours du docteur O'Grady. Paris: Grasset, 1950.

Les Roses de septembre. Paris: Flammarion, 1956.

Romans. Paris: Gallimard, 1961. (Collected novels but does not include *Ni ange, ni bête*)

F. Maurois's Short Fiction and Theater (in chronological order)

Le Pays des trente-six volontés. Paris, 1928.

Voyage au pays des articoles. Paris: J. Schiffrin, 1928.

Les Mondes imaginaires. Paris: Grasset, 1929, and Paris: Gallimard, 1947.

Le Peseur d'âmes. Paris: Nouvelle Revue Française, 1930.

Patapoufs et filifers (with illustrations by Jean Bruller, later known as Vercors). Paris: Hartmann, 1930.

Premiers Contes. Rouen: Desfontaine, 1935. (Extremely limited edition; the first stories Maurois ever wrote)

La Machine à lire les pensées. Paris: Nouvelle Revue Française, 1937.

Toujours l'inattendu arrive. Paris: Editions des Deux Rives, 1946.

Tu ne commettras pas d'adultère. Paris: Albin Michel, 1947.

Aux Innocents les mains pleines. Paris: La Table Ronde, 1955. (Proverbe en un acte—Maurois's only play)

Pour piano seul. Paris: Flammarion, 1960.

G. Maurois's Autobiographical Works (in chronological order)

Fragments d'un journal de vacances. Paris: Emile Hazan, 1929.

En Amérique. Paris: Flammarion, 1933.

Mes Songes que voici (essais et journaux de voyage). Paris: Grasset, 1933.

Discours de réception de M. André Maurois à l'Académie française et réponse de - M. André Chevrillon. Paris: Grasset, 1939.

Etats-Unis 39 Journal d'un voyage en Amérique. Paris: Editions de la France, 1939.

Mémoires. New York: Editions de la Maison Française, 1942. 2 vols. Reissued in one volume. Paris: Flammarion, 1948.

Etudes Américaines. New York: Editions de la Maison Française, 1945. (Maurois's writings in *Pour la Victoire* newspaper during his American exile)

Retour en France. (Journal 1946–1947) New York: Editions de la Maison Française, 1947.

Journal Etats-Unis 1946. Paris: Les Editions du Bateau ivre, 1948.

Journal d'un tour en l'Amérique latine. Paris: Les Editions du Bateau ivre, 1948.

Journal d'un tour en Suisse. Paris: Aux Portes de France, 1948.

Portrait d'un ami qui s'appelait moi. (See above under Useful Bibliographies)

Choses nues. (Chroniques) Paris: Gallimard, 1963.

Mémoires. Paris: Flammarion, 1970. (Revisions of the two earlier versions of the *Mémoires*, brought up to date. Posthumous publication.)

H. Maurois's Historical Works

Histoire d'Angleterre. Paris: Fayard, 1937.

La Monarchie Anglaise de Victoria à George VI. Paris: Flammarion, 1937.

Histoire des Etats-Unis. New York: Editions de la Maison Française, 1943–1944. Reissued in two vols. Paris: Albin Michel, 1947.

Washington, the Life of a Patriot. Paris: Didier, 1946.

Histoire de la France. Paris: Dominique Wapler, 1947. 2 vols. Reissued, Paris: Albin Michel, 1958.

Louis XIV à Versailles. Paris: Hachette, 1955.

Lafayette in America. Boston: Houghton-Mifflin, 1960.

Histoire parallèle: Histoire des Etats-Unis de 1917 à 1961. (Louis Aragon wrote the parallel history of the Soviet Union.) 4 vols. Paris: Presse de la Cité, 1962.

Napoléon. Paris: Hachette, 1964.

Histoire d'Allemagne. Paris: Hachette, 1965.

I. Maurois's Works in English Translation

Adrienne, the Life of the Marquise de Lafayette. Translated by Gerard Hopkins. New York: McGraw-Hill, 1961. (*Adrienne ou la vie de Madame de Lafayette*)

Ariel, The Life of Shelley. Translated by Ella D'Arcy. New York: Ungar, 1952. (*Ariel ou la Vie de Shelley*)

The Art of Being Happily Married. Translated by Crystal Herbert. New York: Harpers, 1953. (*Cours de bonheur conjugal*)

The Art of Living. Translated by James Whitall. New York: Harpers, 1958. (*Un Art de Vivre*)

Aspects of Biography. Translated by S. C. Roberts. New York: Appleton, 1929. (*Aspects de la biographie*)

Atmosphere of Love. Translated by Joseph Collins. New York: Appleton, 1929. In England titled *Whatever Gods May Be.* Translated by Joseph Collins. London: Cassell, 1929. (*Climats*)

Bernard Quesnay. Translated by Brian W. Downs. New York: Appleton, 1927. *(Bernard Quesnay)*

Byron. Translated by Hamish Miles. New York: Appleton, 1930. *(Don Juan ou la Vie de Byron)*

Captains and Kings. Translated by John Lewis May. New York: Appleton, 1925. *(Dialogues sur le commandement)*

Cecil Rhodes. Translated by Rohan Wadham. London: Collins, 1953. *(La Vie de Cecil Rhodes)*

Chateaubriand. Translated by Vera Fraser. New York: Harpers, 1938. *(René ou la Vie de Chateaubriand)*

The Chelsea Way. Translated by George D. Painter. New York: James H. Heineman, 1967. *(Le Côté de Chelsea)*

Conversation. Translated by Yvonne Dufour. New York: Dutton, 1930. *(La Conversation)*

The Country of Thirty-six Thousand Wishes. Translated by Pauline Fairbanks. New York: Appleton, 1930. *(Le Pays de trente-six volontés)*

Dickens. Translated by Hamish Miles. New York: Harpers, 1935. *(Un Essai sur Dickens)*

Disraeli. Translated by Hamish Miles. New York: Appleton, 1928. *(La Vie de Disraeli)*

The Edwardian Era. Translated by Hamish Miles. New York: Appleton, 1935. *(Edouard VII et son temps)*

The Family Circle. Translated by Hamish Miles. New York: Appleton, 1932. *(Cercle de famille)*

Fatapoufs and *Thinifers.* Translated by Rosemary Benet. New York: Holt, 1940. *(Patapoufs et filipers)*

From My Journal. Translated by Joan Charles. New York: Harpers, 1948. *(Journal, Etats-Unis, 1946)*

From the New Freedom to the New Frontier. Translated by Patrick O'Brien. New York: D. McKay, 1963. *(Histoire parallèle des U.S.A. et de l'URSS:* Maurois's section on America)

The Miracle of England. Translated by Hamish Miles. New York: Harper and Brothers, 1937. *(Histoire d'Angleterre)*

A History of France. Translated by Henry L. Binsse and Gerard Hopkins. New York: Farrar, Straus, and Cudahy, 1957. (Histoire de la France)

Illusions. Foreward by Edouard Morot-Sir. New York: Columbia University Press, 1968. *(Les Illusions)*

I Remember, I Remember. Translated by Denver and Jane Lindley. New York: Harpers, 1942. *(Mémoires,* New York edition)

Lelia, The Life of George Sand. Translated by Gerard Hopkins. New York: Harpers, 1953. *(Lélia, ou la Vie de George Sand)*

The Life of Sir Alexander Fleming, Discoverer of Penicillin. Translated by Gerard Hopkins. New York: Dutton, 1959. *(La Vie de Sir Alexander Fleming)*

Lyautey. Translated by Hamish Miles. New York: Appleton, 1931. *(Lyautey)*

Mape. Translated by Eric Sutton. New York: Appleton, 1926. *(Méipe, ou la délivrance)*

Memoirs 1885–1967. Translated by Denver Lindley. New York: Harper and Row, 1970. *(Mémoires,* Flammarion posthumous edition)

My American Journal. Translated by Joan Charles. London: The Falcon Press, 1950. *(Etats-Unis, 1946;* also sections from *Retour en France)*

Olympio, The Life of Victor Hugo. Translated by Gerard Hopkins. New York: Harpers, 1956. *(Olympio ou la Vie de Victor Hugo)*

Open Letter to a Young Man. Translated by Frances Frenaye. New York: James H. Heineman, 1968. *(Lettre ouverte à un jeune homme)*

A Private Universe. Translated by Hamish Miles. New York: Appleton, 1932. *(Conseils à un jeune Français partant pour l'Angleterre; Mes Songes que voici;* sections of *l'Amérique inattendue;* and *Chantiers américains)*

Profiles of Great Men. Translated by Helen T. Patterson. Ipswich (England): Tower Bridge, 1954. *(Destins exemplaires)*

Prometheus, The Life of Balzac. Translated by Norman Denny. New York: Harper and Row, 1965. *(Prométhée ou la Vie de Balzac)*

Prophets and Poets. Translated by Hamish Miles. New York: Harpers, 1935. *(Magiciens et Logiciens)*

Proust, Portrait of a Genius. Translated by Gerard Hopkins. New York: Harper and Brothers, 1950. *(A la recherche de Marcel Proust)*

The Return of Dr. O'Grady. Translated by Gerard Hopkins. London: Bodley Head, 1951. *(Les Discours du docteur O'Grady)*

Ricochets, Miniature Tales of Human Life. Translated by Hamish Miles. New York: Harpers, 1935. *(L'Anglaise et d'autres femmes)*

September Roses. Translated by Gerard Hopkins. New York: Harpers, 1958. *(Les Roses de Septembre)*

Seven Faces of Love. Translated by Haakon M. Chevalier. New York: Didier, 1944. *(Sept Visages d'amour)*

The Silence of Colonel Bramble. Translated by Thurfride Wake and W. Jackson. London and New York: J. Lane, 1919. *(Les Silences du Colonel Bramble)*

The Thought-Reading Machine. Translated by James Whitall. New York: Harpers, 1938. *(La Machine à lire les pensées)*

A Time for Silence. Translated by Edith Johannsen. New York: Appleton, 1942. *(L'Instinct du bonheur)*

The Titans. Translated by Gerard Hopkins. New York: Harpers, 1957. *(Les Trois Dumas)*

Tragedy in France. Translated by Denver Lindley. New York: Harper, 1940. *(Tragédie en France)*

The Weigher of Souls. Translated by Hamish Miles. New York: Appleton, 1931. *(Le Peseur d'âmes)*

Voltaire. Translated by Hamish Miles. New York: Appleton, 1932. *(Voltaire)*

A Voyage to the Island of the Articoles. Translated by David Garnett. New York: Appleton, 1929. *(Voyage au Pays des Articoles)*

Woman Without Love. Translated by Joan Charles. New York: Harpers, 1945. *(Terre promise)*

J. Major Works on Maurois

Chaigne, Louis. *Vie et oeuvres d'écrivains, André Maurois.* Paris: Pierre Bossuet, n.d.

Droit, Michel. *André Maurois.* Paris: Editions Universitaires, 1953.

Fillon, Amélie. *André Maurois, romancier.* Paris: Société française d'éditions littéraires et techniques, 1937.

Guéry, Suzanne. *La Pensée d'André Maurois.* Paris: Deux Rives, 1941.

Kauffmann, Judith. *See* Useful Bibliographies above

Keating, L. Clark. *See* Useful Biographies above

Larg, David G. *André Maurois.* New York: Oxford University Press, 1942.

Lemaître, Georges. *See* Useful Bibliographies above

Sauvenier, Justin. *Mes Amitiés Spirituelles, André Maurois.* Brussels: Editions de Belgique, 1932.

Suffel, Jacques. *André Maurois* (avec des remarques d'André Maurois; portrait-dialogue), Paris: Flammarion, 1963.

Index

Included below are the names of most of the persons and institutions mentioned in the text. I have also listed the references to Maurois's works under the heading of André Maurois.